D0579096

Curriculum Development and Teaching Strategies for Gifted Learners

NATIONAL UNIVERSITY
LIBRARY   SAN DIEGO

Curriculum Development and Teaching Strategies for Gifted Learners

⚘ Second Edition ⚘

C. June Maker

Aleene B. Nielson

With contributions by

Judith A. Rogers

Lannie S. Kanevsky

PHOTOGRAPHS BY

C. June Maker

pro·ed

8700 Shoal Creek Boulevard
Austin, Texas 78757-6897

pro·ed

© 1996, 1982 by PRO-ED, Inc.
8700 Shoal Creek Boulevard
Austin, Texas 78757-6897

All rights reserved. No part of the material protected by this
copyright notice may be reproduced or utilized in any form or by
any means, electronic or mechanical, including photocopying,
recording, or by any information storage and retrieval system,
without the prior written permission of the copyright owner.

Library of Congress Cataloging-in-Publication Data

Maker, C. June.
    Curriculum development and teaching strategies for gifted learners / C. June Maker,
Aleene B. Nielson. — 2nd ed.
        p.   cm.
    Rev. ed. of: Curriculum development for the gifted. 1982.
    Includes bibliographical references and index.
    ISBN 0-89079-631-9 (hardcover)
    1. Gifted children—Education.   2. Curriculum planning.
I. Nielson, Aleene B.   II. Maker, C. June. Curriculum development
for the gifted.   III. Title.
LC3993.M29   1995
371.95'3—dc20   95-9020
                                                                      CIP

This book is designed in Goudy.

Production Manager: Alan Grimes
Production Coordinator: Karen Swain
Managing Editor: Tracy Sergo
Art Director: Thomas Barkley
Reprints Buyer: Alicia Woods
Editor: Cynthia Woerner Halm
Editorial Assistant: Claudette Landry

Printed in the United States of America

    2   3   4   5   6   7   8   9   10   00   99   98   97   96

To Judy and Lannie
for
Friendship,
Great Ideas,
Glorious Humor

Contents

Preface

When I wrote the first edition of *Curriculum Development for the Gifted* in 1982, I wrote alone. I spent countless hours reading what others had written, looked for themes, then added my own ideas. These syntheses of literature, combined with my own experience, were shared with students in my graduate classes. Their suggestions helped me improve the ideas and the way they were presented.

The writing of this book has been different, and much more exciting. When I finally (after much discussion) agreed to revise the book, I was determined that it would reflect my current thinking and the significant changes that have occurred over the past 12 years. A change in my own life has been discovering the joy of thinking, discussing, and writing with colleagues who share a vision and enjoy each other's company.

Aleene Nielson, Judy Rogers, Lannie Kanevsky, and I arranged our full schedules so that we could have uninterrupted, extended periods for thinking and discussing. First, we examined the principles set forth in the first edition to decide if they all were still appropriate. Then, we examined each one carefully, talking about the research supporting its use, how it should be implemented, how it could be explained, and how its meaning should be changed. Throughout this process, we shared stories about children, teachers, and ourselves. The stories were wonderful! We all wished we had turned on the tape recorder early enough to get them all.

We then put the principles to the "acid test." Because we believe that curriculum and teaching strategies should build upon the characteristics that make the children different, we needed to try out these principles and see how they worked. In the first edition of this book, we used an existing behavior checklist based on research on students considered gifted from a traditional viewpoint. In writing this edition, we decided that a different list of behaviors was needed to reflect our current views of the varied forms of giftedness and the many ways giftedness can be exhibited. Starting with a National Research Center publication by Mary Frasier, which was based on work by Sandra Kaplan, we pooled our knowledge, searched for the right words to convey our meaning, and shared more stories, which would make a book of their own!

We all went away exhausted and renewed. Lannie kept thinking. She and Aleene exchanged e-mail messages and did drafts of the chart we had decided to use as a focal point.

During the next visit, we revisited the characteristics and principles, and decided where to put the Xs on the chart. What an intellectually demanding but exciting process! I don't think any of us slept much; we couldn't turn it off. At the end of the visit, we gathered our thoughts and examples and presented our new work at a state conference on education of the gifted. We had rave reviews. The audience could relate well to the principles and could see our personal and professional connections.

After that experience, we all wrote our parts. You can see the results in the pages that follow. We trust you will find the ideas and examples helpful in your teaching. We do. We also know you have many thoughts, experiences, and stories of your own. We'd love to hear them.

C. June Maker

Part 1

Curriculum Principles for Gifted Individuals

Chapter 1

Curriculum, Gifted Learners, and Change

When educators make decisions about the types of learning experiences to provide for gifted students, they must consider several factors. First, they must take into account that the context of the classroom is affected by school system and individual school, including educational philosophies, administrative structures, support services, resources, other students and teachers, the regular classroom program, the community, and the parents. Second, they must assess the theoretical models designed for education of gifted students to discern the assumptions the author(s) made about learning, teaching, and giftedness, or potential for high competence in one or more intelligences, and determine whether the curricular modifications implicit in the model are appropriate for the students identified for the special program. Third, educators must analyze the results of research on the first two decision processes to determine whether one specific teaching–learning model will be adopted or whether a synthesis of two or more models will provide a more appropriate educational program for gifted students in a particular setting.

Theories of Intelligence

When the first edition of *Curriculum Development for the Gifted* (Maker, 1982a) and its companion book, *Teaching Models in Education of the Gifted* (Maker, 1982b), were published, the prevailing theory of education was

3

behaviorist; the prevailing definition of giftedness was psychometric, and many educators differentiated between giftedness (i.e., high general intellectual ability) and talent (i.e., high ability in a specific field). In most school districts, students who had high scores on aptitude or achievement tests generally were selected for participation in programs for the gifted. Because these tests primarily measure aspects of linguistic and logical–mathematical intelligences and because these intelligences are basic to academic success in traditional school programs, the notion of *g* (Spearman, 1904, 1927), or general intelligence, was a dominant factor in the identification of gifted students.

During the ensuing years, these prevailing theories and definitions have been challenged by researchers in fields as diverse as neuroscience, information processing, developmental psychology, anthropology, creativity, linguistics, and evaluation and measurement. A new discipline, cognitive psychology, has arisen and incorporates many of the discoveries from research on the brain, life-span development, learning strategies, comparative cultural anthropology, and talent development. The long-standing debate about nature versus nurture in the development of intelligence is becoming less relevant, if no less heated, as theorists stress the reciprocal effects of heredity and environment on the development of intelligent behaviors. Sternberg (1990) dubbed these new ideas as "inside–outside" theories. He listed his own triarchic theory (Sternberg, 1985), the theory of multiple intelligences (Gardner, 1983), and the bioecological approach of Ceci (1990) as examples of the reciprocity of learner and environment.

Sternberg (1985) discussed three types of intelligence: analytic, synthetic, and practical: "The convergence of my analysis of the research literature and my personal experience convinced me that what was needed was a 'triarchic' theory of human intelligence—one that did justice to each of these three aspects of intelligence" (p. 58). He proposed that the mental processes involved in thinking are of three kinds: (a) metacomponents, or executive processes needed for planning, monitoring, and evaluating problem solving; (b) knowledge-acquisition components, used to gather information necessary to solve problems; and (c) performance components, or processes needed to implement the commands issued by the metacomponents. These three components are highly interdependent. "In effective mental management . . . the metacomponents control or activate the performance and knowledge-acquisition components at the same time that the performance and knowledge-acquisition components provide feedback to the metacomponents" (p. 59). Sternberg also recognized the effect of socialization and noted that although the three components operate in all cultures, some strategies may be more preferred in some cultures than in others and resources may be allocated differently. Therefore, "components vital to success in a society will develop readily, whereas others may tend to be inhibited" (p. 251).

Gardner (1983) posited the interaction of a biological proclivity, learning environments, and cultural values. Further, he defined intelligence as "the ability to solve problems or fashion products that are valued in at least one culture" (Gardner, 1994, p. 4). He argued that individuals may have greater proclivities toward one or another intelligence at birth but that intelligences that are developed depend heavily upon experiential and cultural factors. He also viewed creativity as *contextualized* and *distributed* with performance and products dependent on the interaction between abilities and human and material resources available in a specific setting. Gardner acknowledged the influence of Csikszentmihalyi (1988) and his reconceptualization of creativity as an interaction of three distinct elements: the distinctive intellect or personality of an *individual*; the *domain*, or discipline, in which one works; and the *field* of critics and judges who evaluate whether one's work is indeed creative.

Ceci (1990) argued that nature and nurture comingle to determine individual manifestations of intelligence.

> We believe that the organism is exposed to an array of subtle and not-so-subtle experiences of life, and that these individual experiences set in motion processes that unfold along multiple pathways, all of which are relevant to the crystallization of cognitive competencies that form the bedrock of adult intelligence. . . . Intelligence is posited as contextual; intelligent behavior in one environment may be foolish or dangerous in another. . . . Each biologically influenced potential ability takes on a synergy, some in a positively spiralling fashion that results in its snowballing into ever greater manifestations and others turn inward, atrophying, never to develop to their fullest possible expression.
>
> (p. 272)

These theories and research findings signal a need for change from the definition of giftedness as an IQ score or performance on a standardized intelligence test that is two or more standard deviations above the norm. In this view, only linguistic and logical mathematical intelligences are valued, and the role of context is disregarded. Working from Gardner's (1983) definition of intelligence, Maker (1992) proposed that gifted behavior, in any field, more properly should be defined as the individual's ability to solve complex problems (or simple problems) in the most efficient, effective, and economical ways. To that definition, the second author adds a fourth E: ethical. Ethical systems are culturally determined but generally include a variation of the Golden Rule (e.g., "Do unto others as you would have others do unto you"). Another modification in the definition of giftedness as very high performance across domains is the recognition of very high competence in one domain.

Gardner's (1983) research showed that at least seven separate intelligences—linguistic, logical–mathematical, spatial, musical, bodily kinesthetic, interpersonal, and intrapersonal—can be identified according to eight criteria:

- potential isolation by brain damage
- existence of idiots savant, prodigies, and other exceptional individuals
- an identifiable core operation or set of operations
- a distinctive developmental history, along with a definable set of expert end-state performances
- an evolutionary history and evolutionary plausibility
- support from experimental psychological tasks
- support from psychometric findings
- susceptibility to encoding in a symbol system

Gardner (1983) posited that "Nearly all cultural roles exploit more than one intelligence; at the same time, no performance can come about simply through the exercise of a single intelligence" (p. 207).

Curriculum Implications of Inside–Outside Theories

These new theories of intelligence also have profound implications for educators' processes of schooling. Most school curricula are focused on two intelligences: linguistic and logical–mathematical. Materials generally are presented through language—lectures and textbooks; demonstrating proficiency generally requires ability to use linguistic or mathematical symbols to solve well-structured problems. Bodily kinesthetic intelligence may be developed if individual ability in that area can be exploited in competitive sports, but abilities in other types of bodily kinesthetic intelligence (e.g., jewelry making, dance, needlework, mime, typing) seldom are emphasized in public schools. Classes designed to help students develop musical and visual-spatial skills often are lacking, especially when school district budgets are strained, and students rarely have opportunities to develop interpersonal and intrapersonal abilities unless they are involved in extracurricular activities.

In many traditional classes, the focus is on the transmission of information from teacher (or other expert source) to students. The roles of students and teachers are quite different from the roles of less skilled and more skilled partners as described by Rogoff (1990) in her view of learning as an apprenticeship in thinking. In Table 1.1, aspects of traditional educational paradigms are compared to those in a constructivist, or reciprocal, paradigm.

Curriculum modifications often recommended for gifted students (Clark, 1986; Kaplan, 1979; Maker, 1982a, 1986; Maker & Nielson, 1995) share many principles with constructive theories of learning. Some modifications of traditional curricula recommended for gifted students may, in fact, be appropriate for most students. For example, the learning-environment modifications are appropriate for almost all children. Other modifications are more specific to the needs of children who are potentially gifted in one or more intelligences. Table 1.2 includes the same categories as Table 1.1 but shows qualitative differences in those categories recommended in programs for gifted children.

Qualitatively Different Curricula

When educators recommend that a program for gifted students should be qualitatively different, they imply that a program must be designed (or enhanced) to take into account the qualities that are special about specific children and young people. If the students are different enough (in learning and thinking styles, needs, motivational characteristics, creativity) from their age peers to need a special program, then the curriculum must be built around the characteristics that make the program necessary. Even though this statement sounds like commonsense programming for all children, justifying a qualitatively different curriculum

Table 1.1. Comparison of Traditional and Constructivist Paradigms

Curriculum Aspect	Traditional	Constructivist
Theory of Knowledge	Objective body of facts and time-tested strategies derived empirically or through rational analysis Cultural practices and values Universal truths	Meanings constructed through interaction of a more skilled partner and less skilled partner(s) in authentic environments Meanings based on customs, values, mores, and cultural practices
Theory of Learning	Acquisition of prescribed content and strategies through study and training Automatization of skills through practice Desired responses to stimuli	Cognitive apprenticeship in social context; gaining skills in the use of tools and processes Increased capacity to solve problems through observation, imitation, or interaction Adaptation to one's environments
Nature of Tasks	Teacher (or curriculum) defined Discrete; often context free Finding "right" answers Individually performed Memory intensive Often involves drill and practice Often text based and reading intensive Usually abstract; few concrete experiences Teacher sets time and format for recitation	Jointly defined problem, although more skilled partner may set problem to be solved Contextually embedded Often trial-and-error experimentation Observation and imitation of a model Goal-directed, concrete, active experiences Often playful; learning skills through games Sensitive to learner's prior experiences and level of development

	Little or no student choice of activities	Leads to independent performance
	Same for all students	Learner chooses time to demonstrate skill
	Product oriented	Process oriented
View of Learner	Incomplete or deficient member of community to be shaped or formed by expert agents of culture	Active inquirer and experimenter
	An empty vessel to be filled or a blank slate upon which to write	Joint constructor of knowledge
	A responder to stimuli and reinforcement	Active participant in developing skills and solving problems in sociocultural context
		Observer and imitator of others in environment
Role of Learner	Attend to either or both classroom presentations and communications from adult experts	Participate in a variety of social and cognitive activities with more skilled partners
	Respond to teacher questions accurately and courteously	Jointly construct meanings
	Practice skills and do activities prescribed by teachers	Jointly solve problems
	Publicly demonstrate skills, in recitation or performance, on teacher's demand	Actively experiment with objects and tools in authentic environments
	Work individually, often without access to any cognitive tools other than language	Appropriate social customs, values, beliefs, and skills through interaction with others in the society
	Pass objective teacher-made and criterion- or norm-referenced tests, relying solely on memory, or restudy prescribed objectives	Observe more skilled partners; imitate and practice skills until ready to perform them publicly
		Communicate effectively with others in social contexts

(continues)

Table 1.1. *Continued*

Curriculum Aspect	Traditional	Constructivist
View of Teacher	Agent of the dominant culture Skilled individual who transmits culturally valued information, conducts training skills, and reinforces desired learner behaviors	A guide to learner-participants in culturally valued activities, problem solving, and use of processes aimed toward intelligent adaptation in varied environmental contexts A more skilled partner who frequently sets problems, structures situations, and is sensitive to the abilities and interests of learners A competent participant in social interactions
Role of Teacher	Prescribe content Present instruction Predetermine acceptable pathways from problems to solutions Predetermine acceptable products Determine goals, objectives Select materials and set up activities Prepare and administer tests Evaluate learners Maintain an orderly environment Control student behaviors Be alert for cheating or other inappropriate student collaboration	Be sensitive to perspectives and previous knowledge of learners Choose scenarios, materials, activities, and settings appropriate for learners' abilities and needs Arrange and structure difficulty of tasks and levels of learner involvement Adjust levels of support and participation in relation to learners' skills and task difficulty Allow learners a choice of activities Gradually shift responsibilities for tasks to learners as they grow in skill and understanding Share a vision of how and why the processes work and why a task is important

	Be accountable to principal and other officials	Use games or playful means to facilitate metacognition
		Intervene to redirect learners' efforts, rather than correcting errors
		Use questions or hints to help learners discover how to solve a problem or understand a new concept
Nature of Environment	External influence that affects learners	Focused on relationships
	Shapes behavior of inhabitants	Contains "affordances" relative to the inhabitants; the ways learners perceive affordances affect the ways they behave
	Behavior setting with arbitrarily established rules and patterns of interaction	Dynamic, reciprocal, temporal interactions
	Controlled and managed by teacher	Each environment affords some activities and constrains others
	Self-contained	Nested in educational, social, political, and economic ecosystems
	Centered on teacher and prescribed sources of information	Allows cognitive conflict among peers
		Authentic
Unit of Analysis	Individual	Holistic, contextual, and functional events and relationships
Evaluation	Most frequently by objective tests	Performance of skills; tolerance for learner mistakes during skill development
	Normed achievement tests or similar standardized instruments	Reaching personal goals
	Often keyed to discrete bits of data or explicit objectives	Solving contextual problems
	Teacher or system controlled	Successful adaptation to varied environments
	"Right" answers	

Table 1.2. Qualitative Differences in Education for Gifted Individuals

Curriculum Aspects	Characteristics
Theory of Knowledge	Meanings jointly and purposefully constructed to solve real problems, explain phenomena, or communicate ideas
	Purposeful, structured, abstract and complex concepts, generalizations, principles, and theories
	Contextual; may vary with culture, environment, discipline, paradigm
Theory of Learning	Transactional and integrative
	Making connections between present knowledge and new information derived from varied materials and environments
	Transforming or synthesizing discrete data to solve problems and create new knowledge
Nature of Tasks	Often ill-defined problem individually or collaboratively chosen
	High-interest activities
	Complex and varied
	May require a broad range of resources
	May require collaboration with a mentor in a setting away from the classroom or school
	Open ended; many alternative solutions or products possible
	Often require analysis, synthesis, evaluation, creative problem solving, decision making, or planning
	Process oriented
	Either abstract or contextually embedded
View of Learner	Active participant in the transformation and integration of knowledge, inference maker, problem solver, decision maker
	Joint constructor of knowledge
	Inventor of self, new tools, new ideas
	Reflective thinker
	Analyzer and synthesizer
	Abstractive thinker, categorizer
Role of Learner	Jointly construct knowledge through a variety of interactions—with more skilled partners, peers, cognitive tools, objects

Table 1.2. *Continued*

Curriculum Aspects	Characteristics
	Actively experiment with objects and tools to discover new data, solve ill-defined problems, or construct new knowledge
	Integrate discrete data into coherent perceptions and new ideas
	Analyze situations, define problems, and synthesize possible solutions
	Communicate effectively with peers, "real audiences," and others in a social environment
	Jointly construct rules, procedures, and practices to regulate interactions in a learning community or interest group
	Question existing knowledge, mores, values, and traditions as a means to understand, improve, or supplant them
View of Teacher	Facilitator of activities which meet individual, group, or social needs and interests
	Constructor of learning environments designed to encourage interaction, cognitive growth, and learner autonomy
	Guide to help learners in the acquisition of skills and use of tools needed to process information, solve problems, and create products
	Consultant or mentor
	Partner in learning
Role of Teacher	Accept ideas, observations, opinions; discuss rather than judge
	Pose real (or realistic) problems and set challenging tasks
	Spend less time on concrete information and repetition; work toward abstract concepts, connections, conclusions, and generalizations
	Include a variety of choices
	Structure interactions and pose problems that require high-level thinking processes
	Ask open-ended questions; use probing questions to clarify or extend ideas rather than to test for known information
	Support intellectual and creative risk taking
	Participate with other learners in joint planning, decision making, construction of rules and other practices to ensure

(continues)

Table 1.2. *Continued*

Curriculum Aspects	Characteristics
	effective interaction among members of the learning community
	Trust and respect intelligence and abilities of learners
	Tolerate ambiguity
	Help students plan time for reflection and incubation
Nature of Learning Environment	Contains "affordances" relative to the nature and characteristics of the specific members of the learning community
	Provides sufficient structure for safety and opportunities for self-management
	Physically and psychologically comfortable
	Provides autonomy, private places, and sense of belonging
	Accommodates a wide range of choices
	Has facilities for varied kinds of interaction among peers, more skilled partners, and mentors
	Complex and rich in many types of learning resources
	Affords challenge and variety
	Affords active experimentation
	Affords reflective thinking
Unit of Analysis	Holistic, contextual, and functional events and relationships
Evaluation	Self-assessment in terms of individual goals and objectives
	Shared decision making with peers or teacher or both
	Responses and critiques from real audiences or experts using standards of a specific domain
	Few "right" answers

based on the unique characteristics of gifted children is not easy. Perhaps much of the difficulty lies in disagreement over the purpose(s) and value(s) of special programs for exceptional learners. In many segments of today's multicultural society, *mainstreaming*, or inclusion, is seen as a positive approach to the education of children who are differently abled. In other segments of the society, special programs for gifted learners are considered elitist and, perhaps, the last bastion of segregation in the public schools. These attitudes are the outward evidence of "administrative, bureaucratic, political, and social engineering agenda" (Start, 1992, p. 2) that masquerade as pedagogical arguments against differentiated education for gifted children. Teachers and parents must be politically proactive if they wish to meet the learning needs of children who show promise of superior intellectual or creative achievement. "There are things the current educational system can and should be doing for its able children. But it is not, does not want to, and probably will not, unless it can be shown that the premise on which opposition to the education of the able is based is wrong, not because it is wrong for the able, but because it is wrong for all children" (Start, 1989, p. 1).

When educators show that some modifications will benefit all students (including gifted children), then these changes will be implemented. In several educational approaches now being recommended (e.g., National Council of Teachers of Mathematics [NCTM] standards for mathematics education, 1989; whole language; problem-based learning; interdisciplinary studies), educators advocate an approach to learning that incorporates several of the modifications that Maker (1982a, 1982b) recommended for gifted students. In some schools, the principles advocated for gifted students have been incorporated in an approach to schoolwide reform (e.g., *The Schoolwide Enrichment Model*, Renzulli & Reis, 1985; *Talents Unlimited*, Schlichter, 1986; and *Talents to the Secondary Power*, Schlichter, Hobbs, & Crump, 1988, based on C. W. Taylor's [1967] theory of multiple talents). In a few cases, educators have adopted a multiple-intelligences approach (e.g., Hoerr & Faculty of the New City School, 1994) to improve learning experiences for a variety of children and young people. Gifted students are better served in programs of this kind but still need greater opportunities for learning at their own pace and with their intellectual peers.

Three Types of Qualitative Change

Despite the criticism leveled at special education for gifted students, qualitatively different curricula are necessary to meet the needs of this diverse population. No one program can be effective for all gifted students, who may differ as much from each other as they differ from students not identified as gifted. Within the field, experts disagree on the effectiveness of different approaches. VanTassel-Baska (1994) stated that three relatively distinct curriculum models have proved to be successful with gifted children. A comparison of the three models is shown in Table 1.3.

The content-mastery model is most like traditional forms of education for all children. The major modification for gifted students is that they move as rapidly as possible through disciplinary content. Accelerated and advanced placement programs are examples of this model. Strengths of this approach are that prescribed content is mastered more quickly, proficiency is relatively easy to assess, and a student's progress can be continuous. Disadvantages include a ceiling on how far content can be advanced, questions about the durability of learned information, lack of interaction with others, a high level of pressure perceived by many gifted students, and the limits of prescribed curriculum. The only modifications for gifted students are more rapid pacing and, sometimes, more complex content. Research shows that, in controlled settings, this instructional approach has proved to be effective in math (Benbow & Stanley, 1983) and Latin (VanTassel-Baska, 1982).

In process–product models, emphasis is placed on various research and information processing skills. Learners are viewed as investigators

Table 1.3. Contrasting Curriculum/Instructional Models for the Gifted

	Content	*Process–Product*	*Concept*
Key Descriptor	Fast-paced instruction and advanced content	In-depth work on selected topics	Meaning-based exploration of key concepts
Organization Structure	Organized by intellectual content	Organized around scientific or other process model	Organized by themes and ideas
Dominant Role of Teacher	Facilitator of small-group and individual learning	Facilitator of collaborative process; metacognitive coach	Question poser and prober
Evaluation Approach	Proficiency based	Product based	Holistic

Note. From "The National Curriculum Development Projects for High Ability Learners: Key Issues and Findings," by Joyce Van Tassel-Baska, 1994, in N. Colangelo, S. G. Assouline, and D. L. Ambroson (Eds.), *Talent Development: Proceedings from the 1993 Henry B. and Jocelyn Wallace National Research Symposium in Talent Development*, p. 23, Dayton, OH: Ohio Psychology Press. Copyright 1994 by Ohio Psychology Press. Adapted with permission.

with a problem or problems to be solved through interaction with peers, teachers, and consultants. The *Enrichment Triad Model* (Renzulli, 1977), *Creative Problem Solving* (Noller, Parnes, & Biondi, 1976), and *Teaching Strategies for Thinking and Feeling* (Williams, 1972) are examples of this approach; the models are described in greater depth by Maker and Nielson (1995). A frequent assumption underlying these models is that process-skill development is emphasized whereas content is incidental. That assumption is erroneous; most developers of process models stress that content should be integrated with process and that both content and process be relevant to the needs and interests of gifted students.

Ideas and themes, rather than content and process skills, are stressed in the epistemological concept model. Students and teachers are involved in highly interactive contexts rather than in the more independent or individualistic modes of instruction used in the content and process–product models. "Concern for the nature and structure of knowledge itself is a major underlying tenet" (VanTassel-Baska, 1994, p. 23). VanTassel-Baska also noted that student proficiency is demonstrated in ways that show "evidence of synthesizing form and meaning across areas of study" (p. 23). What she neglected to point out is that the concept model requires the integration of content, process, and product in a specific learning environment; modifications must be made in all four areas if teachers and students are to use this model effectively.

Interdisciplinary Curriculum

Jacobs (1989a) listed four factors that contribute to the need for interdisciplinary curriculum content and organization around broad themes and ideas:

- exponential growth of knowledge in all areas of study
- fragmentation and interruption of classroom schedules
- curriculum irrelevant to life outside of school
- need for balance between increasing specialization and the multifaceted nature of work in the world

She noted that active linkages can be designed between fields of knowledge. "We can teach the works of Shakespeare with an eye to the history of the times, the arts, the values, the role of science, and the general intellectual, moral, and cultural facets of that era rather than simply sticking with specific passages of specific plays. The student who does not possess a literary bent may encounter *King Lear* in another subject area" (p. 5). Curriculum will become more relevant when students find connections between subjects than when each is studied in isolation.

Table 1.4 includes some useful definitions derived by Jacobs (1989a) from the work of Jean Piaget and L. R. Meeth, for terms in current use. Traditional classrooms, especially in secondary schools, tend to be disciplinary. Little or no integration of concepts from one discipline to another is attempted or discussed. Even when innovations are implemented, the approach tends to be multidisciplinary or pluridisciplinary. In most elementary classrooms, the day also is divided into disciplinary study. For example, in a school observed by the second author, students in all 24 classrooms studied math between 9:00 A.M. and 10:00 A.M. Even if students in one classroom were in the midst of a fascinating discovery

Table 1.4. Definitions of Selected Curriculum Terms

Term	Definition
Discipline Field	A specific body of teachable knowledge with its own background of education, training, procedures, methods, and content areas (Piaget, 1972)
Interdisciplinary	A knowledge view and curriculum approach in which language and methodology from more than one discipline are consciously applied to examine a central theme, issue, problem, topic, or experience (Jacobs, 1989a)
Crossdisciplinary	Viewing one discipline from the perspective of another; for example, the physics of music, the history of math (Meeth, 1978)
Multidisciplinary	The juxtaposition of several disciplines focused on one problem with no attempt to integrate them (Meeth, 1978)
Pluridisciplinary	The juxtaposition of disciplines assumed to be more or less related; for example, math and physics, French and Latin (Piaget, 1972)
Transdisciplinary	Beyond the scope of the disciplines; that is, to start with a problem and bring to bear knowledge from the disciplines (Meeth, 1978)

Note. From "The Growing Need for Interdisciplinary Curriculum Content," in H. H. Jacobs (Ed.), *Interdisciplinary Curriculum: Design and Implementation,* pp. 7–8, Alexandria, VA: Association for Supervision and Curriculum Development. Copyright 1989 by Association for Supervision and Curriculum Development. Adapted with permission.

activity in another subject, all materials had to be put away by 8:55 so they would be ready to work on math at 9:00.

Just as students need some "right-answer" problems, they need some curriculum experiences in discrete disciplines. For learning activities to be effective, students need a base of knowledge in each of the relevant disciplines. However, some problems should be open-ended, and many curriculum experiences should have an interdisciplinary orientation. Interdisciplinarity should be used when students need to bring fragmented ideas together to create a more holistic understanding of a concept or general theme. Interdisciplinary activities, when properly designed, help students to break away from traditional views of knowledge and develop perspectives that are more relevant in the world outside the classroom (Jacobs, 1989b). According to *Thinking in the Classroom: Resources for Teachers, Volume 2: Experiences That Enhance Thoughtful Learning* (1991–1993, p. 16), when interdisciplinary activities are characterized by the following features, connections between disciplines and topics are encouraged:

- Tasks are open ended.
- Students' prior knowledge, experiences, and feelings are explicitly engaged.
- Exploring is valued at least as much as the result.
- Tentativeness is encouraged.
- Students have opportunities to collaborate.
- Students have time to pursue and revise their ideas.

Crossdisciplinary studies may be particularly relevant for students who have strengths in intelligences not usually tapped in a discipline. For example, a gifted student who is both highly competent in musical intelligence and passionately interested in musical composition might meet a science requirement by studying the physics of music or sound. A student talented in spatial intelligence might meet a requirement for research on human body systems by creating a series of drawings rather than by writing a research report to demonstrate understanding of physiological and anatomical systems.

When gifted students define their own problems, their problem-solving strategies may require a transdisciplinary approach, that is, the use of knowledge gained from several disciplines to reach and implement a desirable solution. In the *Enrichment Triad Model* (Renzulli, 1977; Renzulli & Reis, 1985), the goals of Type III enrichment activities usually will require transdisciplinary thinking:

- Students investigate real problems or topics using appropriate methods of inquiry.

- Students take an active part in formulating problems and selecting methods by which problems will be investigated.

- Students use *raw data* rather than reporting on conclusions reached by others.

- Students actively direct their inquiry toward a tangible product.

- Students apply thinking and feeling processes to real situations rather than to highly structured exercises.

When students are involved in collaborative activities (e.g., group investigations, productions), transdisciplinary thinking and application of skills from many intelligences are required. These kinds of activities also are closer to the world of work activities pursued by adults.

Descriptions of Qualitative Differences

Despite the difficulties of defining something as value laden and ambiguous as *qualitatively different*, several attempts have been made. The U.S. Department of Education's Office of the Gifted and Talented provided the following definition:

> [Differentiated education or services] means that process of instruction which is capable of being integrated into the school program and is adaptable to varying levels of individual learning response in the education of the gifted and talented and includes but is not limited to:
>
> 1. A differentiated curriculum embodying a high level of cognitive and affective concepts and processes beyond those normally provided in the regular curriculum of the local educational agency;
>
> 2. Instructional strategies which accommodate the unique learning styles of the gifted and talented; and

3. Flexible administrative arrangements for instruction both
   in and out of school, such as special classes, seminars,
   resource rooms, independent study, student internships,
   mentorships, research field trips, library media research
   centers and other appropriate arrangements.

   (United States Department of Education, 1976, pp. 18665–18666)

Virgil Ward (1961), unique in the field of education for the gifted
because of his development of a comprehensive logical theory, defines
differential education for the gifted by presenting a series of formal propositions and corollaries that take into account both the characteristics of
gifted individuals and the impact they may have on society if their
superior intellect is nurtured. His proposal includes the following propositions and corollaries relating to the design of curricula:

1. "that the educational program for intellectually superior individuals
   should be derived from a balanced consideration of facts, opinions
   based on experience, and deductions from educational philosophy as
   these relate to the capacities of the individuals and to the probable
   social roles which they will fill" (p. 81)

2. "that a program of education for the intellectually superior should be
   relatively unique" (p. 86)

3. "that the curriculum should consist of economically chosen
   experiences designed to promote the civic, social, and personal
   adequacy of the intellectually superior individual" (p. 102)

4. "that in the education of the gifted individual considerable emphasis
   should be placed upon intellectual activity" (p. 126)

5. "that the educative experience of the intellectually superior
   individual should be consciously designed as generative of further
   development, extensively and intensively, along similar and related
   avenues" (p. 141)

6. "that the education of gifted children and youth should emphasize
   enduring methods and sources of learning, as opposed to a terminal
   emphasis upon present states of knowledge" (p. 156)

7. "that the instruction of intellectually superior individuals should
   emphasize the central function of meaning in the acquisition of fact
   and principle, and the varieties of reflections of meaning in the
   developed communicative devices of mankind" (p. 161)

8. "that the instruction of the intellectually superior should include content pertaining to the foundation of civilization" (p. 170)

9. "that scientific methods should be applied in the conception and execution of education for personal, social, and character adjustments of the intellectually superior individual" (p. 195)

10. "that instruction in the theoretical bases of ideal moral behavior and of personal and social adjustments should be an integral part of the education of gifted individuals" (p. 201)

Shacal and Rachmel (1993) developed guidelines for Israeli schools, using ideas drawn from several pioneers in the field of education of the gifted. They noted that, although some of these guidelines can also be applied to programs for general student populations, all are important for the population of children who are gifted. They emphasized that (a) unique traits of each gifted child must be taken into consideration in the planning of learning experiences; (b) learning materials should include central ideas and problems combined with thought processes; (c) programs should promote both cognitive and self-teaching skills; (d) programs should afford opportunities for students to use unique research methods and advanced technology and also to use experts as a learning resource; (e) both creativity and excellence should be emphasized in implementation and in final products; (f) the program should be designed to help students gain insights into their own personal strengths, interests, learning styles, and motivation; (g) students should have learning experiences that help them develop sensitivity to other human beings and to develop social and national consciousness; (h) interdisciplinary aspects of a subject should be emphasized and interdisciplinary programs are strongly recommended; (i) real-world problems should be used to help students reach decisions and to enable them to better solve future issues; and (j) students must have opportunities to acquire knowledge as well as learning strategies and research skills.

According to Kaplan (1974), differentiation of curricular activities for the gifted and talented relies on the elaboration of the procedures for presenting learning opportunities, elaboration of the nature of the input, and elaboration of the expectancies for learning outcomes. In relation to differentiating learning as a separate curriculum, she suggested that input should be accelerated or advanced, more complex, beyond the regular curriculum, selected by the students according to their interests, and concerned with the more abstract concepts in each content area. The levels and types of resources used or available to these individuals are different from those available for all students.

Kaplan (1974) also stated that expectations for gifted learners are different from those for all children. Gifted students may become more involved in a project and use a longer time period for learning what they want to know; create new information, ideas, or products; involve themselves in deeper thought or more extensive investigations; show personal growth or sophistication in affective areas; develop new generalizations; develop more complex patterns of thinking; and design and implement their own study programs or projects.

Procedures for Presenting Learning Opportunities

From a synthesis of these recommendations and definitions and from our own research with gifted individuals, several elements can be described as common to most definitions. Differentiated curricula (a) build upon the characteristics unique to gifted students, (b) include concepts at higher levels of abstraction or greater complexity, (c) emphasize the development of varied complex thinking processes and methods of inquiry, and (d) provide administrative or other arrangements necessary to enable gifted students to realize their potential.

Input, processing, and *output* all differ from the regular classroom curriculum in defensible programs for gifted students. These factors also will differ from one program to another and from one individual student to another in the same program. Input is discussed at greater length in Chapter 3, Content; processing is considered in Chapter 4; and output is the topic of Chapter 5, Product. Learning environment modifications, the subject of Chapter 2, are prerequisites for making modifications in content, process, and product. The learning context shapes input, processing, and output. The environment affords certain kinds of learning experiences; when the environment is properly modified, greater opportunities are afforded to its inhabitants. Without needed modifications to the environment, opportunities are restricted and gifted students cannot develop their abilities effectively.

A Comprehensive Approach to Curriculum

In the following pages, we present a comprehensive, organized approach to the development of a qualitatively different curriculum based on curriculum principles recommended for gifted children and on characteristics often attributed to them. Using a broader definition of giftedness, we have selected a simplified set of 12 broad characteristics, suggested by Mary Frasier (Frasier & Passow, 1994), because many of the 36 characteristics listed in the first edition of *Curriculum Development for the Gifted* (Maker, 1982a) were drawn from research conducted at least half a century ago. The context of schooling, as well as of social, political, and economic life, has changed dramatically since that time. The new list of 12 broad characteristics is more flexible and, we believe, more useful to educators planning curriculum for an increasingly diverse population of gifted students.

Table 1.5 is a summary of ideas presented in this section and in subsequent chapters. In addition, the chart is an easy reference for educators, parents, or students who need to justify or explain how a program must be based on the specific characteristics of the gifted individuals involved. This guide can be used for making decisions for curricular modifications for special populations and for individual children in either heterogeneous or homogeneous groups and for planning effective lessons, units, and curricula for the classroom, school, or district. The chart also can be used with students to help them understand themselves better and to make more informed choices about their independent learning experiences.

In Chapters 2, 3, 4, and 5, the principles summarized in Table 1.5 are described in greater depth. After each explanation of a recommended modification, a justification based on the relationship between the curricular principle and the characteristics of gifted children is presented. Specific examples of how the principles of curriculum can be implemented in lessons, units, and K–12 curriculum strands are presented in Chapters 6, 7, and 8.

Table 1.5. A Guide to Selecting Curriculum Modifications Based on a Student's Behaviors

Strength in _____

Characteristics of Gifted Individuals (True)	Content: Abstractness	Content: Complexity	Content: Variety	Content: Organization	Content: Study of People	Content: Study of Methods	Process: Higher-Level Thought	Process: Open-Endedness	Process: Discovery	Process: Evidence/Reasoning	Process: Freedom of Choice	Process: Group Interaction	Process: Pacing	Process: Variety	Product: Real Problems	Product: Real Audiences	Product: Transformations	Product: Variety	Product: Self-Selected Format	Product: Appropriate Evaluation
Humor: Exceptionally keen sense of the comical, bizarre, absurd		X	X			X	X					X					X			X
Motivation: Intense desire to know, do, feel, create, or understand		X			X	X	X		X		X		X		X				X	X
Interests: Ardent, passionate, sometimes unusual, fleeting			X			X			X		X		X		X				X	
Communication/Expressiveness: Extraordinary ability to convey meaning or emotion through words, actions, symbols, sounds, media	X					X				X		X		X		X	X	X		

(continues)

Table 1.5. *Continued*

| | | Principles of Curriculum Modification | | | | | | | | | | | | | | | | | | | |
| | | Content | | | | | | Process | | | | | | | | Product | | | | | |
True	Characteristics of Gifted Individuals	Abstractness	Complexity	Variety	Organization	Study of People	Study of Methods	Higher-Level Thought	Open-Endedness	Discovery	Evidence/Reasoning	Freedom of Choice	Group Interaction	Pacing	Variety	Real Problems	Real Audiences	Transformations	Variety	Self-Selected Format	Appropriate Evaluation
	Inquiry: Probing exploration, observation, or experimentation with events, objects, ideas, feelings, sounds, media	X	X	X			X	X	X	X	X	X		X	X	X				X	
	Problem Solving: Outstanding ability to bring order to chaos through the invention and monitoring of paths to a goal; enjoyment of challenge	X	X		X		X	X	X			X		X	X	X	X	X	X		
	Sensitivity: Unusually open, perceptive, responsive to experiences, feelings, others					X			X				X			X	X			X	X

Trait																				
Intuition: Sudden recognition of connections or deeper meanings without conscious awareness of reasoning or thought	X			X X			X			X X				X						X
Reasoning: Outstanding ability to think things through and consider implications or alternatives; rich, highly conscious, goal-oriented thought	X X	X	X	X		X	X X		X	X X			X	X X			X			X
Imagination/Creativity: Extraordinary capacity for ingenious, flexible use of ideas, processes, materials		X				X X	X X		X				X							X X
Memory/Knowledge/Understanding: Unusual capacity to acquire, integrate, retain, and retrieve information or skills	X X	X	X			X	X	X	X		X		X		X					
Learning: Ability to acquire sophisticated understandings with amazing speed and apparent ease	X	X		X		X X X	X X X		X		X		X				X			X
Number of Xs in column	5	7	5	5	2	7	4	6	7	4	6	3	6	5	5	3	6	3	5	6
Number of Xs highlighted																				

Note. Copyright 1994 by L. S. Kanevsky, C. J. Maker, A. B. Nielson, and J. A. Rogers. Printed with permission.

Chapter 2

Learning Environment

Learning environment modifications are essential if teachers wish to meet the needs of gifted students effectively. A century ago, John Dewey (1956/1900) pointed out that traditional classrooms have no place for children to work:

> If we put before the mind's eye the ordinary schoolroom with its rows of ugly desks placed in geometric order, crowded together so that there shall be as little moving room as possible, desks almost all of the same size, with just space enough to hold books, pencils, and paper, and add a table, some chairs, the bare walls, and possibly a few pictures, we can reconstruct the only educational activity that can possibly go on in such a place. It is all made "for listening"—because simply studying lessons out of a book is only another kind of listening; it marks the dependency of one mind upon another. The attitude of listening means, comparatively speaking, passivity, absorption; that there are certain ready-made materials which are there, which have been prepared by the school superintendent, the board, the teacher, and of which the child is to take in as much as possible in the least possible time.

> (pp. 31–32)

Despite Dewey's biting criticism of traditional classrooms, too many children today spend most of their waking hours in this kind of environment. Little real learning can take place in such a setting. Students cannot *actively* solve problems, do experiments, observe, and construct new knowledge under these conditions. They need materials, tools, and spaces in which they can construct, create, and inquire actively. A class-room might be visualized as a learning laboratory (Tierney, Readence, & Dishner, 1990), a workshop (Resnick, 1987), or a studio (Sutton, 1985) with an emphasis on cooperative, goal-oriented work. The focus of class-rooms for all students must shift toward purposeful activity for all persons. This shift requires several modifications in the learning environment of classrooms and schools.

Changes in learning environment to enhance its effectiveness serve a primarily facilitative function. They enable a teacher to implement the recommended modifications in content, process, and product recom-mended in this volume and the teaching–learning models recommended in our companion book (Maker & Nielson, 1995) more successfully. They also increase students' motivation to learn and their interest in pursuing topics of study and allow students freedom to learn in ways that increase comfort, autonomy, and opportunity. As many of these changes also are important to some degree in programs for all children, the ele-ments of learning environments are conceptualized as continua with opposite extremes. The most appropriate modification for each child is at some place along each continuum. Generally, the modifications are in the same direction (away from the traditional, passive, listening environ-ment) for all classrooms; however, modifications may be more extreme for gifted students. For example, the space in a classroom for gifted students (or activities for gifted students in a heterogeneously grouped classroom) might be modified to include more learning centers; more time would be allocated to individualized activities and less time for whole-class instruction. Students would work more independently in small groups or individually, with the teacher available for aid, guidance, or microteaching as needed.

No one set of modifications can be appropriate for all learners. Gifted students have a wide range of learning preferences, and they differ in their perception of the importance of various environmental elements. For example, some students want sound in their physical environment; others prefer complete quiet. Some students want to work actively with a small group; others prefer privacy. Preferences may change over time or with the nature of learning activities. No general statement can be made about the nature of an effective learning environment for gifted students except that it *must* accommodate a range of choices. All modifica-tions discussed in this chapter are perceived as important because, first, they are preferred by gifted students *as a group*, and, second, they are environmental changes necessary for implementing other curricular modifications.

The following principles for modifications to learning environments for gifted children are recommended:

- *learner centered* rather than teacher or content centered

- *independence* rather than dependence emphasized

- *open* rather than closed to new ideas, innovations, exploration

- *acceptance* rather than judgment exercised

- *complexity* rather than simplicity as a focus

- *variety of grouping options* rather than one grouping as a general organization

- *flexibility* rather than rigid structure or chaotic lack of structure

- *high mobility* rather than low mobility permitted and encouraged

These recommendations pertain both to the physical and psychological environments created for gifted children. Each continuum is discussed in more depth in the sections that follow.

Learner Centered ⟵⟶ Teacher Centered

Classrooms and programs for gifted students must be focused on learners—students and teachers. In a teacher-centered classroom, the focus is on content: the ideas and methods selected by the instructor, who is the final authority when disagreements arise or when decisions must be made. A high proportion of class time is used for the delivery of information, selected by the teacher, through lectures or audiovisual media. Students perceive pressure to produce the right answers or other prescribed evidence of achievement, and the general pattern in discussions involves primarily teacher-to-student-to-teacher interactions.

J. H. Clarke (1990) described a wheel as a metaphor for learning. Experiences precede inductive thinking, or the process of constructing ideas from experience. Ideas, expressed as general statements or broad concepts, are then applied to specific problems through a process of deductive thinking that leads to new experiences. "Inductive thinking involves making meaning, through purposeful scanning of experience, categorization, and theory building. Deductive thinking involves the application of ideas to experience, in prediction, planning, and problem solving" (pp. 3–4). In a learner-centered classroom, these activities continue in an ever-widening spiral. The process is interactive—students, teacher, and learning environment change as a result of converting experience to ideas and ideas to experience.

In learner-centered classrooms, students and teacher(s) form a learning community in which a balance between state-mandated curriculum and students' ideas and interests is achieved. The teacher's major goals are to find out the interests of the students, determine what they already know, and arrange learning experiences that will help them find out both what they need to know and what they want to know. In discussions, students do most of the talking, and the pattern of interaction is mainly learner to learner and learner to teacher. The teacher usually is a more skilled partner (Vygotsky, 1978) who participates in the discussions, responds to students' queries, and asks questions to stimulate higher-level thinking. On occasion, a student with advanced knowledge of a subject or process may be the more skilled partner. Students also feel less pressure to produce teacher-selected ideas or objects for grading purposes.

Teachers cannot teach children to think and they cannot deliver knowledge to students. They can shape experiences (plan activities) that stimulate the construction of ideas and give students opportunities to think about them. They can demonstrate patterns of thinking integrated with the content that students are learning and provide opportunities for students to use varied patterns of thinking to process information gained from experience. Three key indicators of classroom focus are teacher talk, teacher authority, and patterns of interaction.

Teacher Talk

Perhaps the most revealing evidence of a classroom focused on the teacher is a high proportion of class time consumed by teacher talk—lectures, informing or giving directions, asking questions, responding to student answers—or reading texts. The more teachers talk, the more passive the role that students must take. Although active student participation is possible in a classroom in which a teacher does much talking, the chances of students' thinking reflectively, maintaining their interest in the topic, and working productively are decreased. In a learner-centered environment, teacher talk (text reading) is deemphasized whereas active student thinking is encouraged and supported.

Most of the process modifications recommended in this volume are facilitated most easily in classrooms in which students talk more than does the teacher. Open-endedness, discovery, group interaction, and freedom of choice cannot be incorporated to a significant degree in classrooms dominated by teacher talk. Also, the teacher cannot provide appropriate pacing without attending to students' ability to acquire content or strategic information; feedback from students is essential for this modification. Variety in information acquisition, processing, and management can happen only when teachers limit the amount of classroom time used for lectures, textbook reading, or other informing methods.

Teacher Authority

One of the difficulties involved in creating a learner-centered environment is convincing students (and parents) that the instructor is not and should not be the final authority in answering questions or providing information. Gifted students often become frustrated when a teacher does not tell them whether an answer or hypothesis is right or wrong. Even when students have found several authoritative sources of information to support their hypotheses, many of them still want the teacher to affirm that they are correct. Teaching students to have confidence in their own ability to select and use criteria to judge the validity and relevance of references is a slow process. Perhaps one cause for this lack of confidence is students' prior experiences in which they were taught to accept an adult's word as the final authority. Also, children often are taught that it is wrong to doubt or question those in authority.

Even though implementing this change is difficult, movement away from the teacher as authority, especially in the realm of ideas, is an important step toward developing a learning community. When the teacher demonstrates that learning is an ongoing process and discusses the metacognitive ability of the mind to monitor thinking activities and to control or direct mental processes to achieve goals (Presseisen, 1985), gifted students build confidence in their own ability to formulate ideas and check their validity. All learners have innate abilities to learn to manage thinking processes and subject matter but will not focus these abilities unless they are encouraged to do so. An approach that helps students develop their abilities to judge ideas through the use of appropriate methods, such as logical coherence, support through research, comprehensiveness, generalizability, replicability, and other scientific procedures, also will engender other important objectives besides changing the focus of authority in the classroom. Teachers can demonstrate methods of judging and using criteria appropriate to the context that are generalizable to other situations; that allow another member of the learning community, including the teacher, to challenge conclusions to make sure appropriate support is provided; and that improve learners' ability to challenge each other's ideas without hurting the feelings of the person. In other words, this approach moves the focus of judgment from the realm of people and to the realm of ideas and logic.

Changes in content, process, and product all are facilitated by a focus away from the teacher as final authority. To enable students to deal with abstract, complex ideas, teachers must encourage learners to seek out their own sources, provide their own examples, and trust their own judgment. An emphasis on higher levels of thinking also requires that students evaluate their own ideas. Open-endedness, discovery approaches, freedom of choice, and group-interaction activities are more successful if the teacher is considered a more skilled partner in the community rather than the final authority. Implementing all the product changes, especially appropriate evaluation, necessitates feedback from several sources, including an appropriate audience, peers, self, and teachers.

Patterns of Interaction

In a learner-centered classroom in which the focus is on members' ideas, interests, and needs, the interaction pattern will reflect greater student involvement and less teacher direction. This pattern is most notable in discussions. One way to represent the differences in interaction is to show graphically how the patterns of communication occur. In a teacher-centered pattern (Figure 2.1), the obvious focus in the discussion is the teacher, who is the center of attention and through whom all comments to other students are directed. No comments go directly from one student to another. In a learner-centered interaction, the teacher is not the center of attention and intervenes only to offer a comment, to redirect or refocus the discussion, or to seek clarification or extension of students' ideas. Many learner comments are directed toward other students, without being controlled by the teacher.

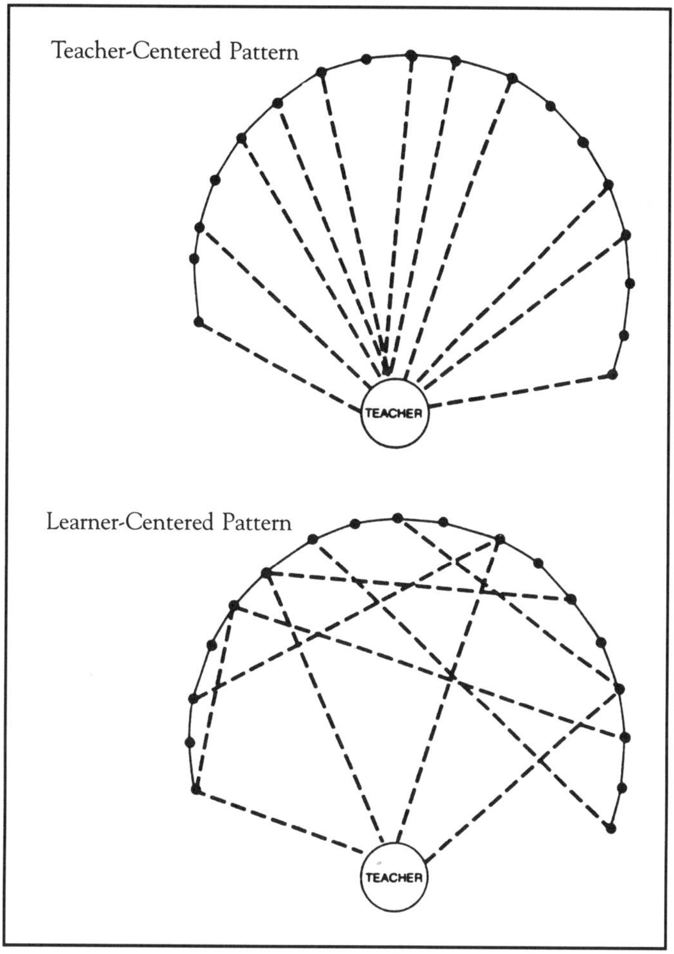

Figure 2.1. Learner-centered and teacher-centered interaction patterns.

Another way of representing patterns of interaction is an observation coding form. One format, developed by Hilda Taba (Institute for Staff Development, 1971a), is shown in Figure 2.2. The observer notes teacher behaviors in the top row and student behaviors in the bottom row. In a simple analysis, only three codes are used: A when someone asks a question, T when someone tells, and SS when students respond to student ideas. The observer can be an outsider watching classroom interaction, the teacher watching a videotape or listening to an audiotape, or a

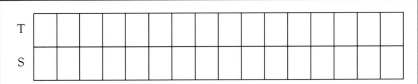

A. Coding System   T = Teacher Behavior, S = Student Behavior, A = Asks, T = Tells, SS = Student Reaction to Student Idea

T	A	T	A	T	A	T	A	T	A	T	A	T	A	T	A	T
S		T		T		T		T		T		T		T		T

B. Teacher-Centered Interaction Pattern

T		A	A						A							A
S	A			T	T	T	T	T	T	T	T	SS	SS	SS	SS	SS	T

C. Learner-Centered Interaction Pattern

Example B
TA = 8
TT = 8
ST = 8
SS = 0
Teacher = 16
Student = 8

Example C
TA = 4
TT = 1
ST = 8
SS = 6
Teacher = 5
Student = 14

D. Analysis of Interaction patterns

Figure 2.2. Coding of classroom interaction patterns.

Note. Adapted from *Hilda Taba Teaching Strategies Program* 1971, Institute for Staff Development. Adapted with permission.

designated student. In the first example (B), the interaction pattern is teacher centered. The teacher asks a question to which one student responds; the teacher comments on the response and asks another question, and another student replies. The pattern continues with no variations. The second example (C) shows a more learner-centered interaction pattern. The teacher opens the discussion with a question, a student responds by asking for clarification, the teacher clarifies and restates the question, and then several students respond. Somewhat later, the teacher intervenes with a question that calls attention to differences in student ideas. This comment results in a long series of student reactions to each other's ideas. To compare the interaction patterns quantitatively (D), the totals are calculated for teacher behaviors and student behaviors. A ratio of student behaviors to teacher behaviors then is calculated. In these examples, the differences are very apparent. In the teacher-centered interaction pattern, the ratio of teacher behaviors to student behaviors is 2:1; in the learner-centered pattern, the ratio is 5:14 (almost 1:3).

To achieve a more learner-centered interaction pattern, teachers can take several basic actions. The first, and perhaps most important, is to ask open-ended questions. The teacher must encourage a variety of responses to each question by asking questions to which many, varied responses can be given (e.g., "In what ways might the problem be solved?"), by avoiding a response to each student answer (e.g., "good," "right," or even noncommittal responses such as "OK"), and by waiting for other students to respond. When a teacher avoids making a comment on student responses, the students will divert their focus from seeking teacher approval (or disapproval) and gradually will stop expecting judgment from the teacher. Because the teacher is waiting, students are encouraged to offer their answers. Another useful tactic is to ask one student to respond specifically to ideas expressed by other classmates (e.g., "Jane, it seems to me that what you are saying about economic discrimination is similar to Susan's earlier comment about political discrimination. How do you see these ideas as similar or different?"). When the teacher participates as a member of a learning community, he or she can model the kinds of questions or comments that stimulate thoughtful responses.

Characteristics of Gifted Students

Development of a learner-centered classroom (program) is most appropriate when educators consider that learners are essentially serving an apprenticeship in thinking (Rogoff, 1990). Because gifted students often have a broad range of knowledge in their area or areas of interest, the teacher must be viewed as a more skilled partner who can design activities or shape learning experiences that facilitate students' thinking and construction of knowledge. A learner-centered environment allows gifted students to use their abilities effectively; facilitates creative thinking, reasoning, and problem solving; and provides opportunities for students to develop their interests and abilities.

Some gifted students have outstanding abilities in reasoning and can consider implications or alternatives of ideas; others may suddenly recognize connections or deeper meanings without being able to explain how they arrived at the intuitive response. Still other gifted students can ask probing questions or communicate meaning very well. In a learning community, each student offers ideas and explanations in a nonthreatening atmosphere. When the focus is on learning, students can discover and pursue their interests, discuss ideas without being overly concerned about being right, and probe more deeply into abstract, complex concepts, generalizations, and theories than they could do alone. Differing student perspectives are complementary and, through sharing, students enrich their own and others' learning.

Contrary to "conventional wisdom," Christensen (1994) found that gifted students strongly prefer collaborative learning experiences in noncompetitive settings. Another finding in her study of 358 gifted students in grades 2 through 6 is that they prefer evaluative feedback, whether positive or negative, to be given privately. The learner-centered environment is structured to allow more collaborative learning and decreased emphasis on individual competition for teacher approval. S. Sharan and Shacar (1988), like Chickering (1969), found that students who work in more open, collaborative settings are more able to solve problems, improve their communication abilities and group membership skills, and show greater motivation and respect for others than do students who are taught in teacher-centered classes. Although Chickering found that teacher-centered classrooms are more effective for teaching specific facts, few gifted students have difficulty in acquiring, integrating, retaining, and retrieving information. The goals of programs for gifted students are to go beyond memory, knowledge, and understanding of facts. Therefore, learner-centered classrooms and programs are preferred for and by gifted students.

Independence ⟵⟶ Dependence

Developing independence is an essential factor in the education of gifted students. Among the process modifications, we stress the importance of freedom of choice and open-endedness. These changes, along with establishment of a learner-centered environment, encourage students to be more independent. A separation of these factors from the elements of a learner-centered classroom is impossible. The learner-centered environment is a necessary prior condition for the encouragement of independence. Most of these recommended modifications are subtle, unstructured strategies that are reflected in teacher attitudes and behaviors.

The basic definition of this dimension is the degree of tolerance for and encouragement of student initiative. Tolerance and encouragement are reflected in many ways in the classroom, including academic factors such as student choice of what to learn, how to learn, and how to evaluate that learning, and in the nonacademic elements of classroom management, social interaction in classroom and school communities, joint construction of classroom rules or regulations (e.g., deadlines for completing assignments, routine chores, procedures for resolving conflicts), and planning of class activities. Because academic aspects are discussed in other chapters, we focus in this section on nonacademic elements and on having students learn ways to prevent or solve their own problems rather than having the teacher or another adult impose solutions.

For example, in one first-grade class for gifted students, the teacher assigns student aides to particular tasks for a week at a time. The class secretary manages the "opening" activities (e.g., pledge of allegiance, opening song, announcements, attendance, lunch count), the messenger delivers information (such as lunch count, etc.) to the office or other school settings, two paper passers take care of distributing materials, and five students are responsible for cleanup at the end of the day. The teacher begins the process by selecting nine students at the beginning of the year and meets individually with them during registration day to teach and model their responsibilities. At the end of the first week during a class meeting, each of the nine students selects his or her replacement for the following week, and then each teaches or models his or her responsibilities to the successor. The regulation is that replacements are chosen from among those students who have not yet had an opportunity to do the job. Students typically serve as class secretary and class messenger only once during the year, paper passers twice or three times, and on a cleanup committee about once every 6 weeks. During the first week, students establish regulations for governing their community. Typically, the rules are few and emphasize courtesy and respect for others.

In almost every class, some students have difficulties getting along with others and may argue or fight. Sometimes most of the class may begin talking at once, with everyone interrupting everyone else. In each of these cases, most teachers intervene, stop the activity, and impose some punishment on the offending students. Some sort of stop action definitely is needed in situations like this. However, if the teacher's goal is to develop student independence rather than dependence, intervention should be aimed toward eliciting a solution for inappropriate behaviors rather than toward imposing penalties. In the right setting, students can propose at least as many solutions to their own problems as can a teacher. Solutions generated by gifted students usually are more effective because the students have bought in to the solution and are more committed to making their ideas work.

Creative problem solving or conflict resolution in a group setting is an excellent means of developing ways to solve social interaction or behavior problems. Issues can be proposed before problems arise, and students can develop possible solutions. Real, immediate solutions can be presented after problems occur. The first author once observed a classroom of 17 gifted students who were reporting on their analysis of artifacts they had collected in a simulation of an archaeological dig. Two teams had analyzed each other's artifacts and developed hypotheses about the other team's culture. All students were eager to present their ideas, and team leaders could no longer control their groups. The teacher almost panicked because she could not reduce the noise level—to even a mild roar. After attempting to control the group, the teacher stopped the action, said they seemed to have a problem, and asked the students if they agreed. They all did. The teacher then asked what they saw as subproblems or contributing factors. In a brainstorming session, they listed several issues, then a variety of solutions to each of them. Next, student volunteers were given the task of developing a plan of action. The original activity was deferred until the following day when the plan could be implemented. The next day, students managed their own discussion and imposed strict penalties on their own group members who broke rules. The teacher reported that her sanity was saved and volunteered that future management problems definitely would be handed over to the class.

Another way of handling classroom management problems is to establish student government through a system in which students develop their own laws or rules and methods of enforcement. Student courts, for example, have proved to be very effective in many schools. The system can include elected officers, appointed committees, and such other roles as the group chooses. Functions of officers and committee members can include management of classroom routines, conflict resolution and problem solving, and activity planning. In the first grade described in this section, students also participated in curriculum planning during the second semester (e.g., making decisions about extending or curtailing a unit of study, special projects). If students are responsible for the planning and coordinating of class activities such as field trips, parties, guest speakers, service projects, and the like, at least two positive outcomes occur: (a) Students learn valuable planning and decision-making skills, and (b) the teacher gains time from having to handle fewer routine details and can use that time more productively. Obviously, much teacher time is needed when students are first learning how to make decisions, solve problems, and plan activities; as these skills are developed, learners can take over a great deal of responsibility.

A dramatic change also takes place in the teacher's role in the classroom. As students become more adept at working together in small or large groups, the teacher really does become a facilitator of learning rather than a delivery system for information and an enforcement officer responsible for controlling student behavior.

One teacher behavior needs to be stressed at this point. When independence in thought and action is the objective, teachers must be prepared to answer questions about their own actions without being defensive. This means the teacher must be prepared to explain the reasoning that led to certain actions and to provide justification for school rules. Teachers also must avoid authoritarian pronouncements or responding to Why questions with statements such as "Because I said so." Teachers must respect students' rights to have honest, reasoned, calm responses to questions that puzzle or frustrate them. Teachers also must be prepared to say "I don't know" when asked a question to which they have no answer. Then teachers might stress the interdependence of learners by asking who else has an answer or ask "What are some ways we could find the answer to your question?"

Certain physical aspects of the classroom also contribute to the development of student independence. Materials for use by students should be readily accessible in centers, on shelves or in drawers that students can reach. Furniture should be arranged so that students can move about the classroom, as necessary, without disturbing others. Finally, unobtrusive routines for going to the rest room, getting a drink, and going to the library or to other learning areas outside the classroom should be established. In another first-grade class, the teacher placed a rest room pass in the chalkboard tray not far from the door. When a student needed to leave, he or she picked up the pass and wrote his or her name on the board. Upon return, the pass was returned to the tray and the name erased. In many hours of observing this classroom over a period of several months, the second author did not see any student who abused the procedure. Of course, the teacher and students had established the rules in advance of the need.

One final point must be made. Although we have alluded to the necessity of teachers' using much time and energy in working with students to establish the self-management skills necessary for independence to occur, this is an essential part of developing autonomous learners. Teachers must remember that the most effective learning takes place when students are doing activities that involve the use (and practice) of decision making, planning, problem solving, and self-management. When students plan an activity, the teacher must let them follow the plan even when he or she knows it has flaws. (A teacher will, of course, suggest alternative actions if any part of a plan is physically or psychologically dangerous to the students or if a part of a plan violates school or community regulations.) Some of the most memorable learning occurs as a result of analysis and evaluation of factors that might have caused the success or failure of their plans. Evaluation, individually or as a class, is an integral part of learning effective self-management.

A phenomenon labeled "learned helplessness" has been used in psychological research to describe a feeling that people are powerless to solve the problems they face (H. Clarke, MacPherson, & Holmes, 1982; Wheaton, 1980). When students learn that teachers or other adults control all aspects of classroom interaction, they feel helpless; they either act out or become increasingly passive and withdrawn. In effect, they come to believe they have no positive means of control over their own lives in school. Conversely, successful problem solving boosts students' self-concept, adds to their feeling of personal power, and expands "the size of the universe in which [they] see themselves as exerting some control" (J. H. Clarke, 1990, p. 235). Thus, for both cognitive and psychological reasons, teachers need to establish a learning environment in which students actively participate in the management of classroom activities and become increasingly independent.

Characteristics of Gifted Students

Gifted students generally want to be independent and exercise some control over their own learning. When an individual has an intense desire to learn, he or she has little patience with interruptions to the learning process. In the midst of a fascinating inquiry, gifted students want to pursue their work in their own way without numerous directions or instructions from the teacher. This principle is true unless a child has been schooled to rely on adult guidance and seek only right answers. Some teachers and parents place an inordinate amount of stress on right answers and grades as measures of learning. Gifted students who have become dependent on external guidance and evaluation need to be reassured that the processes of learning, problem solving, and self-evaluation are more significant educational outcomes than are test scores or grades.

The ability of many gifted students to acquire sophisticated understanding of content with amazing speed and apparent ease and their unusual capacity to acquire, integrate, retain, and retrieve information or skills in their areas of interest justify less emphasis on whole-class instruction and greater emphasis on independent learning experiences. A classroom set up with learning centers, small-group work areas, and individual carrels allows learners the opportunity to explore content materials in a center to whatever depth they wish. Independence is promoted in this kind of environment because students can proceed at their own pace, work in areas of intense interest, and explore objects, ideas, feelings, sounds, symbols, or other materials in preferred intelligence domains. Students can enhance their perceptiveness to their own experiences and their sensitivity to the experiences of others when they are not in competition with each other or doing exactly the same tasks. In a workshop, laboratory, or studio setting, learners can collaborate to achieve bona fide goals through their own talents and efforts added to the talents and efforts of others. The intense desire to know, do, feel, create, and understand is enriched by social interaction and collaborative problem solving. S. Sharan and Schacar (1988) found that collaborative activities stimulate the growth of self-concept, appreciation of others, and independence. When traditional, whole-class instruction was emphasized, how-ever, these desirable results were not found.

Open ←——————→ Closed

In a learning environment, this dimension is closely related to the teacher's development of open-endedness in methods and learning activ-ities, but it is essential also in nonacademic areas. Elements of open-endedness stressed in Chapter 4 on process include encouragement of and tolerance for many ideas, many solutions to problems, many answers to questions, and many, provocative learning experiences that lead to further study. In a learning environment, the basic differentiation be-tween open and closed is the extent to which conditions—physical, psychological, or regulatory—enhance or restrict the learning oppor-tunities of students.

When a physical learning environment is open, new ideas, new people, new materials, and new things are allowed to enter. The environ-ment is not static but can be changed when desirable or necessary. In the psychological aspects of the learning environment, an open climate per-mits new ideas, exploratory discussions, and the freedom to change direc-tions or procedures to deal with different or changing possibilities. In other words, when unexpected or unpredicted factors arise, the plan can be changed. Not only are different student ideas encouraged or permit-ted, but also different behavior. Not all students are expected to conform to the same standards of classroom behavior, meet the same instructional requirements, or complete the same assignments.

The dimension of open versus closed is closely related to indepen-dence versus dependence in that openness is necessary for creating an atmosphere in which students can become independent or autonomous learners (Betts, 1985). This dimension is also related to the dimension of learner-centered versus teacher-centered because openness to student ideas and interests is necessary before a practitioner can focus on them in the development of learning activities. Open versus closed, as a dimen-sion of classroom climate, differs from the two other dimensions in its focus on divergence. Instead of simply accepting differences in learners, the teacher of gifted students should encourage them to be different and to avoid conformity. The focus on divergence also should extend to the teacher. Students (and parents) need to recognize and value different styles of teaching rather than placing unnecessary or unrealistic restrictions on teachers.

An open environment can facilitate the success of product and process modifications that are essential to a program for gifted students. If students are expected to transform data acquired as a result of investigating real problems, to develop original products, or to direct the products toward real audiences, they need to operate with a minimum of environmental restrictions. To provide variety in process modifications, teachers must be able (and willing) to try out a variety of teaching styles and to accommodate a variety of learning styles. New ideas, new people, and new materials must be welcomed. To afford students freedom of choice, to encourage higher levels of thinking, and to facilitate group interaction, the teacher must encourage as much divergence as possible in all aspects of the learning environment.

Characteristics of Gifted Students

Gifted students differ greatly in their interests, abilities, and motivation. They also differ in their strengths in various intelligences and in their preferences for modes of learning. In an open classroom environment, divergence and diversity are valued and accommodated. A student with a bizarre sense of humor is accepted as readily as a student whose reasoning ability is extraordinarily rich. Both students need a climate in which they can safely offer way-out ideas and clever answers to questions or scorn conformity to politically correct thinking. A teacher who is unusually open, perceptive, or responsive to students is needed for those young people who respond to a question with a sudden intuition that may seem unconnected to the subject of discussion until probing reveals the subconscious reasoning that led to the intuitive response. Students who are imaginative or creative and who like to use ideas, materials, and processes to create unique products need an open climate in which teachers and other students value diversity and tolerate ambiguity. Teachers need to remain open to possible changes in direction among gifted students when passionate interests change, for no apparent reason, and are replaced by equally passionate interest in something else. Closure seldom is as necessary to gifted students as it is to their teachers or parents (Clark, 1992). The open learning environment is designed to encourage exploration, risk taking, motivation, and creativity. In an environment that affords

divergent experiences, students gifted in diverse areas can find and exploit the opportunities for optimum development and growth.

Acceptance ←——————→ Judgment

As with other dimensions of classroom climate, the accepting–judging
dimension cannot be separated entirely from the open–closed dimension.
Openness implies acceptance; closed indicates nonacceptance. Perhaps
the best distinction, however, is in the sense that acceptance implies the
absence of judgment. In other words, the acceptance–judgment dimension
is characterized more by the avoidance of value judgments than by the
absence of restrictions and the encouragement of divergence. Although
encouragement of divergence implies avoidance of value judgments, the
environmental emphasis is somewhat different. Three elements are important in the description of the accepting–judging dimension of classroom
climate: attempting to understand, timing, and evaluation rather than
judgment. These elements each reflect a somewhat different emphasis, and
each is important in different contexts.

Attempting to Understand

Adults often jump to conclusions about an idea or a method before
obtaining all the facts or listening to different points of view. This tendency to make judgments takes the focus away from the effortful process
of trying to understand a different point of view. This tendency often
occurs with greater frequency when adults are dealing with children.
Adults tend to believe that because of their wider range of experience
and greater depth of knowledge, their perspective is better or more valid
than a child's. Gifted students, perhaps because of their confidence in
their own ideas, are unlikely to listen to a teacher's perspective if they do
not believe the teacher has made an honest attempt to understand their
point of view.

   This element of attempting to understand is closely related to Jung's
(1923) concept of the continuum of judging versus perceiving as a dimension of every individual's personality. Characteristics of the two personality types were described by Keirsey and Bates (1978, pp. 25–26) as
follows:

Perceiving	Judging
Open options	Closure
Gather more data	Make decisions
Tentative	Decisive
Flexible	Fixed
Adapt as you go	Plan ahead
Let's wait and see	Get the job done
There's plenty of time	Hurry
What deadline?	Beat the deadline!
Something will turn up	Make it happen
Let life happen	Control all aspects of life

A perceiving person prefers to keep options open and fluid, whereas a judging person feels a sense of urgency until a decision has been made. The judging person feels more comfortable after a decision has been made; the perceiving person may resist making a decision because of a need to collect more data and may feel uneasy, rather than comfortable, after a decision has been made.

In a teaching situation, persons with judging personalities should take care in their interactions with children because of their tendency to live by defined standards and beliefs, which is not changed easily (Lawrence, 1979), and because of their desire to be right. These tendencies contribute to teachers' use of their own standards and values to judge student ideas; teachers must attempt to understand another's point of view and to avoid passing judgment on it. Students need to feel that a teacher is making a genuine attempt to understand their feelings, their values, and their beliefs. To convince students that this attempt is genuine, teachers must listen actively to what students are saying. Active listening is, first, nonverbal; the teacher, by physical actions, displays an interest in the student's ideas and demonstrates that those ideas have worth and significance. Nonverbal behaviors include (a) facial expressions, such as smiling; (b) eye contact; (c) spatial distance, such as moving toward or nearer the speaker; (d) body positioning, such as inclining the head; (e) tone of voice; (f) rate of speech; and (g) movements, such as head nodding and gestures. Other behaviors also may indicate interest nonverbally, but those listed are typical of the actions people take unconsciously when they are interested and listening.

After attending to the student's ideas, an actively listening teacher indicates acceptance, implying that the ideas are worthwhile, significant, relevant, pertinent, or sincere. Neither agreement nor disagreement is suggested by this acceptance. To accept an idea is to grant it importance and to recognize its worth for purposes of examining, elaborating, perhaps clarifying, and ultimately challenging.

Expressions of acceptance, unfortunately, can become rote, distracting mannerisms. A teacher must be conscious of this tendency and consciously vary ways of accepting student responses. The following verbal responses are some examples of the almost infinite number of ways of responding to a student in an accepting manner:

Yes, I can understand that.

That seems reasonable to me.

I see what you mean.

I think I see the idea you are getting at.

You are developing some interesting ideas.

That makes a lot of sense.

That's an interesting difference you noticed.

This might work.

I hadn't thought about that before.

Expressions that easily become mannerisms when used too often include the following responses:

Yes.

I see.

OK.

Good.

Fine.

Right.

In addition to acceptance and encouragement, teachers also can request that a student explain, elaborate, and clarify ideas. Not all student ideas require such requests, so the teacher must exercise judgment about the need for additional explanation. Some gifted children, who may give their ideas in abstract or ambiguous terms, need practice in providing concrete examples and offering explanations for them. In this clarification process the speaker restates the ideas in some manner that is acceptable to the speaker and clearer to the listener. Another method, which encourages more student discussion, stimulates critical thinking, and sounds less condescending, is the use of statements such as "Let's explore this idea," "Let's discuss this further," "Let's develop your idea a little more." Two subcategories of questions or invitations that might follow such statements are those that require clarification or elaboration and those that ask for an extension of the idea:

Clarification/Elaboration

Please tell us more about the idea.

What is an example of what you are talking about?

Please explain that in a different way.

When you say ⎯⎯⎯⎯⎯, what do you mean?

Please give us more details.

I'm having trouble understanding. Please tell me more.

Extension

What is an example of that idea in a different area?

What do you think might have been some results of that?

What would be some good and bad points about this?

What kinds of facts can be used to support your idea?

How could you use this (information, strategy) in another context?

Clarification/elaboration and extension behaviors should come after the teacher has displayed attending behaviors and after he or she clearly has accepted a student's idea. Teachers should take care that questions or requests do not have critical overtones. A smile followed by "Yes, that might work; give us some more details" is far less threatening than simply saying "Give us some more details." The difference may seem inconsequential, but our experience has indicated that it is not. Teachers also must remember that tone of voice and nonverbal cues must be appropriate and congruent with the verbal statements. An accepting statement said in a sarcastic tone of voice while the teacher looks at something else does not build a feeling of acceptance among students.

Whereas attending, accepting, and encouraging behaviors are designed to increase the student's *quantity* of expression, the questions and statements of clarification and extension are meant to increase the *quality*. Transitions in student expressiveness take place more readily when the learning environment provides an atmosphere of acceptance and encouragement.

Timing

The element of timing in the acceptance–judgment dimension of classroom climate is related simply to when evaluations are made. In the previous section, we noted that teachers may go through a series of behaviors in an attempt to understand a student's ideas more clearly. These behaviors include attending, accepting, clarifying, and extending. These behaviors are designed to help a teacher and other students understand a student's ideas clearly before the merits of the ideas are considered. When ideas are accepted, stated clearly, and understood, the teacher or another student can pose challenging questions or ask the originator to cite evidence or reasoning to support the ideas.

Too often teachers, in an attempt to urge students to "really think," begin to ask challenging and probing questions that may force a student into a defensive position. Challenging or probing questions can be effective *when* an appropriate student–teacher rapport has been established. This rapport must include respect on the part of both teachers and students. In one sense, the behaviors discussed in the previous section are designed to create this feeling of respect so that open, rigorous debate can take place. When respect has been established, the discussion can proceed to debate through the use of challenging questions such as the following:

What reasoning led you to that conclusion?

How did you reach that conclusion?

What are some facts that support your idea?

What led you to believe that _____?

Why?

Why do you believe that _____?

What are some of your reasons for saying that _____?

Challenging questions help students and teachers better understand the ideas and allow the originator to reorganize, restate, qualify, and possibly rethink her or his response. Properly worded, questions of challenge should not force a student to be defensive. Instead, the originator may begin to qualify the generalization or statement, indicating which parts can be supported and identifying other parts that may be guesses or hypotheses.

Another aspect of timing is relative to certain stages of problem solving and decision making. When the purpose of an activity or stage is to generate a quantity of ideas or possible solutions to problems, evaluation of any kind is completely inappropriate. For example, in the process of brainstorming or productive thinking, the most important principle to enforce is deferred judgment. Some of the most creative, original ideas can be inhibited by evaluation and, thus, will not be available for consideration during later steps in the process if a person cannot avoid the natural tendency to judge an idea as good or bad before saying or writing it. Research (e.g., Parnes, 1975) showed that (1) individuals instructed to defer judgment during idea production tend to produce more unique and useful ideas than those allowed to judge at that time; (2) individuals taught to use deferred judgment produce more unique and useful ideas under deferred-judgment instructions than do people who have not been taught this strategy; and (3) groups using this principle also produce more and better ideas when taught to defer judgment.

In creative problem solving, judgment is not eliminated—it is deferred until a more appropriate time. After the group has produced a quantity of ideas, they then review and evaluate the ideas to select the most promising or most important. Groups also develop and apply appropriate criteria for evaluation rather than simply imposing an initial judgment that may be emotional or based on past experience rather than on open-minded consideration of possible alternatives.

Evaluation Rather than Judgment

Judgment implies rightness or wrongness and goodness or badness as global concepts. When they judge an idea, individuals tend to consider it as entirely good or entirely bad, entirely right or entirely wrong—in terms of black and white rather than of varying shades of gray. Evaluation, on the other hand, implies the consideration of multiple factors including both good and bad (right and wrong) aspects of an idea. In evaluation, criticism also is constructive rather than destructive. Both the manner of speaking and the timing of the critique are important in this context. For example, a teacher says, "Your description of the operation of the state penal system is accurate in that you have said _____. However, that description could be improved if you also included _____." The statement considers both accurate and inaccurate aspects of the idea, but the focus of the critique is on how the description can be improved rather than on how or why it is wrong or bad.

When evaluating students' products, the teacher's focus always should be on both the positive aspects and the possible ways to improve the product. If only the positive aspects are considered, students cannot grow (and may not believe in the value of the critique), but if the positive is not emphasized, the critique will not be constructive. In simple language, the purpose of evaluation is to say, "You have done _____ well in that you _____; you need to improve (add, change) _____ to make your product better." Students also need to practice the same kind of evaluation of other people's ideas. The teacher can be both model and instructor in these situations. "The trick is to place the criticism within a context of positive reinforcements. . . . Begin with two positive reinforcements. . . . (2) insert your criticism. . . . (3) Add one more positive reinforcement. . . . (4) Finish with a ray of hope" (Koberg & Bagnall, 1976, p. 117). For example, a teacher might say, "You have created a powerful image of hope in your poem. The metaphors you used really help me understand your ideas. In a few of the lines, the rhythm is unwieldy. You have an excellent vocabulary. If you work on the lines I've indicated, I believe you will have a truly powerful poem."

Facilitation of Success

The learning environment modification of acceptance versus judgment is necessary for the success of the recommended content, process, and product modifications for gifted students. Abstract, complex ideas cannot be developed without this environment modification. The development of higher-level thinking processes and open-endedness are dependent on an atmosphere in which ideas are accepted rather than judged. Discovery and inquiry processes also necessitate a teacher's willingness to accept and allow learners' trials, successes, and mistakes so they will reach their conclusions and discover their own principles. The series of teacher behaviors from attending and accepting through clarifying and extending are necessary prerequisites to the requirement that students offer evidence of reasoning to support their ideas. Questions of challenge are nonthreatening only if they are preceded by teacher behaviors that indicate acceptance, understanding, and recognition of the worth of the idea.

To be successful, the product modification of appropriate evaluation also requires a climate of acceptance. Emphasis on evaluation and constructive criticism rather than on judgment is necessary to help students develop skills in assessing their own products and in evaluating the products of others. The teacher's own behavior in modeling appropriate methods of evaluation is especially important. In a first grade of gifted students observed by the second author, the teacher used a sentence from an anonymous student's writing as the topic of a daily direct oral language (DOL) activity. The teacher modeled the behavior of saying one thing that the student did well. The students then offered their observations of what the author did well. The next part of the activity began with a question, "In what ways can this sentence be improved?" Students could comment on misspelled words, suggest a more effective word for a trite word, indicate needed punctuation or capitalization, and so on. After these comments, the teacher again complimented the writer and the work of students who had suggested improvements. In another first grade classroom, a similar procedure was followed, but the student who led the activity could choose a sentence of his or her own for evaluation by peers. In both classrooms, the writers felt that the procedure was a positive way to improve both expressiveness and accuracy in their writing.

Characteristics of Gifted Students

Few gifted children are comfortable in situations in which they constantly are judged, yet they also are dissatisfied with high grades and no evaluation. "My teacher gave me an A on this assignment, but I want to know how to make it better" is a statement we have heard often from some of the most gifted students we know. Enhancing the strengths and minimizing the difficulties of gifted students require that teachers develop classroom climates in which all ideas, regardless of how bizarre, unique, clever, or ordinary they may be, are accepted as having value. Teachers do not want to destroy creativity, imagination, or humor by requiring too much evaluation, too early judgment, or too little recognition of the worth of these qualities among gifted students. Teachers must be able and willing to recognize when students are not ready for their ideas or products to be evaluated or challenged; they also must provide an atmosphere in which all students accept the importance of timing in the evaluation process.

Sometimes, gifted students, in their intense desire to understand, may make comments or ask questions that another student is not ready to answer. Their comments or questions may be interpreted as harrassment. These students need to learn the behaviors of attempting to understand, timing, and evaluation so that they can offer constructive criticism to peers and others. Gifted students also can learn to ask challenging questions of adults in nonthreatening ways so that they can question bald statements or authoritarian pronouncements without being perceived as "smart aleck kids." Those gifted students who are unusually open, perceptive, and responsive to others can assist teachers in their effort to develop a climate of acceptance. Other gifted students who have outstanding ability to think things through and to consider implications or alternatives in a situation have qualities that also contribute to effective evaluation in an accepting climate. Those gifted students who have a tendency to make snap judgments with insufficient knowledge or evidence need to have that tendency channeled in such a way that judgments are constructive and timed appropriately. Because gifted students are susceptible to reasoning, presentation of alternative views, modeling, and consistency of expressed values (Hollingworth, 1926), they can be guided to develop acceptance of others' ideas and the behaviors that establish acceptance rather than judgment in the learning environment. Through discussion of this dimension, gifted students also can transfer this attitude and its accompanying behaviors to situations outside the classroom.

Complexity ⟵⟶ Simplicity

Complexity versus simplicity as a dimension of classroom environment includes both the degree of complexity present in the physical environment and the kind of tasks students are asked to perform. Clearly, gifted students should be expected to carry out complex intellectual tasks. They should have learning activities that require higher levels of thinking; they should be expected to consider abstract, complex ideas; and they should transform rather than summarize information acquired from the ideas of others. Interactions, both intellectual and social, also should be complex.

Gifted students need a complex physical environment that includes a balance of hard and soft elements; a variety of materials, textures, and colors; and many types of spaces or microenvironments for learning. A wide variety of informational media is necessary so that gifted students can find data in their areas of interest and in their varying zones of proximal development (Vygotsky, 1978). Reference books of many kinds, videotapes, audiotapes, slides, filmstrips, and other audiovisual media should be readily available in addition to trade books on a variety of subjects. Microcomputers linked to national databases allow students to search for up-to-date and hard-to-find data they need for their own research. Manipulative materials and other tools of learning in each intelligence also should be accessible. Some representative materials, categorized by intelligence, are provided in Table 2.1.

Wall and bulletin-board displays should feature complex, asymmetrical drawings or constructions, examples of student products, and charts highlighting learning strategies such as evaluation criteria and steps in thinking processes. Finally, classrooms for gifted students should include a wide variety of materials of all kinds for use in creative projects. One way to supply this need is to establish "a big box of junk" or other system to store inexpensive, or throwaway, materials (e.g., pieces of wood, fabrics, small hardware items, plastic containers, poster paints, glue, styrofoam, felt) and tools needed for constructions.

Characteristics of Gifted Students

Creatively gifted students often have extraordinary abilities to use ideas, processes, and materials to make ingenious products. During a visit to the Hirshorn Gallery of the Smithsonian Museum in Washington, D. C., the second author saw two impressive wall murals that were created entirely from colored, plastic pieces recycled from detergent and fabric softener bottles. In a first-grade class, gifted students used plastic six-pack holders, turkey skewers, and spray paint to create flowers as gifts for residents of a nearby nursing home. The flowers turned out so well that the project was extended to an effective study of economics in which students produced flowers in many colors, calculated the cost of making one, set a price, and advertised them for sale to schoolmates and other interested persons.

Table 2.1. Representative Materials and Tools for Gifted Students

Intelligence	Representative Materials and Tools
Linguistic	A variety of dictionaries; thesaurus; word-processing software and computer; guides to writers' markets; cassette tape recorders; how-to books for various genres of writing
Spatial	A variety of art papers, paints, pencils (color, charcoal, and drawing), pastels; clay and modeling tools; building blocks and construction kits (e.g., Capsela); grids, maps, navigation instruments; drafting tools; computer-assisted graphics software and computers; how-to books for a variety of spatial processes
Logical–Mathematical	Manipulatives such as attribute and pattern blocks, Cuisenaire rods, graphing tools and graph paper; database software and computers; scientific equipment; taxonomy charts; scale models; calculators, measuring devices; how-to books and charts for varied scientific and mathematical processes
Musical	Rhythm instruments (e.g., drums, bells, castanets); recorders and other wind instruments; stringed instruments (e.g., guitar, mandolin, violin); keyboards; karaokes; tape recorders; cassette tapes or compact discs of many, varied musical styles, sound effects; amplifiers and microphones; sheet music; varied how-to materials on music composition or production
Bodily Kinesthetic	Open space for movement, manipulative materials, needlework and craft materials, hoops, scarves, balls, varied athletic equipment, typewriters, modeling clay and tools, precision tools, mazes, templates for tracing
Interpersonal	Simulations, activities, leadership opportunities, discussions
Intrapersonal	Journals, reflection time, personality inventories, books

MacKinnon (1962) found that creative individuals show a marked preference for complex drawings that are dynamic and involving. Generally, the more creative the individual is, the stronger is the preference for complexity. MacKinnon concluded:

> It is clear that creative persons are especially disposed to admit complexity and even disorder into their perceptions without being made anxious by the resulting chaos. It is not so much that they like disorder per se, but that they prefer the richness of the disordered to the stark

barrenness of the simple. They appear to be challenged by disordered multiplicity which arouses in them a strong need which in them is serviced by a superior capacity to achieve the most difficult and far-reaching ordering of the richness they are willing to experience.

(p. 489)

Although most studies showing that creative individuals prefer complexity to simplicity have been conducted with adults, research of others (Khatena, 1978; Khatena & Fisher, 1974; Torrance, 1972, 1979) shows that most of the perceptual and personality characteristics of creative children parallel those of adults. Preferences are not as strong at younger ages but become more marked as gifted students mature. From research and from teaching experience, we have found strong indications that gifted students prefer complexity, especially when we consider that they tend to become bored quickly when required to do routine activities, drills, and other unchallenging tasks.

Gifted learners who have ardent interests in a subject and those who prefer to learn through inquiry processes, such as experimentation or observation, need a more complex learning environment. Standard texts simply do not have enough information to meet their needs. When information can be found in many different ways and in many, diverse sources, gifted students are more likely to transform data into new knowledge rather than merely summarizing or paraphrasing information found only in one source.

A complex learning environment includes displays or other materials that show the connections between varied subjects or disciplines; gifted students who are intuitive have greater opportunities to recognize connections between concepts and processes and can share their insights (e.g., such as how metaphors are used for similar purposes in language, art, and science). The richness of the connections these gifted students can make is enhanced by interaction with a complex environment.

Varied Groupings ←——————→ Similar Groupings

Grouping arrangements in programs and classes for the gifted should be varied and fluid rather than identical and static. Groupings should approximate real-life situations and students should be able to make choices about how groups will be set up. Teachers should consider several factors when planning learning activities and coordinating them with the physical elements of the learning environment. These include the nature of the activity or task to be done, the cognitive and affective purposes of the activity, and the learning styles and preferred intelligences of students.

Some activities, such as the joint construction of rules and practices to regulate interactions in the classroom, require input from all members of the class. Other activities, such as journal writing, are individual pursuits. Many other activities, however, can be done in ad hoc small groups, and students often can determine the group in which they want to work. Y. Sharan and S. Sharan (1992) recommend that students have the opportunity to join a group on the basis of interest in a topic or of friendship. Students also should have the option to change groups very early in an investigation if the topic initially chosen is not involving. David (1982) equated opportunity in the classroom with a variety of grouping options. He suggested that if a student wishes to work alone, rather than in a group, that option should be available at all times. Group sizes may vary from dyads to whole classes. As a general rule, however, when students are working on projects or small-group investigations, the number of persons in a group probably should range from three to five. Simulations or productions may require more students and an emphasis on a balance of preferred intelligences or talents.

Cognitive and affective objectives for group work can affect group membership. If members of a class choose to focus on an affective goal, such as improving relationships among different ethnic groups in the class, each group should include representatives of each ethnic group. If the cognitive objective is development of deeper understanding of a complex generalization, students should join groups on the basis of similarity in zones of proximal development (Damon, 1984). If the objective of a lesson is to improve performance in a specific skill, a student may choose to seek help from a more skilled peer.

Learning Styles and Multiple Intelligences

Research on learning styles (e.g., Dunn & Price, 1980) shows that there is wide variation in learning preferences and that learning styles may change over time. Preferences also may be contextual; a gifted student may prefer to work alone in solving mathematics problems and prefer to work with partners in discovery activities. Some gifted students may need more time to develop independence; one student may need more structure and support than does a student who is capable of setting goals and planning ways to meet them. The former student will be more comfortable working in a group whereas the latter may prefer to work alone.

More sophisticated research techniques in the latter part of the 20th century have allowed researchers to show that intelligence is multifaceted and that students may be highly competent in one area of intelligence (e.g., spatial, linguistic) and less competent in other areas. In his theory of multiple intelligences, Gardner (1983) described core capabilities in seven different intelligences—bodily kinesthetic, interpersonal, intrapersonal, linguistic, logical–mathematical, musical, and spatial. He asserted that, although most activities draw upon more than one intelligence, most individuals are highly competent in only a few. C. W. Taylor (1986) also described multiple talents that are derived from those needed in the world of work. In addition to academic talent, he listed communication, productive thinking, planning, forecasting, decision making, discerning opportunities, implementing, and human relations as talents that occur in varying degrees in individuals. Gifted students should have opportunities to work in groups with other students who have different and complementary intelligences or talents. The focus, then, is on what students *can* do and *how* they can develop those talents through group interaction. Use of varied grouping arrangements and a multiple-talent approach also give students opportunities to choose activities in areas in which they feel most competent or in which they want to develop greater competence.

Characteristics of Gifted Students

Gifted students differ from each other almost as much as they differ from students not identified as gifted. Some are so passionately interested in a subject or area of study that they prefer to work alone or with one other student who shares that passion. Other students who have outstanding ability to solve problems and those who have extraordinary communication abilities may prefer to work mostly in groups with their peers. No one method of grouping is appropriate for all gifted students at all times. Although some research (e.g., Dunn & Price, 1980; Li & Adamson, 1992; Restow, Edeburn, & Restor, 1985; Ricca, 1984) shows that gifted students often prefer to work alone, Christensen (1994) reported that students in grades 2 through 6 in a school for gifted children preferred to work collaboratively.

Gifted students have a need to work in one or more intellectual peer groups. Developing individual strengths, learning attitudes and skills for effective social interaction, and planning cooperatively often are goals of gifted students. Cognitive, social, and emotional growth occur as a result of interaction in small groups. "Any problems encountered in living together as a group can be resolved by the group to give a natural setting for the development of leadership skills" (Clark, 1986, p. 292). Through small-group work, gifted students also can build positive personal interaction skills and create a minienvironment in which they feel free to attempt new learning.

Those gifted students who are unusually open, perceptive, or responsive to experiences, to feelings, and to others, those who have strengths in interpersonal intelligence, and those who have extraordinary ability to use words to communicate meaning often have a natural tendency to work with others. Experience with a variety of groups enhances their natural talents and gives them opportunities to demonstrate their giftedness in ways that often are not revealed in traditional programs.

Gifted students need opportunities to develop their strengths and attempt new learning in psychologically safe environments. Making this modification allows most gifted students to work at least part of the school day in their preferred style of learning and area of intelligence. They benefit from opportunities to see themselves in relation to others and to evaluate the effects of their interaction style. Clark (1986) stated that the needs of gifted students in relationship to society fall into four categories: "the need to be an effective member of a group; the need to understand what is going on in a group and to be able to influence the group process; the need to extend one's feelings of membership from family and small group to the community at large; and the need to extend identification with one's community to identification with the human community" (p. 252). Modifying the learning environment to provide varied groupings for learning activities gives gifted students varied opportunities to learn different group process skills and helps them make connections from the classrooom environment to the community at large and, ultimately, to the human community.

Flexibility ⟷ Rigidity

The learning environment for gifted students should be flexibly structured to meet the varying needs of diverse individuals. Making the physical structure of the classroom more flexible is essential. Furniture should be easy to move so that spaces can be arranged for a variety of activities. Tierney, Readence, and Dishner (1990) suggested that a classroom be arranged to include (a) an area for teacher-directed group activities, (b) areas for small group work, (c) areas for independent work, and (d) areas for learning centers. H. Feldhusen (1993) identified several components that contribute to flexibility in learning environments:

- A cluster-seating arrangement using flat-topped student desks that can be pushed together so that gifted children can have a place to keep their own materials. These desks can be moved easily to form cluster groups of varied sizes; they also can be moved out of the way when a large floor space is needed for activities such as dramatic productions, dance, simulations, or constructions.

- Extensive use of learning centers and resource materials. Learning centers for varied intelligences or theme studies can be placed around the perimeter of the room, in corners, on bulletin boards, on tops of counters, or even on the floor. A balance between the arts and language, mathematics, social studies, and science disciplines should be maintained.

- Student involvement in planning their own daily learning activities.

- Individualized arrangements for learning needed skills and strategies.

Centers organized around self-expression might include activities in many different intelligences designed to stimulate oral expression: impromptu speaking, storytelling, creative writing, dramatics, art expression, music, puppetry, or movement. Other centers can be set up for students to use audiovisual media, to browse through books, to use manipulatives, and to employ other tools for learning.

Whenever possible, time constraints should be relaxed so that students can pursue subjects of interest in depth or move rapidly through more routine curricular requirements. The management of classroom time also should be structured to allow students to choose the time they wish to work on particular activities. In one classroom that we observed, a variety of individual activities were listed on the board as "Invitations." During all parts of the day when students were not directly engaged in work with the teacher or in small-group activities, they could choose a specific invitation, such as "Write a thank-you letter to Mrs. Grant for sharing her knowledge about New Zealand with us," or "Illustrate and/or describe the changes you observed in the terrarium this week." Initially, the teacher wrote all the invitations on the board. During the latter half of the year, students often added items to the invitation list. In another self-contained class for gifted students, the teacher listed six required tasks for the day on a bulletin board; Task 7 was "choose ahead." The choices that followed varied with the time of year and the sophistication of the particular class, but generally included from 6 to 12 options that appealed to students' different interests and intelligences. Students did the required tasks in whatever order they chose and then selected one or more of the optional tasks as time permitted. In both classrooms, young, gifted children were learning the self-management skills needed to become autonomous learners.

A second way that time structure can be made more flexible is to allow students to use more time than initially planned for an inquiry or discovery activity or, if their work has proceeded more rapidly than expected, to move on to another activity sooner than planned. Preparing time schedules is a complex forecasting process. When the forecast turns out to be wrong, the time schedule should be flexible enough to be altered.

Teachers in secondary schools often have to be ingenious to achieve any flexibility in time schedules. Certainly, collaboration with other teachers is essential. Betts (1985) suggested that gifted students, with the help of the teacher or coordinator of programs for the gifted, work out a plan with one or more content area teachers that will allow the students to complete the required course work in a shorter period of time. The time saved then could be combined and used for investigation, creative projects, or data collection activities that require more than the typical 50-minute class period. Another option that has been used successfully in many secondary schools is a two-period block of time (i.e., combining two subject areas into one course or scheduling longer classes that meet on alternate days).

Flexibility is related also to an open environment. As classrooms are embedded in schools and schools in communities, events that occur outside the classroom may affect students dramatically. A home fire in the neighborhood, the kidnapping and murder of a schoolmate, a devastating storm, or a shooting on campus require that teachers put aside the planned curriculum for a period of time and allow students to talk about what has happened and how the event made them feel. Good news, too, must be shared. When a school team wins the state debate championship, the regional drama meet, or takes first place at the state track meet, or when individual students win state or national awards, time for celebrating and talking about the accomplishment is sufficiently important to justify a disruption of routine activities.

Flexibility and a sense of humor can turn a potential discipline problem into a valuable learning experience. A 6th-grade teacher was demonstrating the movement of air masses and discussing their effects on weather patterns when a paper airplane came sailing toward his head. Instead of becoming angry and seeking to find out who had thrown it, the teacher incorporated paper airplanes into the lesson. Before the end of the class period, students were excitedly comparing different paper airplane designs, observing the effects of wind (supplied by a portable fan), and learning principles of aerodynamics and their relationship to various weather conditions.

Flexibility, in essence, is demonstrated by a willingness to change—either room arrangements or routines—so that students will feel they are an integral part of an effective, functional, learning community. Flexibility allows teachers to find a student's "point of personal interest and shape it into a learning experience or a living experience occurring within the school day. . . . Every child needs to know that he or she is filling an important space in the world. They all need desperately to feel connections, to themselves, to teachers and to peers and parents" (Artabasy, 1991, p. 14).

Characteristics of Gifted Students

Gifted students vary so much that teachers must be flexible in order to provide learning experiences that are generative. Students who are highly motivated and who are passionately interested in some area of study profit from flexibility in timing so that they can pursue inquiries in depth. Gifted students with extraordinary imaginations need flexibility in space arrangements so that they can construct products or prepare for performances. Students who have an unusual capacity to acquire, retain, and retrieve information and those who learn rapidly can take advantage of their memory and learning abilities in some subjects to "buy" time to work on projects when the learning environment is flexible. Without that flexibility, they may waste valuable learning time while they wait for the next scheduled activity.

Students who have extraordinary ability to convey meaning or emotion through words, actions, symbols, sounds, or media often need to rearrange classroom space to accommodate dramatic productions or to explore various instruments and tools of production. Time for exploration and rehearsals also is important to allow them to prepare products for presentation to various audiences.

Students who are unusually open, perceptive, or responsive to experiences, feelings, others, or events particularly need opportunities to discuss what is happening in the world outside the classroom. The occurrence of events with great emotional impact, either positive or negative, must be recognized; flexibility in curriculum requirements allows students and teacher to discuss these events and consider their possible impact on students' lives.

Flexibility offers challenges and opportunities to students who are highly competent problem solvers and reasoners. Students who have outstanding ability to bring order to chaos, to invent and monitor paths to a goal, and to consider implications of their actions gain valuable experience when they examine the elements of curriculum that must be balanced with student interests or when they consider effective ways to arrange classroom space for a specific purpose. With the modification of flexibility in the learning environment, gifted students can try out their ideas, evaluate the results, and gain valuable experience in real-world talents.

High Mobility ⟵⟶ Low Mobility

Mobility refers to the amount of movement needed by the student and allowed or encouraged by the teacher. Mobility is related closely to independence and flexibility and includes the physical movements of students within the classroom and movement in and out of the classroom. Gifted students need an environment that is flexible enough to allow a great deal of movement in and out of the classroom, access to a variety of learning or investigating environments, and access to a variety of materials, references, equipment, and people (Renzulli, 1977). High mobility also includes administrative arrangements that allow a gifted student to move to another classroom (or another school) for instruction in an area of high competence.

Gifted students may be served full time in regular classrooms, may spend a few hours per week in a resource room for bright students, or may be in a self-contained classroom with intellectual peers. Others may be accelerated for some or all classes, and a few may attend special magnet schools for gifted students or for students with strong interests and talents in a particular area, such as science or fine arts. Regardless of the administrative arrangement, the most important element in the environment that relates to mobility is the understanding that allows freedom of movement in and out of the classroom as well as within it. To enable gifted students to learn varied methodologies, develop abstract and complex concepts, be true investigators, and have freedom of choice in their activities, administrative arrangements must be flexible enough to allow these students to study outside the confinement of the classroom. For example, gifted students may need to collect data on a street corner, collect specimens from a local river or pond, interview officials in their places of business, or use community television facilities. Perhaps most important, gifted students may need to study in an area of interest with a mentor or scholar who can help them learn methodologies for research or performance and develop skills and systems of thought in that discipline. Because of social conditions, school district policies, and liability laws, mobility outside the classroom may be the most difficult of the environmental modifications to make. Careful planning is essential, and students must be monitored by teacher, parent, or approved mentors to ensure that time away from school is used in a safe, productive manner. As regulations vary from state to state and among school districts within a state, teachers of gifted students must know district policies and work with administrators to make arrangements for field trips, projects away from school, and individual study with a mentor.

Within the classroom, gifted students need to have the freedom to organize themselves and direct their own activities. They also need the freedom to consult or work with one or more classmates on a project of interest. High mobility within the school is related closely to the modification of independence. Procedures for going to the library/media center and to other sites in the school should be established so that students understand clearly what is expected of them when they are outside the classroom. High mobility is a key to the success of other learning environment modifications as well as many of the product, process, and content changes recommended as important for gifted students.

Characteristics of Gifted Students

Gifted learners, like other students, have a variety of learning styles and intelligences. Perhaps the modification of high mobility is most important for bodily kinesthetic learners who use movement as an integral part of content and skill learning. For those students with strengths in other than linguistic and logical–mathematical intelligences, freedom to move to various learning centers and to use a variety of information media is critical. They may need to use many different resources, work on a variety of constructions or products, and consult with peers in order to obtain maximum benefit from learning experiences.

Gifted students who have passionate interests in some area or who have progressed far beyond a teacher's ability to provide meaningful instruction need to work with mentors or attend accelerated classes at a higher level of education. Arrangements for these very gifted students must be made with experts in a field; public schools seldom have the personnel or facilities needed for a highly talented dancer, painter, musician, or gymnast. Research facilities seldom are adequate for an aspiring physicist or neuroscientist, nor are most elementary or secondary schools prepared to enable a mathematical prodigy to progress as rapidly as needed. For these extraordinarily gifted students, high mobility in and out of the school is a critical need.

High mobility is needed also by imaginative and creative students and those who have extraordinary ability to convey meaning through some kind of communications channel. These students often choose to be involved in dramatic or artistic performances and need the freedom to move to different parts of the school to practice, to design and construct scenery and costumes, and to conduct the business of a production company. High mobility helps to support their efforts and allows them to seek guidance from professionals in their areas of interest and talent.

Summary

Our purpose in this chapter has been to describe the dimensions of classroom and school environments that are important in a program for gifted students. Each dimension discussed is perceived as a continuum, with the most appropriate environments for gifted students arranged near one extreme. An environment for gifted students should be learner centered, facilitative of independence, open, accepting, complex, facilitative of varied groupings, flexible, and facilitative of high mobility. These dimensions are supported by research on the preferences of gifted students as a group, are necessary to facilitate the success of other curricular modifications in a program for gifted students, and build on and extend the characteristics of these young people. A learning environment so modified affords gifted students the comfort, autonomy, and opportunities they need for optimum growth and development.

Chapter 3

Content

The content of a curriculum includes concepts, ideas, strategies, images, and information presented to students. Content can occur in a variety of forms (Guilford, 1967): *figural* (concrete objects, shapes, pictures, diagrams, etc.), *symbolic* (letters, numbers, mathematical symbols, representative of something), *semantic* (words or ideas with abstract meaning), and *behavioral* (information related to actions, perceptions, intentions, and emotions of people). To make content more appropriate for gifted learners, educators can select or modify content so that it is more abstract, more complex, and more varied than the standard curriculum; include the study of creative and productive people and cultures; and use methods of inquiry and develop generalizations basic to various scholarly disciplines. Content also should be organized differently for gifted students so that maximum learning value can be derived from each learning experience. Perkins (1992) recommended "generative topics" that are central to a discipline, that are accessible to deep understanding, and that encourage rich connection making. Using broad themes that integrate several disciplines also helps students to create powerful mental images to build cohesive understanding of the interrelations among varied disciplines.

Abstractness

Objects, shapes, and noises are concrete. They can be seen, touched, or heard. Very few people disagree over their existence or their physical properties. Concepts such as love, hate, prejudice, honor, and truth are abstract. Although most people would agree on the existence of such abstractions, few individuals agree on their meaning or their manifestations. Within every subject taught and within every content area, information can be ordered on a rough continuum from concrete to abstract. Gardner (1992) distinguished between *first-order knowledge*, gained from direct experience with concrete objects, and *second-order knowledge*, gained through representations of reality such as pictures, dance, music, and symbol systems. J. J. Gallagher et al. (1966) use a classification system with three levels—*data*, *concepts*, and *generalizations*—in an attempt to classify content according to its abstractness. Banks (1990) proposed a similar system using four levels—*facts*, *concepts*, *generalizations*, and *theories*.

Levels of Knowledge

Data or Fact Level

Facts or data consist of specific information about a particular event, object, action, or condition that can be verified by the senses. The emphasis is on things, people, and events rather than on ideas without concrete referents. Data may be represented in statements or contained in tables, charts, maps, or other graphic formats. This level includes only actual data; inferences or interpretations of data, such as trends, or statements that include value judgments are not data or fact-level information. The following are examples of fact-level knowledge:

A description of an industrial robot and its actions

A story of how I fell into the creek while trying to catch a fish

A descriptive report of the election process

Using a map to discover which of two cities is farther from Phoenix

Drawings of plants and animals observed during a field trip to a marsh

Teacher's demonstration of how to use a specific tool or method for a classroom experiment or exercise

A musical theme and its notation

Graphic notation or a demonstration of a dance step

Concept Level

At this level, discussion is focused on ideas and classes of objects, events, processes, and so forth. Specific data may be used in the topic for illustration, but the focus is on class inclusion or exclusion and is thus an abstraction. The following classification of animals is an example:

Mammals	**Not Mammals**
Primates	Birds
Whales	Fish
Rodents	Amphibians
Felines	Reptiles
Canines	Insects
Cattle	Shellfish

Concepts help humans make sense of the vast amount of sensory data they encounter daily and allow the brain to organize and store information in a manageable format. Concepts also can range from relatively concrete to highly abstract. For example, *family* is a more concrete concept than is *nation*, and the concept of *girl* is more comprehensible than is the concept of *humankind*. The following topics are examples of concept-level knowledge:

Discussion that deals with the definition and attributes of a virus, a bacteria, and a parasite

Discussion of the positive and negative features of a social contract

Relationships of such topics as day, week, month, year, century

Design systems such as spiral, vertebraic, cluster, radiating, branching

Consideration of the topic of poverty from local, national, and international perspectives

Possible changes in future farming practices

Reflection on the characteristics of one's personal learning

Characteristics, exemplars, and nonexemplars of pendular movement

An examination of key characteristics and variations in waltz music

Generalization Level

Statements of the relationships among two or more concepts may range from relatively simple to very abstract and provide a useful way to represent the connections within a body of information in a systematic and highly organized manner. Banks (1990) described generalizations as "verified hypotheses" (p. 98). Generalizations also may be referred to as principles or laws. Differentiating between a concept and a generalization can be facilitated by applying the following criteria for generalizations:

1. Two or more concepts are involved. The topic focus thus represents a complete sentence or statement in a logical sense. The presence of data in the topic focus automatically eliminates the topic from consideration as a generalization.

Generalization	Nongeneralization
Great men make history.	Thomas Jefferson was a great man.
Frustration breeds aggression.	Billy rebels when rules are strict.
Water seeks its own level.	The Mississippi floods low-lying land.

2. The two or more concepts are interrelated as a set of component parts in a system (e.g., the telecommunications network, the balance of trade) or as part of a larger generalization. Comparisons must be made and relationships established between the important concepts or variables. An emphasis on a piece of a system, in the absence of a focus on the system itself, would not be a generalization. Verb phrases such as *is influenced by, is associated with, varies with, causes changes in, modifies, declines, reflects,* often are used in generalizations.

Generalization	Concept Level
Discussion of the balance of powers in a federal system	Discussion of the nature of the presidency
Discussion of the relationship of crime to punishment	Discussion of the death penalty

3. The topic focus in a generalization is on a large idea having broad applicability. Another way of stating this idea is that the concepts making up the generalization do not, themselves, have concrete referents. For

example, In the generalization, "*Beauty* is in the eye of the beholder," *beauty* is an abstract noun.

Care must be taken to differentiate between a generalization and a summarizing statement. All three criteria listed above are necessary for a generalization; a summarizing statement is an organized review of an accumulation of facts, no matter how complex. In addition, a summary can be drawn from the organization of data from a single sample; a generalization requires data from many sources and must have broad applicability.

A generalization requires high-level mental functioning, although that high level may not be sustained throughout an entire discussion. A topic should be classified as a generalization if that high level of thinking is clearly reached, however briefly, during the topic discussion and can be considered the topic focus. For example, in a discussion of seaports on the Atlantic Ocean, a student notes that all major metropolitan areas are located on or near navigable waterways. Because all other parts of the discussion can be subsumed under this statement, the generalization is clearly the focus of the discussion of Atlantic seaports, even though the student's statement took only a small part of the total discussion time.

Generalization may be observed as representing an upward conceptual step in the discussion. Students may move from the weather patterns of a specific region to weather systems in general, or from a discussion of classroom rules to consideration of social controls and individual rights. After students work with multiplication problems in base 5 and base 10, they may move to a discussion of number bases in mathematics.

To assess whether gifted students reach the generalization level during discussions, teachers can use the following criteria. If, through *explicit* statement, a student draws an implication from a generalization, the discussion is moved to the generalization level despite the lower conceptual focus from which it may have begun (e.g., the statement, "If color affects human behavior, then classroom designers must consider psychological as well as aesthetic qualities of a color scheme"). In the same way, discussions can move to a higher level when provocative questions are posed: If we accept the idea that great men make history, what does that imply for our responsibilities in choosing a president?

Generalizations vary in levels of abstractness and in levels of application. Low-order generalizations may be based on data from a limited number of samples and apply only in certain cases (e.g., "Temperatures that are either too low or too high will prevent the growth of yeast in food mixtures."). Low-order generalizations usually are closer to a learner's experience and more tangible. Intermediate-level generalizations are based on greater quantities of data or samples from many parts of the world, from different cultures, or from different periods of history. They have broader application than low-order generalizations and are somewhat distanced from a learner's personal experience but still may be limited by the selection of regions, cultures, or historical periods involved. High-order generalizations apply to all people at all times; they have universal application. High-order generalizations often are called *laws* or *principles* and serve as essential structures in scholarly disciplines, social relationships, and other areas of human endeavor.

Within each of these levels, of course, are additional levels of abstraction. A generalization may be stated in different degrees of abstraction even when the same underlying principle is involved. Womack (1966) provided the following example of four levels of statements of the same general idea:

1. All families divide the work among the family members so they can meet their basic needs.

2. A division of labor takes advantage of the best skills of each member of the family or any working group.

3. A division of labor produces specialized workers, thereby leading to an increase in the production and quality of goods.

4. A division of labor leads to increased productivity and a rising standard of living. (p. 8)

As can be seen by inspecting these statements carefully, the level of abstraction is determined mainly by how far away the statement is from a student's concrete experience. Most children are part of a family in which chores are divided among its members; division of labor in a nation, leading to an increase in the standard of living, is much further from their experience.

Theory

The highest form of knowledge is *theory* (Banks, 1990), a "set of testable interrelated lawlike statements or high level generalizations. Theories are highly abstract and must show the relationship between clearly defined variables or concepts, constitute a deductive system and be logically consistent (unknown principles must be derivable from known ones), and be a source of testable hypotheses" (p. 102). A theory often contains several theorems or ideas accepted or proposed as demonstrable proofs and a systematic statement of the relationships that underlie certain phenomena. The purpose of theories is to "explain, relate, and predict wide varieties of experimental and observational findings in the simplest and most efficient ways" (Carin & Sund, 1980, p. 9) and to provide guidance for research and practice.

A new theory often is proposed when existing theories fail to explain the results of systematic observations. For more than a century, for example, theorists have argued whether intelligence is purely genetic or purely environmental. In recent years, several researchers have hypothesized that mature intelligence is a result of interaction between inborn characteristics, cultural characteristics, and environmental factors (Sternberg, 1990). For example, Gardner (1983) proposed his theory of multiple intelligences as a result of research in several fields: neuroscience, psychology, anthropology, linguistics, artificial intelligence, art education, and philosophy. He reviewed studies of "prodigies, gifted individuals, brain-damaged patients, idiots savants, normal children, normal adults, experts in different lines of work, and individuals from diverse cultures" (p. 9). Based on the three criteria recommended by Banks (1990), an evaluation of Gardner's theory is shown in Table 3.1.

These systems for classification of content provide a useful way of looking at curriculum. The point is that, although specific facts and concrete or descriptive information are necessary components that provide the raw material for development of ideas, the content focus for gifted students should be abstract concepts and generalizations. Gifted learners need to spend much less time on concrete information and little time in drill and practice in their area or areas of giftedness. The development of abstract concepts, derivation of generalizations, and induction of unknown principles is a much more effective use of their learning time.

Characteristics of the Gifted

Abstract content is appropriate for all gifted students; however, this modification is particularly appropriate for certain groups of gifted students, as shown in Table 1.5. Learners who have extraordinary ability to convey meaning or emotion through words, actions, symbols, sounds, or

Table 3.1. Banks's (1990) Criteria Applied to Gardner's (1983) Theory of Multiple Intelligences

Criteria	Evidence
Shows the relationship between clearly defined variables or concepts	The theory encompasses a reasonably complete set of the kinds of abilities valued by human culture.
	Abilities in an intelligence are a means of acquiring information.
	An intelligence is a *useful fiction* rather than a physical entity; each is a potentially useful scientific construct for the discussion or consideration of abilities and processes that are essentially continuous.
	An intelligence consists chiefly as *sets of know-how* (tacit knowledge or procedures for doing things).
	Each intelligence operates according to its own procedures and has its own biological bases.
	An intelligence is most accurately thought of as a *potential.*
	Specific intelligences are linked to carry out complex, culturally relevant tasks.
Constitutes a deductive system and is logically consistent	An intelligence potentially can be isolated by brain damage.
	Idiots savants, prodigies, and other exceptional individuals can exhibit a highly uneven profile of ability in one intelligence and deficits in others.
	Each intelligence contains an identifiable core operation or set of operations.
	Each intelligence has an evolutionary history and evolutionary plausibility.
	The relative autonomy of each intelligence can be supported by experimental psychological tasks.
	Each intelligence is susceptible to encoding in a symbol system.
Is a source of testable hypotheses	Provides a framework for assessing intellectual profiles
	Allows more specific planning and assessment of individual educational programs.
	Allows evaluation of the efficacy of matching materials and modes of instruction to a student's individual profile.
	Provides a framework for research on talent development.

media and those who have outstanding problem-solving and reasoning ability are apt to learn most efficiently and effectively when they work with abstract ideas. Even when gifted learners have an insight into cause-and-effect relationships, they may need opportunities to work with abstract ideas to clarify and deepen their understanding of underlying principles. Other gifted students have a desire to reason things out, to look for similarities and differences, and to find out what makes things work. Gifted children who learn rapidly and have good memories often have a large quantity of readily accessible information about a variety of topics related to their area or areas of giftedness. They also may pursue adult topics or projects in their areas of interest. Little emphasis is needed on the actual acquisition of factual data, but these gifted learners do need an emphasis on abstract ideas as a way to integrate and make sense out of conflicting, disparate, or disconnected bits of information or experience. A curricular emphasis on abstract ideas enables them to make sense out of their storehouse of information and to use it productively. Emphasis on enduring abstract ideas and general principles, less likely to become obsolete than specific data and factual information, is necessary for gifted children to promote their intellectual growth and to prepare them to become outstanding contributors in some area of human endeavor.

Complexity

Complexity, as a content modification, is closely related to abstractness. Some abstract ideas may be rather simple, but a complex idea also is abstract. Complex ideas are made up of many interconnected or interrelated parts woven into an intricate or complicated whole. Much study is needed to analyze and understand complex ideas. Generalizations, by definition, are more complex than concepts (Banks, 1990) because they involve relationships among two or more concepts. Compared to a less complex generalization, a more complex generalization (a) involves more concepts, (b) contains more abstract or complex concepts or both, (c) involves more relationships between concepts, (d) involves more complex relationships, (e) cuts across more disciplines or fields of study, and (f) integrates knowledge or concepts from fields or areas of study that are more diverse. Consider, for example, the following two generalizations:

1. Whenever a state of matter is changed (e.g., from a gas to a liquid or from a liquid to a gas) a large quantity of energy must be emitted or added in the process.

2. Energy is equal to the mass of matter times the speed of light squared.

Each generalization involves several concepts. The first includes *state of matter, change, gas, liquid, energy,*and *process*. The second includes the concepts of *energy, equality, mass, speed of light,* and *squaring a mathematical quantity*. However, the relationships among the concepts in the second generalization are more complex than those of the first in which the concepts are quite similar. A second difference between the two generalizations is the number of disciplines or fields of thought involved. The first takes concepts only from physical sciences. The second involves concepts primarily from the fields of mathematics and physical sciences. Yet the two generalizations, vastly different in level of complexity, seem to involve a similar level of abstraction.

Taba (1962) combined the characteristics of abstractness and complexity to classify curriculum content into four levels. The first level includes specific facts or descriptive ideas. The second level includes basic ideas or principles, or what Bruner (1960) called the *structure* of the discipline. The third level includes constructs such as democracy, motivation, intelligence, social change, and themes or *motifs* (in the arts). The fourth level contains systems of interrelated principles, concepts, and definitions (thought systems) and is most important for gifted learners. According to Taba, the academic disciplines represent thought systems "composed of propositions and concepts which direct the flow of inquiry and thought" (p. 178). Thought systems, or paradigms, affect the types of questions asked, the kinds of answers sought, and the methods by which answers are found. According to Taba, by learning the structure or thought system of a discipline such as mathematics (i.e., the system consisting of the separate subjects of arithmetic, algebra, and geometry), the individual can acquire effective mathematical thinking. A thought system can be defined as a set of interlocking low-level, intermediate-level, and high-order generalizations and theories (Banks, 1990) that form the basic structure of an academic discipline or field of inquiry. This system is much more complex, but not necessarily more abstract, than any of the individual generalizations that are a part of it.

Curriculum content for gifted learners should have a global focus (Passow, 1989) and prepare students to adapt to rapidly changing technology and a crowded world. A global focus provides opportunities for in-depth study of the problems faced by humankind, such as hunger, and should include moral and ethical dimensions of problems and events, emerging concepts such as regional development and global planning, economic inequalities, and peace. Gifted students should have opportunities to network with students in other parts of the world so they can gain an appreciation of the feelings, lifestyles, and hopes of their peers in a variety of international settings.

Gifted students need to learn more about systems of knowledge (Ward, 1985) rather than particular bits of information. Complex issues, embedded in content, facilitate the development of a holistic, global perspective and a systems approach to the construction of knowledge.

Characteristics of the Gifted

Gifted students who have an exceptionally keen sense of humor, who make unusual connections, and who have an intense desire to know, do, feel, create, or understand are particularly able to profit from the curricular modification of complexity. These students, and their classmates who love to explore, observe, or experiment in numerous ways, can use complex content to deepen their understanding of ideas, concepts, and generalizations from diverse fields. When a learner has an unusual capacity to acquire, integrate, retain, and retrieve information or skills, an extensive pursuit of adult-level materials in one or more areas of interest and the development of complex ideas are necessities. These ideas provide a structure for organizing, remembering, and using that store of information and experience; important, complex ideas in their areas of high competence are a source of challenge for gifted learners. The more complex the generalizations or thought systems are, the greater is the challenge to those students who enjoy figuring out how things work and how things or ideas are related. The teaching of complex content from a variety of disciplines and experiences with the tools for evaluating or communicating in ways that are appropriate to specific disciplines also provides gifted learners an opportunity to attempt to organize and bring structure to the seemingly disparate information they have accumulated.

For students who have outstanding ability to bring order to chaos through the invention and monitoring of paths to a goal, who enjoy challenge, and who suddenly recognize connections or deeper meanings without conscious awareness of reasoning or thought, the study of complex ideas and thought systems seems essential. The importance of this emphasis lies in their needs both to understand a discipline and to have a working understanding of several disciplines. Through this exploration, they can make informed decisions about areas of interest to pursue. Unfortunately, most students do not begin to understand thought systems in a field until they are involved in advanced studies. At that point, they may have invested so much time and effort in gaining admission to advanced study that they often resign themselves to continuing in a field that is less personally satisfying than they had anticipated. The inclusion of complex content in the curriculum is one way to ensure that gifted individuals have the tools to become outstanding contributors in some area of human endeavor.

Variety

The content modification of variety is one that is included frequently in programs for gifted students. In some programs, *variety* seems to be synonymous with the word *enrichment*. While most children are learning basic skills, children in some programs for the gifted are taught conflict resolution, oceanography, geology, futuristics, astrophysics, robotics, anthropology, media arts, unusual languages (e.g., Arabic, Hindi, or Chinese), mime, topology, polling techniques, chaos theory, or more exotic subjects. Many teachers of gifted learners, who may see a particular group of students only a few hours per week, use content such as this to avoid conflict with the curriculum of the children's classroom teachers. By avoiding traditional subject areas, one can reduce the frustration of a subsequent teacher who hears a student say, "But I learned that last year in the class for gifted kids."

However, content can and should be selected to broaden and deepen students' understanding of diverse fields of study and practice and also to enhance their motivation, curiosity, and interest rather than merely to provide novelty. In addition to the consideration of whether a subject area is taught, the concept of variety also includes systematic sampling of different types of content and methods that nurture the intellectual and artistic strengths of the students. Learners need opportunities to explore and manipulate tools (e.g., real, figural, and symbolic), media, techniques, and ideas in multiple intelligences (Gardner, 1983) as well as opportunities to sample varied fields of endeavor such as music, architecture, mechanics, drama, and human relations. Any abstract theme and most topics can be used for designing a matrix of problems in multiple intelligences. Several examples are presented in Chapter 8.

Variety in problem types is important for gifted students so that they have an opportunity to use both convergent and divergent thinking. Maker (1992) and Schiever (1991), building on the work of Getzels and Csikszentmihalyi (1967), developed a continuum of five problem types ranging from highly structured, single-right-answer problems to completely unstructured situations that require problem definition before selection from among many, possible solution strategies and that allow many, diverse solutions. In Table 3.2, the continuum of problem types is described by whether or not the definition of the problem, method of solution, and solution are known by the presenter and the problem solver.

By using the problem-solving continuum, teachers can strike a balance among problem types and allow students to demonstrate memory, knowledge, or understanding of ideas and creative thinking in their areas of interest and ability.

Characteristics of the Gifted

For students who have ardent interests, a passion for inquiry, and the ability to make sudden recognition of connections or deeper meanings, variety of content is an important modification to help them use and

Table 3.2. The Maker–Schiever Continuum of Problem Types

Type	Problem		Method		Solution	
	Presenter	Solver	Presenter	Solver	Presenter	Solver
I	K	K	K	K	K	U
II	K	K	K	U	K	U
III	K	K	R	U	R	U
IV	K	K	U	U	U	U
V	U	U	U	U	U	U

Note. K = known; U = unknown; R = range.

extend their abilities. Gifted students' imagination, creativity, and sense of humor are important determinants of their ability to benefit from this modification. In areas of interest, these students tend to become absorbed in subject matter and involved in projects to the extent that they need little external motivation to follow through on work that proves to be engaging. Whereas gifted students are easily bored with routine tasks, they are interested in many "adult" topics and often will work independently with little teacher direction. By providing a wide range of content, a teacher has a greater chance of finding areas of intrinsic interest that will engage gifted learners' passionate desire to find out more about an issue or topic. Creativity, curiosity, and willingness to take risks in learning help to identify gifted students who like to be involved in very different content areas. Gifted students' characteristics of creativity and problem solving are enhanced by making seemingly remote associations of ideas from disparate disciplines (Davis, 1989).

Their sensitivity to the aesthetics of a topic or situation as well as their possible involvement in many of the fine arts is a key to the need for the arts among the varied content areas in the curriculum. Also, if gifted children are to become creative producers in any field of endeavor, knowledge of a wide range of disciplines can contribute to their thinking in a chosen field and assist them in choices of vocational and avocational fields.

Gifted scientists may be gifted also as artists, musicians, or poets; authors may be artists, mathematicians, or musicians as well. Root–Bernstein (1987) pointed out that many gifted adults have "correlative talents" (p. 19). In other words, they often use what they have learned in one area of study to support their investigations in another. An individual's intuition, imagination, humor, and creativity seldom are limited to one field of endeavor.

Organization for Learning Value

Content should be integrated or multidisciplinary to help learners who have a wide range of abilities and interests to explore and clarify relationships within and among varied areas of investigation. "The goals of integrative curricula are: (a) to unify a student's educational experiences across subject-matter boundaries and (b) to focus the direction of teaching on the integrative processes which students must utilize if they are to organize knowledge" (Kersh, Nielsen, & Subotnik, 1987, p. 57). This holistic approach supports learners' efficient organization of information and enables them to construct richer and more efficient schemata for processing new information.

Ward (1961) was perhaps the first to suggest the principle of organization for learning value in his third proposition: Individuals select learning experiences with the greatest potential for transfer or generalization. However, Taba (1962) suggested that rather than arranging content according to *chronology* (e.g., time periods of history), *functional similarities* (e.g., tools, equipment, strategies), *categorical groups in a classification* (e.g., chemical elements, biological classes of plants and animals), or *descriptive similarities* (e.g., geographic environments, types of government), teachers should organize content around the basic concepts or abstract generalizations that "represent the most necessary understandings about a subject or field" (p. 177). An example of basic concepts and abstractions in a field is presented in Table 3.3.

By organizing and integrating the content taught (including data, concepts, and generalizations) around central ideas or themes, educators can provide a setting in which the specific facts are chosen carefully to illustrate abstract ideas. Information gathered must be related and interpreted in the context of the ideas they serve. Content can be sampled so that sharp contrasts and comparisons are available as examples and nonexamples of the ideas. In addition, content from related fields can be analyzed for connections to reveal how ideas and generalizations are similar and how they differ. Further, the methods of presentation of content materials and strategies can reveal the thought systems in varied disciplines. For example, one can learn the essential ways of being a historian, not by studying all of history, but by studying some historic phenomenon in sufficient depth to "discover the essential ways of thinking, of discovering appropriate causalities, of handling generalizations, and of establishing conclusions" (Taba, 1962, p. 180). Taba provided the following example from history: "It should be possible, for example, to study a few crucial social phenomena, such as wars, by asking all the questions a historian might ask: What are the factors that create wars; how are wars affected by conditions, such as the tools of warfare and the political institutions that surround them; what is the history of causation of wars, and so on" (p. 180).

Basic principles or abstract generalizations in an area of study can serve as a guide for selecting content and organizing learning activities and as major curriculum strands. Maker (1986) suggested that curriculum be organized around interdisciplinary themes with content goals to be

Table 3.3. Key Concepts and Generalizations Related to Conflict

Generalization	*Related Concepts*	
In every era of human history, conflicts between individuals, groups, and nations have arisen. Conflicts may have negative effects on a society, but they also are the stimulus for effective change.	Conflict Groups Change	Individuals Nations Society
No social group can remain completely harmonious; in all societies, varied forms of social disorganization exist.	Harmony	Disorganization
Conflict develops between individuals and groups in every social organization. Controlled conflict sometimes leads to the attainment of desired social goals.	Control Desires	Social goals Civil rights
Social classes are a result of varied levels of prestige and power.	Prestige Social class	Power
Prejudice due to differences in age, gender, race, religion, or cultural practices often leads to discrimination against groups or individuals.	Discrimination Cultural differences	Prejudice Social status
Social control is the regulation of human behavior by outside social forces. When regulation becomes oppressive, individuals may rebel against the social controls.	Social control Power Oppression	Force Regulation Rebellion
Civil disobedience is caused by autocratic and selective enforcement of oppressive rules or procedures.	Autocracy Civil disobedience Procedures	Oppression Rules Selective enforcement

stated as abstract principles, with generalizations to be discovered, and with key concepts to be learned. With these content goals, guidelines for the selection and organization of content to achieve maximum learning value "while also allowing flexibility to both the teacher and student in the selection of specific examples or areas of study" (p. 153) are readily developed. From an authoritative body of theory and ideas, Womack (1966) suggested that educators (a) choose those generalizations most likely to be discovered from the planned content of the course, (b) place the selected generalizations in order of priority from those that *must* be learned through those that are nice to know, (c) select from the list of *must* generalizations those that students can discover in specific units of study, and (d) arrange units so that the *absolutely must* generalizations are included in the sequence of activities students will do within the unit of study.

Both Womack's (1966) and Taba's (1962) suggested ways of using generalizations to articulate curriculum for kindergarten through 12th grade depend on the concept of a spiral curriculum, in which an idea is introduced again and again and expanded each time the idea is revisited. The degree of abstractness is increased as children become more capable of handling concepts and more familiar with the ideas and as they have a wider range of experiences to bring to the classroom. The following example (adapted from Womack, 1966) of the idea of supply and demand restated as it might be taught at various grade levels provides guidelines for choosing and organizing content for a spiral curriculum.

Grade 3	Some workers make more money than others because their services are needed more.
Grade 5	Both the supply of workers and the demand for workers determine the wages paid for particular kinds of work.
Grade 7	The more income one has, the greater his or her claim on the goods available, and thus the higher is one's standard of living.
Grade 9	The standard of living one has is a major criterion for determining the social class to which one belongs.
Grade 12	The supply and demand of particular categories of workers leads to wage and standard-of-living differentials and thereby to stratification of social classes.

An extension of this example of the generalizations related to the law of supply and demand is illustrated in Table 3.4, which gives the

Table 3.4. Use of Generalizations to Help Select and Organize Content and Learning Activities

Substantive Generalization

The supply and demand of particular categories of workers leads to wage and standard-of-living differentials and thereby stratification of social classes.

Related Generalizations	Concepts	Sample Data	Sample Learning Activities
In a capitalist country, the regulator of supply and demand is the marketplace (low-level generalization).	Capitalism Regulator Supply Demand Marketplace Free trade Commodities	A study of the North American Free Trade Agreement (NAFTA). A study of a major trade center such as Los Angeles or Mexico City with particular emphasis on its economic development. A study of stock, bond, and commodity markets in North America.	Students examine both primary and secondary source materials describing the North American Free Trade Agreement and the economic development of major trade centers. Students play a simulation game such as *Boxcars* or *The Stock Market Game*.[a] Students set up a sales operation to supply selected materials needed or desired by students at the school. Market analysis, advertising, personnel selection, and accounting systems are structured and generated so the effectiveness of the operation can be evaluated.
Few events have single causes or single effects (methodological generalization).	Cause Effect Events	An analysis of the perceptions of different people from different countries of the causes and effects of the formation of the North American Free Trade Agreement.	Class discusses the possible causes and effects of the formation of the North American Free Trade Agreement. Students brainstorm (without self-judgment or teacher judgment) a number of the possible causes and effects of NAFTA; each student then selects and describes, in some medium, what she or he perceives as the most important cause and the most important effect of free trade.

Generalization	Concepts	Objectives	Activities
Throughout history, man's incentive to take risks and progress has been the desire to attain material wealth rather than to serve the causes of humanity (normative generalization)	Incentives Desires Values Cooperation Humanitarianism	An analysis of the different causes and effects of the development of major trade centers in North America. An analysis of the different causes and effects of labor strife in major trade centers in North America. An examination of the possible values or motivations of different people involved in or opposed to the formation of the North American Free Trade Agreement. An examination of the differences in values or motivations of people engaged in various occupations in a major North American trade center and a contrasting area such as a rural agricultural region.	Students share conclusions in small groups, then compare and contrast their ideas. Students decide on issues and roles, then write speeches and slogans, paint posters, write jingles for advertising, plan demonstrations, and design other products for a simulation of a strike or lock-out in a major international industry. Students examine the list of causes and effects generated through brainstorming to determine how many involve values and desires; they then analyze and classify these values as related to a) desire for material wealth, or b) humanitarianism. Students discuss their participation in the simulation games and the underlying motives for their behavior. In small groups, students develop a point of view about the formation of NAFTA and create a 30 to 60 second television commercial, or other advertising campaign, to promote their point of view. Students write and produce a play or musical illustrating the differences between values of a prosperous, urban businessman and his family with those of young people from a rural area who work in occupations that supply commodities to the businessman.

[a] A complete catalog of simulations, including *Boxcars* and *The Stock Market Game*, is available from INTERACT, P. O. Box 997, Lakeside, California 92040.

(1) related generalizations, (2) concepts that must be taught or understood before the generalization can be understood, (3) the data (e.g., specific facts, information) to be used in developing the concepts and generalizations, and (4) some sample teaching activities that can be used to promote the development of an underlying thought system. With this procedure, content and learning experiences can be selected and organized to enhance learning value while important abstract and complex ideas necessary for understanding a particular discipline or a group of related disciplines are being developed.

Characteristics of the Gifted

The learning characteristics of gifted children that contribute to the need for organization for learning value include (a) intuition and insight into relationships; (b) ability to acquire sophisticated understandings with speed and ease; (c) extraordinary ability to communicate and express ideas; (d) unusual capacity to acquire, integrate, retain, and retrieve acquired knowledge; (e) outstanding reasoning ability and goal-oriented thought; and (f) outstanding problem-solving ability. These attributes imply that gifted children need fewer experiences with presented information and less practice with data than children not identified as gifted to enable them to understand significant ideas. Because they are bored easily with routine yet potentially will become producers in a variety of fields, the principle of organizing learning experiences for maximum value is a critically important content modification.

Organization and integration of content according to broad themes and abstract generalizations are built on the belief that when content is richly connected, gifted students gain more from their learning experiences. Gifted students who have an analytical learning style may try to understand complicated materials and ideas by breaking them down into component parts; they have a need to organize and bring structure to situations. Gifted students who have an intuitive style need more opportunities to examine similarities and differences across disciplines to reach insightful conclusions. Because the strengths of gifted students are so varied, content should be organized not only according to significant ideas but also to support diverse topics and methods of inquiry.

The Study of People

Gifted students often are painfully aware of differences between them and their age peers. Many of them also are self-critical and perfectionistic. Their heightened sensitivity and their awareness of differences can cause severe stress unless they learn to understand traits of creative, productive people (Betts, 1985; Silverman, 1986). Teachers should guide gifted students in the study of creative individuals (including themselves), how such individuals interact with each other and how they function in a career or avocation. The study should include an examination of (a) personal characteristics, motivations, and coping skills of creative, productive individuals and how they adapt to change; (b) career characteristics, including the creative processes, leadership styles, learning styles, types of products developed, and how these individuals respond to success or failure; and (c) their social characteristics. In all three of these areas, the study of people should be concentrated on the actual processes or skills used, the development of the individual, and the interaction among the personal, vocational, and social aspects of their lives. For example, the development of personal characteristics should be examined at several points in time to infer how those traits developed—how parents, siblings, peers, teachers, or others contributed to motivation in the effective adult; how the social and political setting of the community or nation influenced personality or motivation or both; and how events and unexpected experiences (i.e., luck, tragedy) affected their development. A study of the career traits of the successful adult also should include the development of the person's leadership style or creative abilities (e.g., characteristic ways of interacting with people, artistic expression) and how personal and social aspects of their lives interacted with their environments during their life span.

A definite focus on problems unique to gifted or creative individuals is essential. How did successful or creative adults solve their problems? How did they resolve conflicts between high self-expectations and the expectations of others? Other issues worthy of study include how the individual reacted to fame, failure, or the lack of social recognition of the value of creative products; whether success is defined in a personal rather than a social sense; how the individual coped with the perception of being different or abnormal or with having a handicapping condition; how he or she dealt with envy, prejudice, or anti-intellectualism; and how the individual reacted to social pressures to conform. Many other problems can be identified by students from their own personal experiences, through their relationships to the lives of others, and through their reading or observations.

In a study of individuals, numerous methods are possible, ranging from (a) in-depth examination of a specific person's life through biographies, autobiographies, personal case studies, and interviews; (b) comparison of several different individuals in one avocation or field of study as well as those in different areas of endeavor who have characteristics in common (e.g. those adults who have achieved success in disparate fields or who exhibit multiple talents); (c) observation and analysis of problem-solving processes and strategies used by exemplary performers in a field; and (d) the effects of mentorships with other gifted individuals. When studying a specific person, for example, students can examine all the products of that individual, noting similarities and changes in products as the person matured or changed focus. Students can note periods in which products are similar as well as events or personal factors that might have caused a transposition from one period to another. Students can do an in-depth study of one historical individual in a certain field and a living individual in the same field. For example, students can compare the two lives, noting anomalies that might be the result of differing sociopolitical contexts and other external conditions as well as similarities that might relate to human nature and the creative process. Comparisons of people considered successful and those not viewed as being at the same level of career success would be valuable experiences to include. Students also might compare individuals in similar careers who are from different cultural or ethnic groups, assess gender differences in selected career areas, examine the effects of various handicapping conditions on career choice, or study the effects of economic background in the development of career goals.

The study of creative, successful individuals certainly should include direct contact with one or more gifted, talented, or creative persons. Opportunities to interview and interact with persons who have met the challenge of developing their talents and using their intellectual abilities in productive ways provide gifted learners with possible role models and opens windows on career fields they may not have considered for themselves.

In addition to reading biographical materials, examining the works of individuals, and having contact with gifted, creative persons, students also can use film, videos, recordings, dramatizations, and fictional works about the lives of talented individuals. In fiction or performance media, students often can make connections with the affective aspects of the lives of artists, scientists, leaders, and other individuals who have struggled to develop their talents and intelligence in spite of difficult circumstances and lack of social approval or support.

Characteristics of the Gifted

The study of people should build on the natural interest of gifted students in how people think and feel, how they develop, and how they deal with their problems. Students whose strengths are in the personal intelligences will find particular fascination and probably will be highly interested in content that is learned in the context of the lives of real people. Gifted learners who have a ready grasp of underlying principles regarding events, people, and things and who desire to look for similarities and differences in events and people also enjoy and profit from an in-depth study of individuals who have achieved success in creative, intellectual, or social fields. Students who are gifted in interpersonal and intrapersonal intelligences often show a definite interest in reading or viewing biographies and autobiographies of famous people. They seem to have a need to study creative people and leaders as though, by analyzing the characteristics and experiences of other gifted persons and relating them to their own lives, they may be able to understand and cope better with their own uniqueness.

The intense motivation of some gifted students also contributes to the need for this content modification. They tend to be self-critical (or strive for perfection) but also may have a tendency to evaluate or judge other people who are less motivated than themselves. The study of the lives of others contributes a more humane perspective to the latter tendency. The imagination and creativity of gifted learners are enhanced through a study of creative individuals; this experience can help students understand and deal more effectively with their own originality. In addition, gifted students' sensitivity may lead to a need to examine their own characteristics to discern how they are different from or similar to those of creative producers in an area of interest or ability. Gifted students' future participation in a career is enhanced by consistent study and observation of others and by reflection on how they can use what they learn to enhance their own talents.

The Study of Methods

A final content modification is the inclusion of the study of the methods of inquiry with substantive information in various fields. This idea was discussed in two previous sections in relation to Taba's (1962) concept of thought systems, but further emphasis is needed. To construct knowledge from data and information, students need to know how data are classified and how generalizations, principles, and laws are derived in a discipline. They also need to know how research is conducted and what constitutes evidence or support to validate conclusions. Although a "common body of skills underlies imaginative thought in all disciplines from the sciences and technology to the arts and literature" (Root–Bernstein, 1987, p. 18), each domain has certain conventions, strategies, methods of inquiry, and rules of evidence that are unique to that field. "In the context of reasoned thought, for example, this means that in addition to deriving a surface knowledge of information, students must learn to understand the ways in which evidence is presented and arguments are developed" (Langer, 1994, p. 81) in the media from which they gain information and in products that they create. Gifted students also must learn how to critique products in a field and to construct knowledge in appropriate ways. Langer and Applebee (1988) and Langer (1992) found through interviews with both university professors and high-school teachers that in the four subject areas examined (American literature, American history, biology, and physics), an increasing focus on the tentative nature of "truth" led to an emphasis on more active questioning and interpretation rather than on simply acquiring a body of information—in essence, on the construction of knowledge.

Perkins (1986) posited that knowledge in a field has a purpose, a structure, and arguments to explain and evaluate it and that model cases of that knowledge can be demonstrated or displayed. As an example, he suggested the consideration of Newton's laws:

> One certainly can ask after purpose—to integrate and explain data about the motions of bodies from baseballs to planets. A useful rendering of structure would be the laws themselves, considered one by one. . . . you can ponder under argument how each law contributes to the ensemble. . . . Model cases include the solar system and how the laws explain the orbits of the planets. Arguments include an explanation of how the laws work together to give a complete account of a

range of dynamic phenomena and an evaluation of the evidence for and against Newtonian mechanics.

(pp. 7–8).

J. H. Clarke (1990) pointed out that Perkins's design questions can be the basis of concept mapping. "If we combine Perkins' questions with a mapping technique for arguments, we get an advanced form of concept mapping that students could use to create or evaluate ideas" (p. 277). Figure 3.1 is a concept map developed by Clarke to show how a paragraph might be analyzed through the use of Perkins's design questions. Gifted students need to learn how knowledge is designed and how to recognize the uniqueness of a domain, particularly in their area or areas of ability and interest. Gifted students need knowledge of how professionals learn and work in a particular field to enable them to become independent investigators. "Teaching students the methodologies and processes of a discipline can result in greater challenge and a truly differentiated education appropriate for gifted students" (Schack, 1988, p. 219).

Characteristics of the Gifted

Because many gifted students want to understand the complexities of an area of study and make creative contributions in their area or areas of talent, opportunities to master the methods of a field are essential. "It is the teaching of the methodologies of practicing professionals that can escalate both the ambitions and the abilities of our students in their pursuits" (Schack, 1988, p. 219). Some gifted students are intensely motivated to inquire, understand, and create in their area or areas of interest; others have the ability to communicate expressively through their talent or talents and must have the support provided by a thorough study of the methods in their areas of endeavor. A study of methods also is necessary for gifted students who have strengths in problem solving, reasoning, intuition, and motivation (i.e., desire and ability to structure their own inquiries in appropriate ways). Gifted learners who have adult interests (an enjoyment of studying phenomena in the ways that an adult does and an interest in ways of thinking about ideas), imagination and creativity, a sense of humor, and a tendency toward constructive criticism also respond positively to learning the unique ways that knowledge is construed and products are developed in different fields. Other gifted

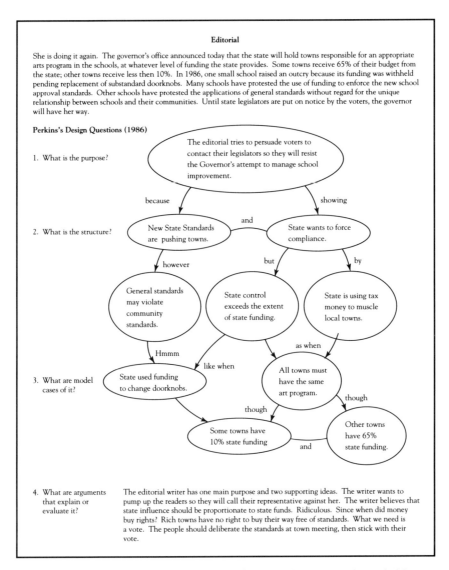

Editorial

She is doing it again. The governor's office announced today that the state will hold towns responsible for an appropriate arts program in the schools, at whatever level of funding the state provides. Some towns receive 65% of their budget from the state; other towns receive less then 10%. In 1986, one small school raised an outcry because its funding was withheld pending replacement of substandard doorknobs. Many schools have protested the use of funding to enforce the new school approval standards. Other schools have protested the applications of general standards without regard for the unique relationship between schools and their communities. Until state legislators are put on notice by the voters, the governor will have her way.

Perkins's Design Questions (1986)

1. What is the purpose?

The editorial tries to persuade voters to contact their legislators so they will resist the Governor's attempt to manage school improvement.

because   showing

2. What is the structure?

New State Standards are pushing towns.

and

State wants to force compliance.

however   but   by

General standards may violate community standards.

State control exceeds the extent of state funding.

State is using tax money to muscle local towns.

Hmmm   like when   as when

3. What are model cases of it?

State used funding to change doorknobs.

All towns must have the same art program.

though

though

Some towns have 10% state funding

and

Other towns have 65% state funding.

4. What are arguments that explain or evaluate it?

The editorial writer has one main purpose and two supporting ideas. The writer wants to pump up the readers so they will call their representative against her. The writer believes that state influence should be proportionate to state funds. Ridiculous. Since when did money buy rights? Rich towns have no right to buy their way free of standards. What we need is a vote. The people should deliberate the standards at town meeting, then stick with their vote.

Figure 3.1. Advanced concept map—Evaluation of a paragraph guided by Perkins's design questions.

Note. From *Patterns of Thinking: Integrating Learning Skills in Content Teaching* (p. 278), by J. H. Clarke, Boston: Allyn and Bacon. Copyright 1990 by Allyn and Bacon. Reprinted with permission.

students use their leadership abilities to assume responsibilities for the direction of activities in which they are involved. These attributes suggest that they need and can profit from an analysis of the methods used by creators, scholars, and leaders in various fields or occupations.

Summary

In this chapter, we have described principles to guide the modification of content in the basic curriculum. Some of the modifications are also appropriate in heterogeneous classrooms, as suggested by some of the literature in school reform (e.g., Ackerman, 1989; Jacobs, 1989a, 1989b; Nielsen, 1989; Perkins, 1989, 1992; Quattrone, 1989; Rothman, 1989). Other ideas, such as the study of universal perspectives or "the common assumptions underlying different scientific and social theories" (Ward, 1985, p. 9) may be appropriate only for highly able learners (Shore, Cornell, Robinson, & Ward, 1991).

The recommended changes in ways to structure curriculum are designed to enhance and extend the learning characteristics that distinguish gifted learners from other learners. The changes are designed also to develop the skills required by adaptable, self-actualized individuals. Most of these content changes build upon varied characteristics that distinguish gifted learners from other learners. However, because all gifted students do not have the same characteristics, teachers must plan for individual strengths, interests, and needs. All the content modifications listed in this chapter may not be necessary for all gifted students all of the time; a comprehensive, well-articulated program should include most of the modifications most of the time to provide challenging opportunities for gifted learners to magnify their individual talents.

Chapter 4

Process

P rocess, or methodology, is the *way* educators teach and the ways students use information. Process involves the ways materials are presented to students, the questions asked of them, and the mental or physical activities expected from them. Although the way information is used cannot be separated completely from content, especially if the content modifications suggested in Chapter 3 are implemented, this discussion of process provides another set of modifications needed in curricula for gifted students.

Among the modifications suggested by educators of gifted children, process has received the most attention. Higher-level thinking, critical thinking, creative thinking, creative problem solving, and real-world skills such as decision making, planning, and forecasting are recommended, not only for gifted children but for all children. In the past decade, numerous books about the teaching of thinking have been published, various critical and creative thinking models have been proposed, and varieties of organizing schemes have been advocated to improve students' ability to think effectively. New theories of intelligence have arisen from research in information processing (e.g., Baron & Sternberg, 1987; Sternberg, 1988, 1990) and from coordinating research in a variety of areas (e.g., Ceci, 1990; Gardner, 1983); in these theories the importance of developing varied strategies to use information in varied intelligences is emphasized.

To make learning and thinking processes more appropriate for gifted students, teachers can modify the level or type of thought processes (i.e., mental activities) emphasized, the pacing of instruction, and the overall approach to reasoning (inductive as well as deductive). Other associated changes teachers can make include using a variety of methods and encouraging students to express both the products of their reasoning (i.e., answers, predictions) and the logic or reasoning processes they used to arrive at the products. Another key modification is structuring learning activities that allow students to choose content or projects for study. Finally, teachers are encouraged to promote group interaction among gifted students. We explain each of these principles in the sections that follow, using the same format as was used in Chapter 3.

Higher Levels of Thinking

Higher levels of thinking, or higher-order thinking skills, are one important modification for all students. Changing instructional emphasis from the so-called lower levels of thinking, such as memory or recall, to the so-called higher levels of application analysis, synthesis, and evaluation is an important step in building greater student involvement in learning. This change essentially involves increasing the emphasis on the *use* of information rather than on the acquisition of facts and skills. A second result of the change involves the planning and implementing of progressively more complex mental activities. Classic studies of classroom interaction (e.g., J. J. Gallagher, Aschner, & Jenné, 1967; Taba, 1966) and more recent research (Brooks, 1987; Schiever, 1986) have shown clearly that, when it comes to mental activity, teachers get what they ask for. If they ask a low-level question, they receive a low-level answer; if they ask a question calling for a high-level analysis, that is what they receive. Learning activities also can provide the setting for an emphasis on higher levels of thinking, but instructor questions and the kinds of problems posed play a major role in moving students from simple recall of memorized data to the use of data for complex reasoning.

Although a number of classification systems have been devised for analyzing levels of thought and for guiding teacher questions, the most commonly used is the *Taxonomy of Educational Objectives* proposed by Bloom and his colleagues (Bloom, 1956). Bloom's Taxonomy describes six levels of thinking in a hierarchical arrangement in which each higher level includes and depends on all those below it. In this taxonomy, thought processes are classified into (a) knowledge or recall, (b) comprehension, (c) application, (d) analysis, (e) synthesis, and (f) evaluation. In a related project dealing with affective behaviors, the same group of educators (Krathwohl, Bloom, & Masia, 1964) developed a taxonomy of affective objectives consisting of the categories of (a) receiving, (b) responding, (c) valuing, (d) organizing values, and (e) characterization by a value complex.

Other systems have been developed in which strategies for the use rather than the acquisition of knowledge also guide students toward higher-level thinking:

- Bruner's (1960) three aspects of a learning episode: acquisition, transformation, and evaluation

- Parnes's (1966) Creative Problem-Solving process, modified recently (Isaksen & Parnes, 1985), to include six steps in which information is generated and used in the process of solving problems: objective finding, fact finding, problem finding, idea finding, solution finding, and acceptance finding

- Taba's (1964) four types of thinking-skill clusters (concept development, interpretation of data, application of data, conflict resolution) that include sequences of skills within each cluster

- C. W. Taylor's (1967) six talent areas (academic, creative thinking, decision making, planning, forecasting, communication), modified in 1984 (C. W. Taylor, Allington & Lloyd, 1990) to add three additional talent areas (implementing, human relations, discerning opportunities) that include varied levels and types of thinking skills

- Guilford's (1967) five operations (cognition, memory, divergent production, convergent production, evaluation)

- Williams's (1972) thinking processes (fluency, flexibility, originality, elaboration) and feeling processes (curiosity, risk taking, complexity, imagination)

- Kohlberg's (1966) six levels of moral reasoning or orientations (obedience and punishment, instrumental relativism, interpersonal concordance, "law and order," social contract, universal ethical principal)

- Sternberg's (1988) triad of mental self-management (knowledge acquisition components, performance components, and metacomponents) that each include subcomponents within the cluster

- J. Feldhusen and Kolloff's (1978) three-stage inquiry process (preinquiry, methods of inquiry, interpretive inquiry) with several skills at each stage

- the four elements of Perkins's (1986) knowledge as design model (purpose, structure, model cases, explanatory and evaluative arguments)

- Maker and Schiever's (Maker, 1992) continuum of five problem types ranging from highly structured convergent to ill-structured divergent

- Short's eight-step inquiry cycle (Short & Armstrong, 1993) that leads from previous experiences through focused inquiry, data collection and organization, collaboration, rethinking and revising ideas, presenting ideas publicly, reflecting on strategies for inquiry, to identifying invitations for further inquiry

Several of these systems have been modified over the years; others are an elaboration (or simplification) of ideas suggested in earlier literature. Howley, Howley, and Pendarvis (1985) traced the antecedents of many of the process-oriented programs to works by early progressive educators (e.g., Stedman's, 1924, *Education of Gifted Children*, and Bruekner's, 1932, *The Nature of Problem Solving*). Some of the approaches (e.g., Guilford, 1967; Parnes, 1966; C. W. Taylor, 1967; Williams, 1972) resulted from midcentury work in creativity and the processes of creative thinking. Generally, all the model developers stressed the importance of integrating thinking and learning processes with significant content.

Another useful concept in the context of higher levels of thinking is that of *critical thinking* as opposed to an uncritical analysis (i.e., acceptance without examination) of information. Critical thinking might be characterized as evaluative decision making. Ennis (1964) provided a practical listing of aspects of critical thinking derived from his cross-disciplinary study of literatures in education, philosophy, and psychology. Students who learn and use the following skills increase the probability that they will become critical thinkers as adults:

- Judging whether a statement follows from the premises

- Judging whether something is an assumption

- Judging whether an observation statement is reliable

- Judging whether a simple generalization is warranted

- Judging whether a hypothesis is warranted

- Judging whether a theory is warranted

- Judging whether an argument depends on an ambiguity

- Judging whether a statement is overvague or overspecific

- Judging whether an alleged authority is reliable (Ennis, 1964, pp. 600–610)

Within each of these skill areas, Ennis presented a series of criteria to be applied to information in making judgments of its validity. For example, a hypothesis is warranted to the extent that it meets the following criteria:

- It explains a bulk and variety of reliable data. If a datum is explained, it can be deduced or loosely derived (in the fashion of the application of principles) from the hypothesis together with established facts and generalizations.

- It is itself explained by a satisfactory system of knowledge.

- It is not inconsistent with any evidence.

- Its competitors are inconsistent with the evidence. This principle is the basis of controlled experiments.

- It is testable. It must be or have been possible to make predictions from it. (Ennis, 1964, p. 605)

Criteria such as these can be used for the related purposes of teaching students the component skills involved in critical thinking, evaluating student progress, and systematically planning learning activities to develop the component skills of critical thinking.

Although higher-level thinking skills are advocated in all disciplines, thought systems vary and a common language seldom exists to allow, for example, literature teachers to talk with sociologists or sociologists with biologists (J. H. Clarke, 1990). J. H. Clarke advocated the use of visual organizers as a graphic means to clarify thinking processes and to help students make connections between disciplines. His "thinking wheel," which integrates the complex processes of inductive and deductive thinking as two interacting fields, is illustrated in Figure 4.1.

Using each chunk or phase in the six parts of his model, students process information using a particular management skill:

- *scanning and focusing:* purposefully searching for meaningful information

- *creating categories and classes:* using grouping techniques to increase mental efficiency and power

- *inducing propositions from facts:* using what the senses know to create new ideas

- *activating conceptual knowledge:* hypothesizing relationships between concepts and events

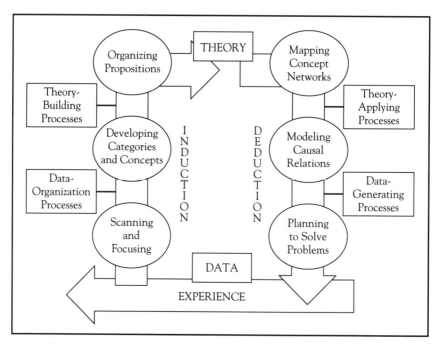

Figure 4.1. Clarke's thinking wheel.

Note. From *Patterns of Thinking: Integrating Learning Skills in Content Teaching* (p. 278), by J. H. Clark, Boston: Allyn and Bacon. Copyright 1990 by Allyn and Bacon. Reprinted with permission.

- *predicting and planning*: using mental models to predict, plan, or decide on the future

- *developing procedures*: creating problem-solving steps appropriate to a specific decision or plan (p. 13)

Another model in which the circular nature of scientific inquiry is explored and the processes and products are identified was created by Costa, Hansen, Silver, and Strong (1985). In Figure 4.2, the connections of data to theory are illustrated through inductive and deductive phases.

According to Costa et al. (1985, p. 167) when one begins with data, the *inductive phase* of the inquiry process proceeds as follows:

- *data organization*: listing, rank ordering, sequencing, comparing, classifying

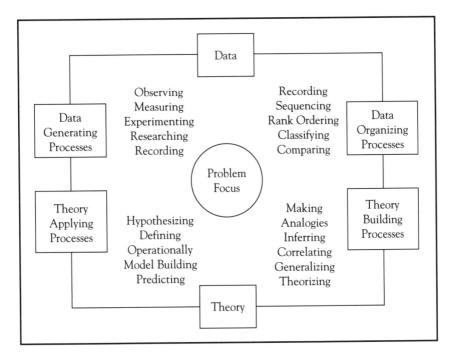

Figure 4.2. Scientific processes and products.

Note. From "Other Mediative Strategies" by A. L. Costa, R. Hanson, H. F. Silver, & R. W. Strong, 1985. In A. L. Costa (Ed.), *Developing Minds*, p 167. Alexandria, VA: Association for Supervision and Curriculum Development. Copyright 1985 by Association for Supervision and Curriculum Development. Adapted with permission.

- *theory building*: making analogies, inferring, theorizing, generalizing, correlating

The inductive phase results in theory from which the *deductive phase* of the process proceeds as follows:

- *theory applying*: hypothesizing, defining operationally, model building, predicting

- *data generation*: observing, measuring, experimenting, researching, recording

Although the language of creative producers and scholars in diverse fields often differs, the necessity of teaching higher-order thinking skills and strategies is a common concern. Data are acquired to be used purposefully, not simply stored in memory for regurgitation on tests or trivial games. No one thinking strategy is sufficient; every learner should have a repertoire of higher-level thinking strategies to be used as needed. "We would do well to equip learners with a menu of their possibilities and, in the course of their education, to arm them with procedures and sensibilities that would make it possible for them to use the menu wisely" (Bruner, 1985, p. 8).

Characteristics of the Gifted

Although abilities and interests of gifted students vary widely and all students can benefit from an emphasis on higher-level thinking, this emphasis is particularly important for those gifted students who have strengths in inquiry skills or problem solving, who have an unusual capacity to acquire, integrate, retain, and retrieve information or strategies, and who have the ability to acquire sophisticated understandings with amazing speed and apparent ease. Because of their usually excellent memories and ability to understand concepts and principles quickly, these students need little practice in the acquisition of knowledge. They do need to learn and practice effective strategies for using, analyzing, synthesizing, and evaluating knowledge. They do need to learn and practice critical thinking and inquiry processes, and they need practice in using various models and strategies for inquiry and problem solving. Although they are more proficient in these kinds of thinking than are most other students (Scruggs & Mastropieri, 1988; Scruggs, Mastropieri, Monson, & Jorgensen, 1985), gifted learners certainly can improve their strategy use; they also need challenge in these high levels as evidenced by their less-than-perfect performance on tests of critical or higher-level thinking (Ennis & Millman, 1971; Ross & Ross, 1976; Taba, 1964, 1966; Watson & Glaser, 1964).

Gifted students who have strengths in inquiry and problem-solving processes need guided practice in making informed, logical, and appropriate uses of information rather than practice in simply acquiring it. They like to explore, observe, and experiment with objects and ideas; they enjoy challenges; and many have an unusual ability to acquire, integrate, and structure information. As their goals often tend toward scholarly or creative pursuits, they benefit from a curricular emphasis on more complex levels of thinking.

Open-Endedness

A critical modification, often discussed in the literature, is asking questions and providing activities that encourage *open* rather than *closed* thinking. One way of describing the difference is through the definitions of convergent and divergent thinking. In convergent thinking, an individual attempts to reach the right or best answer; in divergent thinking, an individual or group attempts to generate many, varied, and unique possibilities or answers. In this context, convergent thinking is sometimes seen as a lower level of thought and a process to be avoided. Such a perception is harmful and should be avoided. Both types of thinking have an important place in everyday life.

Many types of complex thinking require a balance of divergence and convergence. Decisions are, and must be, made every day; everyone is required to judge the adequacy, usefulness, or appropriateness of information, products, or actions daily. Making judgments or decisions requires convergence on the best answer, but the process is facilitated through the divergent process of generating and considering many, varied, possible alternatives. Possibilities then are judged according to criteria that help to guide a thinker toward the most appropriate decision for a given situation. The point is that one type of thinking—convergent or divergent—should not replace the other in a curriculum for gifted children.

The concept of open-endedness is different from and more important than the convergent–divergent dichotomy stressed in the popular literature, however. Open-endedness implies a difference in teacher attitude reflected in (a) questioning techniques and content of questions, (b) the design of learning activities and materials, and (c) evaluation of student responses to questions. When they ask questions, many teachers often have preselected the responses they want to hear and go through a probing or fishing process with students until they obtain the favored response. At times closed questions may appear to require divergent thinking, as in a situation in which a teacher asks a question such as "What are some other ways we can evaluate this solution?" When the teacher continues to ask the question until some student comes up with the one answer the teacher thinks is most important, the question really is closed. The question constitutes a test, and students are required to discern what answer the teacher is seeking. High-level divergent, or even high-level convergent, thinking simply is not valued. This closed attitude on the part of the teacher serves only to stimulate the mental process of figuring out what the teacher wants. As most educators know, many gifted students are experts at giving the teacher what he or she wants but may be less expert at doing their own thinking. Closed questions also are inappropriate or irrelevant in many cultures (Deyhle, 1983; Heath, 1982). When a teacher holds up a ball and asks, "What color is this ball?" the question makes little sense. The teacher can see the color of the ball. Questions in many cultures (e.g., Navajo) are used by an individual to obtain information that is not currently known. A more appropriate question would be, "What can you tell me about the object I am holding?" This query allows students to share many attributes of the object, and responses probably will include color. As a way of assessing preexisting knowledge before beginning a lesson, the latter question is much more powerful.

The content or phrasing of questions can be critically important and is easier to modify than are teachers' attitudes. An open-ended question must satisfy two basic requirements: It cannot be answered yes or no, and it has no predetermined right answer. In the following examples, closed questions are presented first, then are followed by a corresponding open question.

CLOSED   Do you think that increased use of computers has a positive effect on student achievement?

OPEN   What effect on student achievement, if any, do you feel the increased use of computers has produced?

CLOSED   What are the seven intelligences described by Howard Gardner (1983)?

OPEN   What are some of Howard Gardner's significant ideas about intelligence?

Although open questions often require higher levels of thinking than do closed ones, even recall questions can be expressed in an open-ended manner. When recall questions are phrased carefully, students have opportunities to share personally evaluated responses.

CLOSED   Does anyone else have a different idea?

OPEN   What other ideas do you have?

CLOSED   What dance steps were performed in this selection?

OPEN   What are some of the things you noticed and felt about this performance?

CLOSED   What did Travis do when his dog was killed?

OPEN   What are some of the things you noticed about the behavior of the characters in *Old Yeller* (Gipson, 1956)?

Open questions have added advantages. They (a) encourage many students to give responses; (b) encourage student-to-student rather than teacher-to-student interaction patterns; (c) elicit more complete and more complex responses; (d) allow students to give knowledgeable answers; (e) encourage students to question themselves, their classmates, and their teachers; and (f) stimulate further thought and exploration of a topic. Williams (1972) recommended asking "provocative questions" and described them as "inquiry to bring forth meaning; inquiry to incite knowledge exploration; summons to discovering new knowledge" (p. 95). Provocative questions generally are one of three basic types:

What do you think might happen if _____?

What effect might _____ have on _____?

How might _____ have changed if _____?

Provocative questions also may be those that call for a quantity of ideas, those that stimulate students to assume a viewpoint different from their own, or those that encourage speculation, such as the following examples:

What do you think might happen if citizens of the United States ratified a constitutional amendment to limit the terms of members of Congress?

What effects do you think closing the U.S. borders to all immigrants would have on the world?

How would the world of art have been different if Picasso had never lived?

What do you think might happen to the world if all fossil fuels were depleted?

How might music be produced in the 21st century?

What effect do you think ending the "War on Drugs" would have on drug abuse in your community?

How is learning like a bridge?

Open-ended questions are generative in nature and encourage exploration of ideas. Closed questions are evaluative and tend to restrict students to safe answers that their teachers or texts have given to them. According to what is known about the phenomenon of curiosity, a teacher who always provides all the required information and asks only closed questions limits opportunities for the joy of discovery. Teachers need to arrange experiences and ask questions that necessitate the analysis of ideas, generalizations, and theories, but not in a didactic manner. The use of an inductive or discovery approach is, in fact, one of the process modifications for gifted learners suggested in this chapter.

Open-endedness is more than questioning techniques or design of learning activities. Open-endedness implies that having students more expert than a teacher about some subjects is okay. It also describes a teacher attitude in which students' unique contributions and the expression of their varied talents are valued more than skill at the game of pleasing the teacher or of getting the right answers.

Perhaps the most important justification for open-endedness is the stimulation of creative characteristics such as fluency, flexibility, originality, and elaboration, and affective characteristics such as playfulness, imaginativeness, lack of inhibitions, openness to new experiences, and sensitivity to self and others. More complex creative thinking also is stimulated through open-endedness. The abilities to find likenesses in dissimilar structures, to develop empathic projections, and to use analogies for symbolic thinking are essential for creative production. "By making mental comparisons, or analogical links, known relationships between dissimilar elements can be transferred to each other—and a whole new world of insight, thought, and imagery is possible" (Roukes, 1982, p. 2).

Characteristics of the Gifted

The ability of many gifted students to acquire sophisticated understandings rapidly and easily in their area or areas of ability and interest and their quick grasp of underlying principles mean that testing for acquisition of information seldom is necessary. Students who show strengths in inquiry and problem solving can ask open-ended questions of themselves and their informants, can extend the scope of an inquiry, or take greater intellectual risks in open-ended learning situations. During the generative phase of idea or question finding, no idea, question, or comment is valued more than another and none are rejected without consideration. Fluency, flexibility, and originality are valued, and students can "piggyback" on ideas suggested by classmates. Each idea or question then is examined to discern its value in meeting the objectives selected for the inquiry.

The modification of open-endedness also is justified for gifted students who have an exceptionally keen sense of humor and often see unusual connections between apparently unrelated concepts, for students who have an extraordinary capacity for the flexible use of ideas, and for students who are unusually open, perceptive, or responsive to experiences, feelings, and other people. Students who make humorous comments often see aspects of a subject that others have not considered, or they may interject a comment to break the tension of a learning situation. In open classrooms, those comments are accepted rather than rejected as inappropriate. The connections between apparently unrelated concepts and the flexible use of ideas contribute to creative thinking and greater understanding.

Open-endedness is appropriate also for students who have active imaginations and communicate expressively in any medium. When educators provide an atmosphere in which learners are encouraged to do their own thinking, regardless of what the teacher might have had in mind, and a setting in which all students are encouraged to offer ideas and to interact with each other, gifted learners can share and examine ideas in ways that stretch the boundaries of their knowledge.

The Importance of Discovery

Discovery teaching is designed to help students learn and "acquire knowledge that is uniquely their own because they discovered it themselves" (Carin & Sund, 1980, p. 100). The process requires the use of data as a tool for inductive thinking to find the meaning, structure, and organization of ideas. Socrates, John Dewey, Jean Piaget, and Jerome Bruner all have emphasized the importance of learning by doing. Learners must use primary mental processes such as observing, classifying, labeling, describing, and inferring. They also must draw conclusions and form generalizations based on analysis of the results of these processes.

Through doing, rather than listening, students learn to think inductively; to see a pattern among items, events, or phenomena that are presented (or observed); and to discern reasons why a particular pattern occurs. This pattern may be based on some criterion such as size, shape, quantity, order, distance, or other specific attribute.

Once a pattern has been discovered, a learner also can make predictions about new items based on knowledge of previous items, events, or phenomena and how they fit together. *Deductive thinking* is the process of predicting future events or patterns, whereas *inductive thinking* is the discovery of the rule or principle underlying the perceived pattern. For example, in a problem involving numbers in a series, (e.g., 1, 1, 2, 3, 5, 8, 13, 21, 34), inductive reasoning is used to find out the rule that governs the pattern. In the case of the Fibbonacci sequence illustrated, each number after 1 is produced by adding the two preceding numbers; deductive reasoning is used to predict the next number ($21 + 34 = 55$) in the pattern. The use of formal logic also is an example of deductive thinking.

Discovery (or inquiry) learning is facilitated when teachers guide students through the process of inductive thinking. Students are encouraged to use the available data and their own mental processes to discover a target concept, generalization, or principle. The product sought is recognition of a relationship between data, concepts, two or more concepts, or two or more observations. In its most extreme form (often found in law school classrooms), the process is called "hiding the ball."

Bruner (1960) posited four reasons for the use of a discovery approach:

- Intellectual potency develops only by using one's mind.

- The rewards of discovery are intrinsically motivating.

- Students learn how to organize and carry out an investigation.

- Memory is enhanced through reasoning out concepts or principles rather than simply hearing them.

In a discovery or inquiry approach, teachers set up situations or activities so that students are faced with decision-problem questions that may have several possible outcomes. As their "prior learning is inadequate to find an appropriate solution or explanation" (Coleman, 1985, p. 368), students must follow the steps in an inquiry process. Banks (1990) suggested that social inquiry might proceed from (a) doubt or concern through (b) problem formulation, (c) formulation of a hypothesis, (d) definition of terms and conceptualization of the inquiry, (e) collection of data, (f) evaluation and analysis of data, and (g) testing hypotheses and deriving generalizations and theories. Both authors pointed out that social inquiry is cyclic and that generalizations in social sciences never are regarded as absolute. Short and Armstrong (1993) and Banks (1990) emphasized the social context of inquiry or discovery learning. In Figure 4.3, the cyclic and social nature of the inquiry process is illustrated by Short's Inquiry Model. The experiences and values that each learner brings to the inquiry affect decisions at almost every step of the process. Problem formulation, hypothesis generalization, and conceptualization of an inquiry are particularly susceptible to the influence of values and beliefs.

Guided discovery provides enough structure so that students can discover concepts and principles. Initially, much of the planning must be done by the teacher until gifted students have learned some strategies such as methods used to collect and record data, methods for analyzing

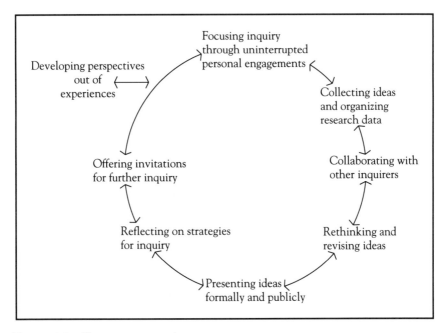

Figure 4.3. Short inquiry cycle.

Note. "Moving Toward Inquiry: Integrating Literature into the Science Curriculum," by K. G. Short and J. Armstrong, 1993, *The New Advocate*, 6(3), p. 194. Copyright 1993 by K. G. Short. Reprinted with permission.

data, and ways to communicate findings. Womack (1966) suggested a sequential order as one way of using a guided-discovery approach to help students develop generalizations:

1. Decide what generalization or generalizations should be discovered from the content of the study.

2. Organize the activity or activities so that all the important concepts and relationships are available to the students.

3. Have students organize the content.

4. Have students trace sequences or identify patterns of events.

5. Ask students to synthesize the patterns or sequences identified into one comprehensive statement.

6. Ask students to provide evidence that their statement fits the requirements of a generalization by giving examples of its applicability to varied times, places, events, or peoples.

This sequence of steps has a definite concentration on generalizations that should be discovered from the content of the inquiry. With this approach, teachers must avoid overcontrol of the process, pre-programmed answers, and expectations of only certain kinds of generalizations. In other words, students must be allowed to discover generalizations different from those identified by the teacher. Students also should be encouraged to examine generalizations developed by others, including the teacher, to determine whether they are accurate and pertinent to the inquiry.

Taba (1966) and Banks (1990) also recommended careful planning for discovery learning. According to Banks, the teacher's plans proceed from generalizations to inferences to concepts to facts and observations; student learning proceeds in the opposite direction. In the *Hilda Taba Teaching Strategies Program* (Institute for Staff Development, 1971a, 1971b), lesson planning also begins with generalizations and key concepts. The teacher develops a cognitive map to identify possible data and possible inferences that might be drawn from the data. However, the teacher's cognitive map is merely a tool for the teacher's thinking about the content of the lesson; students must have the opportunity to reach their own conclusions and generalizations about a topic based on the data they study and the inferences they make. Equally important, students must provide an explanation of the logic they used to reach their conclusions and defend their position in discussions with other students. Two of the four teaching strategies developed by Taba are guided-discovery tech-niques. The structure and procedures of the second strategy, called *Inter-pretation of Data*, are summarized in Table 4.1.

Throughout the *Interpretation-of-Data* process, the teacher asks ques-tions to focus students on the task; to induce them to clarify, extend, and elaborate on their ideas; and to give them opportunities to cite evidence or reasoning in support of their ideas. In all of the strategies, a focusing question calling for a variety of possible responses is asked of the entire group; no one student is required to respond. The teacher attempts, through questioning, to stimulate students to think on as abstract a level as possible but accepts all responses whatever the level of abstraction. The teacher does not judge or criticize students' ideas nor allow other students to criticize ideas. Although students may challenge ideas offered by other students, they do so by asking questions to clarify meanings or by offering other ideas for consideration. No student is ever required to verbalize an idea when she or he is not ready.

Some controversy exists about whether verbalizing the principle is the same as understanding the principle (Coleman, 1985). For example, J. J. Gallagher (1985) recommended that students demonstrate their understanding of general principles through applying ideas or solving problems. He cautioned against having students verbalize their discovery on the basis of two factors: (1) Too-early verbalizations may be poorly stated, and evaluation may be concentrated on the form and organization of the statement rather than on its meaning; and (2) too-early verbaliza-tion of the underlying principle by one student may "short circuit" the thinking processes of other students who work more deliberately. A third reason for using alternative means to demonstrate student understanding of general principles is that some students have difficulties verbalizing principles even though they understand them very well. For students whose strengths lie in spatial or logical–mathematical intelligences, a diagram or model might serve the purpose of demonstrating understand-ing of underlying principles.

The discovery method requires teachers to select materials or exam-ples carefully, to have a clear conception of the relationship of the gener-alization or generalizations to the curriculum, and to possess a familiarity with the major principles that are essential to a field of study. The process also requires time, special materials, and organization. In his discussion of the merits of a discovery approach, J. J. Gallagher (1985) noted the existence of arguments both for and against this method of teaching. On the pro side, discovery learning generates enthusiasm and excitement

Table 4.1. Summary of Steps in Taba's Interpretation of Data Strategy

Step	Students' Behavioral Objectives	Students' Thinking Objectives	Teachers' Focusing Questions
1	Enumerate data relevant to the topic focus of the discussion	Recall data from prior knowledge or new experience Differentiate relevant from irrelevant data	What did you read? see? hear? What do you recall about . . . ? What can you tell me about . . . ?
2	State inferences about causes and/or effects State evidence or reasoning to support inferences	Infer causes (effects) of events or phenomena (items of data) Identify evidence or reasons to support inferences	What are some causes for [*data*]? What have been some effects of [*data*]? Why do you think [*inference*] is a *cause* (*effect*) of [*data*]?
3	State inferences about prior causes and/or subsequent effects State evidence or reasoning to support inferences	Infer causes (effects) of previously inferred causes (effects) Identify evidence or reasoning to support inferences	What are some causes of [*cause*]? What are some effects of [*effect*]? Why do you think [*inference*] is a cause of [*cause*] (*effect*) of [*cause*] (*effect*)?
4	State conclusions based on cause/effect inferences State evidence or reasoning to support conclusions	Synthesize inferences to form conclusion(s) Identify evidence or reasoning to support conclusion	What could you conclude about . . . ? From what you know and what we've discussed, what would lead you to make that conclusion?
5	State generalization based on conclusion State evidence or reasoning to support generalization	Generalize about all of the inferences and to other like situations/phenomena Identify evidence or reasoning to support generalization	What could you say generally about the causes (effects) of . . . ? From our discussion and from what you know, what would lead you to make that statement?

Note. From *Hilda Taba Teaching Strategies Program: Unit II* (p. 8), by Institute for Staff Development, 1971, Miami, FL: Author. Copyright 1971 by Institute for Staff Development. Adapted with permission.

among students while their active involvement in the process increases the likelihood of learning the key concepts and generalizations. Students experience an intellectual thrill when they learn they can solve problems autonomously, and they appreciate the freedom they have to actively direct the investigation.

Arguments against discovery learning usually involve the costs in teacher preparation and student learning time. In a typical discovery lesson, students may take four or five times as long to discover a rule or principle as it would take the teacher to state the rule and give half a dozen examples to illustrate the point. Time certainly is an important element for students and teachers. Teachers who believe that teaching is knowledge transmission and who are captive to a "bloated curriculum" (Onosko & Newmann, 1994) often forget that it takes time for students to think, reason, compare, and gain insight into important concepts and generalizations. In discovery learning, the teacher covers less content, but the students retain more important knowledge and are more able to transfer that knowledge to solve related problems in other contexts. Given the learning abilities of gifted students, combined with carefully chosen content selected to illustrate broad concepts and generalizations, the extra time spent using a discovery approach with gifted children is well worth the cost. "Discovery helps students become more autonomous, self-directed, and responsible for their own learning" (Carin & Sund, 1980, p. 75). They become more self-motivated and learning becomes intrinsically rewarding.

Research on discovery learning has accumulated slowly and generally shows the value of this approach over didactic methods. Taba's (1966) research shows that the inductive approach both helps students to increase academic achievement and enhances reasoning skills. In a summary of research on discovery learning, Shulman (1968) reported to a Conference on Learning by Discovery that in controlled experiments, guided discovery generally has been effective for both immediate learning levels and later transfer of learning. Discovery-oriented curricula improve students' inquiry abilities and help individuals to become better learners. Children with behavioral problems, such as learning anxiety or rebellious acting out, also benefit from nondirective, nonauthoritarian environments in which students have opportunities to explore materials and to discover new ideas. This kind of environment promotes greater achievement and lessens behavior problems.

Throughout most of this section, we have stressed formal inductive thinking processes of discovery learning. Equally important for discovery are problem-solving processes. Creative Problem Solving (Noller, Parnes, & Biondi, 1976), "Problem-Based Learning" (S. Gallagher, Stepien, & Rosenthal, 1992), and "Thinking Actively in a Social Context" (Adams & Wallace, 1988, 1991) are examples of excellent models for the development of problem-solving heuristics and discovery among gifted learners. Less formal discovery learning, such as exploration of the tools and methods of a discipline or a specific intelligence also are fruitful learning experiences for gifted students.

One final point needs to be made. We do not suggest that teachers emphasize inductive reasoning to the exclusion of deduction, nor do we recommend that teachers always use a discovery approach. We are recommending a balance between inductive and deductive reasoning, and the use of a guided-discovery approach whenever appropriate. A discovery approach is both appropriate and necessary when the objectives are to simultaneously develop complex, highly abstract ideas and higher levels of thinking with gifted learners. If these students simply are "given" the ideas, neither will they understand them fully nor will they have an opportunity to develop their own inductive reasoning processes. "Beyond substantive knowledge of the topic, students need analytic knowledge (e.g., the structure of well-reasoned arguments; distinctions between empirical, conceptual and normative claims; criteria to judge reliability of evidence) and metacognitive knowledge (i.e., awareness and self-monitoring of one's thought processes)" (Onosko & Newmann, 1994, p. 29).

Characteristics of the Gifted

Many gifted students are intuitive and may recognize connections or deeper meanings without conscious awareness of reasoning; others have outstanding abilities to think things through and to consider alternatives. Some are goal oriented or highly motivated in their areas of interest, whereas others seem to acquire sophisticated understandings with ease. For all students who have these characteristics and for those who love to explore, observe, and experiment, discovery learning is a most appropriate process. These are students who will be able to carry out independent and group investigations after some guided experience with inquiry processes, and the time costs of implementing inquiry activities will be minimal compared to the benefits these students will derive from these opportunities. Those who enjoy bringing structure to seemingly disparate data also enjoy learning through the discovery approach. Discovery-learning processes facilitate productive research, synthesis of results of research, and graphic representations of results. Valid inductive thinking is essential for formulating theories and creating new knowledge. Students who acquire high competence in discovery processes are more apt to become creative, productive adults and lifelong-learners.

Evidence of Reasoning

An integral aspect of a discovery approach and a critical element in the development of higher levels of thinking is the fundamental requirement that in expressing their conclusions, students also express the logic or reasoning they used to arrive at those conclusions. With one exception,[1] each time students give answers (i.e., inferences, conclusions) or make statements arrived at through a thinking process, they should be asked to explain or cite evidence to support their statements. Explanation can involve diagrams, demonstrations, pictures, and other nonverbal methods as well as verbal ones. Explaining the logical analysis or reasoning process behind an answer is important for gifted students for at least three reasons. First, learners can benefit from hearing or seeing how another person analyzed a problem; methods chosen by others may be different from their own processes. Theoretical support for the learning of reasoning from intellectual peers can be found in the research and writing of Piaget (Piaget & Inhelder, 1969), Vygotsky (1978), and Damon (1984). Students can profit from expressions of reasoning by students at a slightly higher level than their own but cannot profit from expressions of reasoning at significantly higher levels because it is too sophisticated. Damon (1984) pointed out that when a learning task is hierarchical and involves discrete steps or skills, a student can learn more effectively from an adult or more able thinker; when the learning task involves concept or principle development, learning is most effective through interaction with intellectual peers.

A second reason for asking students to explain their reasons is that others have an opportunity to evaluate the process as well as the products of their thinking. Support for assessment of process, or *how* students know what they know, comes from the work of J. H. Clarke (1990), Gardner (1992), Goodman (1989), D. Taylor (1991), and others. The development of varied effective thinking processes is an essential component of

---

[1] The exception to this rule is during the divergent thinking steps of various thinking processes.

curriculum, but products (e.g., writing, pictures, tests) may be as much the result of bodily kinesthetic skills as of intellectual processes. In traditional school products, logical–mathematical and linguistic intelligences are most frequently stressed. Reasoning probably results from a combination of several intelligences and may represent a richness of thinking that is not evident in a product.

A third important purpose for asking students to provide evidence of their reasoning is that "students need to be aware of their own mental processes in order to learn to control them" (J. H. Clarke, 1990). Several critical and creative thinking processes depend, to a large extent, on sound reasoning. Problems to be solved often have multiple solutions, each with certain costs and certain benefits; decision making and evaluation require interpretation and informed judgment through the application of multiple, sometimes conflicting criteria (Resnick, 1987). Higher-order reasoning also involves self-regulation of thinking processes and awareness of purpose. J. H. Clarke (1990) pointed out the need for attention to higher-order reasoning in the curriculum:

> Left to its own devices, the human mind may not be inclined to refine its own strategies. It can reason automatically, but it can also dispense with reason automatically. It can ignore the facts, fail to recall, infer incorrectly, leap to unreliable conclusions, get the wrong idea, fail to set goals, devise shoddy plans, endlessly repeat a fruitless procedure, and carry out an approach without checking for accuracy. . . . It can work better—to a greater number of purposes and with greatly increased power—if we teach students how to control the work it does by nature.
>
> (p. 25)

Too many teachers ask students for reasons or evidence only when they disagree with a response or think a student is wrong and wish to call the attention of the class to the faulty reasoning process as an example of what not to do. Parents, too, often ask for reasons only when a child apparently has done something wrong. For these reasons, students often consider "why" questions to be a threat rather than a tool for reflective thinking. This modification of the curriculum is one way to enable students to refine their higher-level thinking skills in all subjects and in a variety of contexts. To illustrate the application of this idea, consider the use of open-ended questions such as those presented earlier.

Question calling for an inference:	What effects, if any, do you feel the war on drugs has had on the abuse of drugs in your community?
Student response:	I think it may have contributed to the increase in teenage murders.
Question calling for clarification:	What do you mean by "contributed to"?
Question calling for elaboration:	What is an example of a contributing cause?
Question calling for support:	How did you arrive at the conclusion that the war on drugs has contributed to an increase in teenage murders?
or	What are your reasons for thinking that the increase in teenage murders is related to the war on drugs?
or	What was your thinking in reaching that conclusion?
or	Why do you think the increase in teenage murders is an effect of the war on drugs?

These types of questions and thinking aloud give students opportunities to examine their own thinking processes and to listen to the processes used by others. Experiences of this kind help students to focus awareness and to direct mental processes toward achieving goals, the linked capabilities that psychologists call *metacognition* (Presseisen, 1985).

Characteristics of the Gifted

The characteristics of gifted students most closely related to the need for this modification are (a) extraordinary ability to communicate ideas and feelings through words, actions, symbols, sounds, or other media of expression; (b) outstanding ability to think things through and consider implications or alternatives; (c) goal-oriented thought; (d) abilities to use ideas, processes, or materials ingeniously; and (e) an unusual capacity for information acquisition and retrieval. Gifted students with these abilities need opportunities to express in some form the thinking processes that led to their ideas, problem solutions, or conclusions and to make connections to previous knowledge or experience. Reflective thinking, or reasoning, is an essential component of learning (Dewey, 1944/1916). "Knowledge is not just something which we are now conscious of, but consists of the dispositions we consciously use in understanding what now happens. Knowledge as an act is bringing some of our dispositions to consciousness with a view to straightening out a perplexity, by conceiving the connection between ourselves and the world in which we live" (Dewey, 1944/1916, p. 344).

The justification for this modification is similar to that for teaching higher levels of thinking and for using a discovery approach. The purpose is to have students go beyond simple acquisition of information to the active and purposeful construction of knowledge. Another reason for this modification is that gifted students may have only a surface knowledge of important concepts that they cover up by using big words and ideas they really do not understand. Teachers often are fooled by this apparent sophistication and, clearly, the student's intellectual development is not facilitated when he or she is allowed to get away with intellectual bluffing.

Too much of what passes for "wisdom" in conversation and in media outlets is little more than unsupported opinion. Because many gifted students are apt to become creative producers in some area or to hold positions of public confidence, they must be able to explain clearly in some expressive mode the processes that led to their conclusions and decisions.

Freedom of Choice

Gifted students need freedom to choose topics to study, methods to use in the process of manipulating and transforming information, the type of products to create, and the context of the learning environment in which to pursue their studies. This modification facilitates their success with other systems and provides a means of building upon the interests and motivation of these learners. Practices that allow varying degrees of freedom of choice include learning centers, contracts, projects, independent study, computer-mediated learning, and self-directed learning. "All of these alternatives, when used correctly, have the advantage of providing gifted students with advanced-level materials and opportunities to work in areas of interest. However, overuse of independent or individualized study arrangements for gifted students limits access to interaction with teachers and other students" (A. Howley, C. Howley, & Pendarvis, 1985).

Many successful programs for gifted children depend almost entirely on independent study. Others, such as Renzulli's (1977) *Enrichment Triad Model* and Betts' (1985) *Autonomous Learner Model* have significant independent-study components. Regular classroom teachers often use this method as a way of extending the learning of gifted students and allowing them to pursue topics of their choice in greater depth than is possible in the classroom curriculum.

Three crucial aspects that must be considered in the implementation of this method are (a) the degree and kind of freedom allowed, (b) the student's ability to manage or profit from the freedom given, and (c) the teacher's ability to relinquish control of a part of the student's learning activities. Each of the practices mentioned previously can be designed to allow different levels of freedom. A learning center, for example, can be designed so that a student has only two possible activities, a defined period of time to work in the center, and a specified product (e.g., a report or drawing) that is evaluated according to predetermined criteria by the teacher. In contrast, a more flexible learning center may contain a variety of tools and materials appropriate to a specific discipline or intelligence, a menu of suggestions for ways that the tools and materials might be explored, and complete freedom to use the center for whatever purpose and for whatever length of time the gifted student deems worthwhile. In the latter case, the student has the option of developing any product she or he desires or no product at all; the product may be evaluated by anyone or by no one. Between these two extremes, various levels of freedom are possible. In the Autonomous Learner Model (Betts, 1985), for example, students initially participate in structured investigations. As they become more adept at research and self-management, they initiate in-depth studies that may involve working with a mentor or at a site away from the school.

Treffinger (1975) designed a useful model for assessing the degree and kind of freedom that a specific gifted student can manage. He included four areas: (1) identification of goals and objectives, (2) assessment of entering behaviors, (3) identification and implementation of instructional procedures, and (4) assessment of performance. Within each of these areas, varying degrees of freedom can be established. For example, in the first area, identification of goals and objectives, four levels of freedom or self-direction can be identified:

Teacher-directed	Teacher prescribes activities for all students
Self-directed, Level 1	Teacher provides choices or options for student(s)
Self-directed, Level 2	Teacher involves student(s) in creating options
Self-directed, Level 3	Learner controls choices; teacher provides [facilitates acquisition of] resources and materials

Coleman (1985) defined independent study somewhat differently: "The independent study method occurs when a learner pursues a topic of personal interest within an area of study by setting the objectives of the inquiry, specifying the procedures, organizing and reporting the results, and evaluating the experience under appropriate, minimal supervision. Teacher and student have joint responsibility for the experience" (p. 370). He merely suggested that the amount of supervision necessary is dependent on the student's previous experience in independent studies and familiarity with the topic. Our belief is that familiarity with the topic is less important than familiarity with inquiry methods appropriate to the topic and access to relevant resources.

Reis and Schack (1993) designed a procedure to help students learn the process of independent study and the development of differentiated products. They stressed the importance of teaching students *how* professionals learn to work in a particular discipline. "This 'knowledge how' not only will enable students to better understand the content of the discipline, but also will teach them the process of becoming independent investigators in their own right" (p. 162). Twelve steps are recommended to teachers:

Step 1	Assess, find, or create student interest
Step 2	Conduct an interview to determine the strength of the interest
Step 3	Help students find a question or questions to research
Step 4	Develop a written plan
Step 5	Help students locate multiple resources and continue working on the topic

Step 6   Provide methodological assistance

Step 7   Help students decide which question(s) to answer

Step 8   Provide managerial assistance

Step 9   Identify final products and audience

Step 10   Offer encouragement, praise, and critical assistance

Step 11   Escalate the process

Step 12   Evaluate

These steps are helpful, but the system contains too much teacher direction. These ideas may be appropriate for students beginning independent study but fail to include options that help students to move from beginners to adept, self-directed learners. The degree of freedom of choice needed by gifted students seems to be somewhat compromised in this model.

In the learning skill component of the individual development dimension of the Autonomous Learner Model (Betts, 1985), students can learn several skills necessary for self-directed learning: (a) goal setting, (b) organization, (c) library research procedures, (d) journal writing, (e) portfolio development, (f) planning, (g) decision making, (h) problem finding, (i) writing, (j) media production, (k) forecasting, and other skills that can be used in a variety of self-directed activities. In addition, students have opportunities to conduct explorations of topics that may be of interest to them so they can develop a proposal for an investigation or an in-depth study. This method is less hierarchical than the model designed by Reis and Schack (1993).

Comparison of the Reis and Schack (1993) model, the Betts (1985) model, and the Treffinger (1975) model reveals that the Betts and Treffinger models include a level of self-direction somewhat higher than that in the Reis and Schack model. In the Reis and Schack model, the teacher continues to impose some restrictions on the student or at least maintains control of choices through the development of criteria for selecting options. In both the Treffinger and Betts systems, students are encouraged to go beyond this level and to develop the self-direction to be completely responsible for their own learning. Students can seek the help of a teacher or mentor when they feel a need for assistance, but the teacher does not supply assistance if it is not requested.

Underlying the need for degrees and types of freedom are several characteristics observed in many gifted individuals. Risemberg and

Zimmerman (1992) noted that gifted students "exhibit preferences for learning that correspond with various features of what we would term self-regulation" (p. 98). Some key features of giftedness, according to Sternberg and Davidson (1986), include intellectual superiority and abilities to choose strategies that will help the students achieve desirable goals, to regulate self-talk and environmental context so as to focus on the execution of a task, and to monitor progress to discern whether goals are being met. Zimmerman and Martinez-Pons (1990) compared the responses to eight hypothetical learning situations of 90 gifted students at grades 5, 8, and 11 with 90 control students from the same grade levels. They found that gifted students reported using more strategies than did control participants and that four strategies—organizing and transforming, self-consequating,[2] seeking peer assistance, and reviewing notes—differentiated gifted students from their grade-level peers. In 10 of the 14 self-regulating learning strategies, however, gifted students did not report significantly greater strategy use than did their grade-level peers. In view of this result, the implication is that gifted students could benefit from self-regulatory strategy training.

Although gifted students need to be guided to progress to a high level of self-direction, educators must make individualized decisions about how much freedom to allow. Even though they have many of the attributes necessary for a self-directed approach, these students still lack the experience to manage complete freedom without preparation. Especially because students have been told what to learn, and how, when, and where to learn it beginning with their first day of school, they should not be expected to know how to completely structure and direct their own learning experiences. Other students, such as those taught with the Whole Language Approach, who have had greater freedom of choice in deciding what is to be learned, selecting methods and materials for learning, communicating with others about what is being learned, and evaluating achievement of goals need less direction. For example, the skills or competencies required for effective participation at the highest level of self-direction in Treffinger's (1975) model are that the student

- can determine criteria for evaluation of progress with teacher advice only when needed,
- can closely match self-evaluation with the assessment made by others,

---

[2] Defined as arranging for rewards or punishment for success or failure.

- can pinpoint general and specific areas of strength and weakness in her or his own products, and

- can determine criteria that would be used by various audiences in evaluating a product.

At that level, (a) the learner controls choices of what to study, and the teacher provides resources and materials; (b) the learner controls diagnosis of needs and consults the teacher for assistance when unclear about some need; (c) the learner defines the project and lists activities; identifies resources needed; and makes scope, sequence, and pace decisions; and (d) the learner conducts self-evaluation. In independent study, this is the ultimate level of freedom of choice.

The discussion of freedom of choice has been focused on its implementation during independent study. However, the element of choice also is crucial in many teacher-directed activities. The use of authentic literature, as in theme sets (i.e., four to five copies of each of several trade books on related subjects) or text sets (i.e., several single copies of trade books about the same subject), allows students to choose to read in an area of interest about a topic rather than having all students read the same information in a text. (For more information about literature-based learning, see Short & Pierce, 1990.) The *Group Investigations* model (Y. Sharan & S. Sharan, 1992) also is an excellent method for facilitating freedom of choice within the scope of classroom curriculum. A broad theme or big idea is introduced to students through a variety of media; then students brainstorm subtopics of the theme for possible investigation. Once subtopics are identified, students sign up for the one of their choice and work with a small group to develop a plan for research that includes individual responsibilities for each group member. Thus, all students in the class are learning about different aspects of the big idea, using methods and materials of their choice, coordinating their work with their small group, and contributing to presentations of findings to all class members. Although initial topic generation and final evaluation are whole-class activities, students have extensive freedom within that structure.

Characteristics of Gifted Students

Students who are highly motivated and who have passionate interests in a topic require freedom of choice of what, how, when, and where to study.

This process modification also is extremely important for students who prefer probing explorations to a broad survey of a topic, who like to bring order to the chaos of information that can be found about issues or themes, and who are aware of connections among data and want to discover the deeper meanings or implications of those connections. These students need little external motivation when they are excited about an area of interest, and they like to accept responsibility and take charge of their own learning. Freedom of choice also is indicated for students with an exceptionally keen sense of humor, who are apt to see aspects of topics that are bizarre or comical. With their ability to play with ideas and deftly illustrate the absurdities intrinsic to a situation, these students need freedom from highly structured courses of study. Students who are highly creative need freedom to choose, particularly in the ways to study or to demonstrate mastery of a topic. They need to be able to work in their preferred intelligences and areas of special interest.

Zimmerman and Martinez-Pons (1990), from their review of research on independent study programs, self-regulatory strategies, and metacognitive development, concluded that such free-choice programs have a positive influence on (a) motivation and increased excitement about learning; (b) helping students choose future careers and college majors; (c) study habits and thinking processes, such as organizing and focusing thoughts, developing study strategies, increasing critical and creative thinking; and (d) the development of a highly challenging and satisfying learning environment.

Group Interaction

Group-process and group-interaction activities[3] should be an integral part of curricula for gifted students. These activities can be used as tools for building group effectiveness and for unlocking the potential of individuals by developing their abilities to relate to others more constructively. Group-process activities may range from simulated social situations or other games in which group interactions are observed and discussed to an extreme form of self-critique and critique of other participants as is found in sensitivity groups in psychological counseling. A

---

[3] For readers interested in simulation games and group-process activities, the following resources are helpful: the entire issue of *Gifted Child Quarterly*, Summer, 1979; Cohen (1986); Foster-Harrison (1994); N. Graves and T. Graves (1990); catalogs from INTERACT.

facilitator trained in the skills needed to establish an atmosphere of trust, to foster the willingness to self-disclose, to encourage honesty, and to develop a group support system is necessary to structure these group-process activities.

In the extreme form, these activities would not be appropriate in a classroom. However, Betts (1985) contended that group-building activities are an essential strand in a program for gifted students. These structured, group-interaction activities provide a setting in which gifted students can learn valuable social and leadership skills, develop interpersonal intelligence, and become more empathetic. Through these activities, students learn by interacting and by reflecting on how to do so more effectively. The essential elements of such activities are (a) a structured simulation (e.g., a game, role-playing situation, discussion) in which individuals follow a set of rules and must interact with at least a small group of other students; (b) self-analysis through verbal critiques, viewing of videotapes, or listening to audiotapes; and (c) critiques of performance by others in the group. These critiques are much more effective if the students actually watch or listen to themselves on a tape; the self-evaluations are much more powerful than are others' criticisms.

One method that is very useful in a wide variety of situations is called the "fishbowl technique." Students are seated in two concentric circles. The inner circle participates in a structured activity, simulation, or discussion. Members of the outer circle serve as observers and are unable to participate or to interfere with the inner circle in any way. In some cases, observers are asked to look for specific behaviors or are assigned to watch certain individuals. When the structured activity ends, the inner circle discusses the activity and critiques itself. The outer circle of observers then adds its comments. The two groups then change places, and the process is repeated.

Another strategy called "think–pair–share" (McTighe & Lyman, 1988) is designed to have students share their knowledge and understanding of a topic in a short discussion. Teachers use some type of signal to help students move smoothly from step to step:

1. Students listen while the teacher poses an open-ended question.

2. Students are given time in which to think about their responses individually.

3. Students then talk with a partner about their responses.

4. Each group shares responses with the whole class.

When teachers encourage students to talk together, they make interaction a legitimate vehicle for learning (Y. Sharan & S. Sharan, 1992). Students learn to view each other as sources of ideas and information, rather than as competitors for the highest grades.

Among the goals of structured group interactions are (a) the development of discussion skills (e.g., conciseness, listening, reflecting, contributing); (b) reaching consensus, making decisions, or both; (c) encouraging participation; and (d) reflecting on group process. Students *identify* what happened in the interaction, *analyze* why the events happened, *generalize* about how they can apply what they learned to new situations, and *set goals* for task completion and group maintenance (N. Graves & T. Graves, 1990).

In role-playing activities, each member of a group is given a specific role. When the group discusses a topic, each individual must assume that specific role. Possible group roles may include the following (Gage & Berliner, 1979):

- unifying roles, or those concerned mainly with climate and harmony in the group (e.g., encourager, harmonizer, compromiser, gatekeeper, energizer);

- task roles, or those concerned with accomplishing the job (e.g., initiator, information seeker, information giver, opinion giver, coordinator); and

- antigroup roles, or those concerned with meeting the needs of an individual at the expense of a group (e.g., aggressor, blocker, attention seeker, dominator, noncooperator).

Members can be assigned randomly to a certain role, or teachers also can choose roles that are opposite to a student's usual style of interaction so that person can experience a different way of participating in a group.

Some simulations are short term, such as *The Murder Mystery* (Stanford & Stanford, 1969) in which each of the participants is given one or more clues to help solve a murder. The group must solve the mystery by compiling their clues *orally*. They may not give all clues to someone to organize. Observers watch for group roles, cooperation of members, and other aspects of interaction. They also note the problem-solving approach taken by the group.

Other simulations, like *Liberté: A Simulation of the French Revolution* (Brasefield, 1970), may take days or weeks to complete. In *Liberté*, students are grouped as royalty, clergy, nobles, bourgeoisie, or peasants.

Students keep balance sheets of the "Revolutionary Influence Points" (RIPS) they gain or lose through researching historical roles and responding to expected and unexpected events (represented by historical bulletins that change financial, social, and political status) that push the participants toward revolution and the Reign of Terror.

In addition to structured games and activities, any activity that includes group collaboration, self-analysis, and critique from others should be included in this modification. Long-term games, committee work, student government, and literature discussion circles can help students develop interaction abilities and provide a setting in which students can assess, change, and reevaluate their own behavior. Self-analysis and group critique should be a frequent and continuing part of the process. An important point to remember is that evaluation of students generally should be done on an individual basis. The assignment of group grades for collaborative activities, particularly in classrooms of heterogeneously grouped students, often does not recognize the contributions of individual members of the group.

Characteristics of Gifted Students

Group-process activities and simulation games generally build upon and develop the leadership and interpersonal characteristics of gifted students. Students who are unusually open, perceptive, and responsive to the feelings of themselves and others, those who express themselves well in a chosen medium, and those with a keen sense of humor particularly benefit from group interaction. In these structured settings, students can develop their skills in cooperating with others and influencing and motivating others. They also can practice their problem-solving skills. Simulations require the exercise of inductive and deductive thinking, analysis, synthesis, decision making, planning, evaluation, and predicting consequences of alternative actions. Because of the high degree of participation and the rapid pace of most games, gifted students usually maintain their interest in them. Simulation games may be particularly effective with gifted students (Cline, 1979) and may help to develop leadership skills among gifted girls (Addison, 1979).

In sharp contrast to "traditional wisdom," Christensen's (1994) findings from a survey of more than 350 students in a school for gifted children indicated that they overwhelmingly preferred collaborative experiences rather than individualistic experiences. Across all grade levels,

2–6, both male and female students showed statistically significant preferences for noncompetitive, collaborative settings. With a few exceptions (e.g., team competitions), "gifted students more frequently favor noncompetitive settings; they [the findings] also support the conclusion that these students generally favor collaborative types of settings whether or not competition is involved" (p. 506).

Pacing

Pacing may be one of the most important process modifications recommended for gifted students. The pace of instruction is how slowly or how rapidly information is presented in learning situations. Gifted students generally do not need as much time as do other students to assimilate information and strategies or to commit them to memory. In the Study of Mathematically Precocious Youth (SMPY) program at Johns Hopkins University, for example, $4\frac{1}{2}$ years of precalculus mathematics was taught successfully in 120 hours of instruction (George, 1976). The classes at Johns Hopkins initially were held for 2 hours each Saturday morning for 13 months. With these talented students, the material was mastered in approximately one-fifth the usual time. The concept subsequently has been adopted in numerous school systems throughout the country. Acceleration and fast-paced instruction also are intrinsic to the *Enrichment Triad Model* (Renzulli, 1977; Renzulli & Reis, 1985). Curriculum compacting, or moving more rapidly through required content by using such techniques as pretesting for mastery, organizing around broad themes, and using less time for drill and practice, buys time for students to work on projects of particular interest to them. Acceleration, as illustrated by the SMPY model, refers to moving students through the standard curriculum in as short a time as is both possible and profitable to students. As practiced in the *Enrichment Triad Model*, acceleration means moving through a year's required curriculum in a few months and using the rest of the year to do activities in areas of study that particularly interest individuals or small groups of students. Both types of acceleration have proved to be effective in the education of gifted students (Rogers, 1993).

The notion of accelerated pacing refers primarily to the introduction of new material; it should not be construed as cutting short the time students have to think (*wait time*). After asking a question that calls for complex thinking, teachers often feel compelled to fill the silence with words or questions; if a student has not answered the question in a few seconds, these teachers either answer the question themselves or pose it in another way. As a child, the first author often complained to her mother that teachers always asked tough questions and then kept talking so she could not answer. Indeed, that childhood observation has been supported by research. Taba (1964, 1966) cited research showing that the average amount of time teachers wait for answers to their questions is 2 seconds! Rowe (1986) found that when teachers wait at least 5 seconds, the level of thinking reflected in students' answers is significantly increased.

Rapid pacing of the required curriculum is facilitated by the content modification of organizing for learning value. When content is inter-disciplinary and organized around broad themes, gifted students can learn complex ideas and their connections to many disciplines in a relatively short period of time. K. Smith (1992) pointed out that American history can be organized around two broad themes: exploration and conflict. Those themes also are central to literature and other areas of the human-ities and arts.

When gifted students are in heterogeneous groups, one form of pac-ing that works effectively is to suggest that they complete the most complex questions in an assignment; if they solve the problems in a satisfactory manner, they can use the remaining practice time to work in an area of their choice. Another option is implicit in the use of materials of varying levels of complexity. In their areas of interest and strength, gifted students can be encouraged to choose more challenging tasks and materials—acceleration through choice of content rather than through the speeding up of traditional content.

Characteristics of Gifted Students

Two of the most frequently observed characteristics of gifted students are how quickly they learn and remember new ideas and how quickly they become bored if learning activities are not challenging. Students who are highly motivated in an area of interest, students who thrive on inquiry and exploration of ideas, events, and materials, and students who are intuitive and quick to recognize connections need to have learning expe-riences that are paced appropriately. "Drill and kill" exercises should be eliminated, and most review sessions need be little more than brief reminders.

In an attempt to show that even those classified as "slow learners" are capable of abstract thought, Taba (1964, 1966) introduced the concept of pacing assimilation and accommodation activities. The Piagetian concept of assimilation is defined as incorporating information into an individual's existing cognitive structures; accommodation is changing the cognitive structures so that new information that does not fit into present structures can be properly classified and stored. Students who learn particular content more slowly need many assimilation activities with concrete materials before they can begin to modify structures to accommodate ill-fitting data and progress to a more abstract level of thinking. Students who learn rapidly in a certain content area need far fewer assimilation activities to enable accommodation to occur.

Speeding up the rate of instruction in classrooms for gifted children, condensing year-long courses into a semester or less, and providing various levels of activities and materials are elements of appropriate pacing for meeting the needs of gifted children and facilitating the other process and content recommendations.

Variety

Variety of process refers to the number and types of learning procedures used. To ensure variety, teachers can use many different information presentation strategies such as lectures, films, television programs, demonstrations, field trips, computer-assisted instruction, and learning centers. Students may participate in discussions, learning games, simulations, committee work, independent research, small-group activities, and discovery activities.

A key element in this modification is that teachers discard the erroneous belief that *all students must do the same thing at the same time.* At least seven types of intelligence are known (Gardner, 1983), and several different learning styles have been identified (Dunn & Griggs, 1988; McCarthy, 1990; Milgram, Dunn, & Price, 1993; L. Smith & Renzulli, 1984). Variations in problem types, ranging from highly structured to ill structured, also have been described (Maker, 1992). Students should be able to choose from among many options and design their thinking processes in their preferred formats. For example, some students prefer to organize their ideas in a traditional outline format; others prefer to use a graphic device, such as a cognitive map. Some students prefer to collect most of their data through reading, others prefer experiments, and still others prefer techniques such as interviews and surveys. Although all students should work on the same process as they are learning its steps, students also should have the option of choosing the process or processes they wish to use during small-group or individual investigations. Even when activities are teacher directed, those activities should be sufficiently varied so that each student has opportunities to work in a preferred learning style or a preferred intelligence.

Characteristics of Gifted Students

Gifted students vary from each other in preferred intelligences, learning styles, interests, and experiential backgrounds. The principle of variety in processes is essential to ensure that students have an opportunity to solve problems in their preferred modes, express their ideas in a way that is compatible with their talents, and take advantage of their strengths (e.g., reasoning ability, intuition, creativity). However, gifted students also need to learn *how* and *when* to use a variety of thinking and information management processes. Because gifted students may enter a variety of fields of productive endeavor, they also need to compare and contrast inquiry methods, problem-solving models, and higher-level thinking skills to discover the similarities and differences among the varied processes and to discover when one process is more appropriate than another (and why).

Summary

Process, or the ways that people do mental and physical activities, cannot and should not be separated from content to be learned. However, the processes used often affect the level of content learning that takes place. Perhaps more than any other modification, the processes recommended for gifted students also can benefit almost all students. Certainly, all students should learn to use higher-level thinking skills and problem-solving processes, have opportunities to participate in responding to open-ended questions, and to be involved in discovery learning. All students should be asked to explain the reasons they came to a specific conclusion or made a specific prediction. Almost all students should be able to make choices and use preferred processes while solving problems or managing information. Perhaps the only process modifications that truly should be reserved for gifted students are rapid pacing of content presentation and the most self-directed levels of independent study.

In too many programs for gifted students, the only modifications made have been in process. As a result, curricula for gifted students often has been criticized as "fun and games." Critics have charged, not unreasonably, that these programs would be appropriate for almost all students.

The key to differentiated education for gifted students is the astute combination of modifications in all four dimensions of the curriculum, not in process alone. The processes discussed in this chapter contribute to the joy of learning but also represent crucial methodologies for manipulating content information and transforming it into personal knowledge. Although process is only one dimension of the curriculum that needs to be modified, these changes must not be deemphasized. Process methodologies continue to be an essential aspect of curriculum for gifted students.

Chapter 5

Product

The nature of products expected from students is a third area of the curriculum that can and should be modified for gifted learners. Products (output) are a natural result of the content (input) and are the end result of processes used to develop knowledge. Although output cannot be separated entirely from input and process, most people rely heavily on products to evaluate students and to evaluate the effectiveness or validity of an educational program. Ideas, problem solutions, research reports, dances, musical compositions, displays, constructions, slides and photographs, television productions, computer programs, books, athletic demonstrations, speeches, mime, and dramatic productions are examples of the myriad kinds of products that result from active use of content and process.

Each of these products involves the use of a particular type of information, is directed toward a particular audience, and is formally or informally evaluated or judged by someone. Products can result from teacher-directed activities or from activities selected, planned, and implemented by one or more individuals. A research report, for example, could involve a student's reading about a teacher-selected topic in two or more encyclopedias and then paraphrasing the content. On the other hand, the product could be a report of original research, with topic area and research methods chosen by the investigator or investigators, in which data related to some phenomenon is collected and analyzed with the resulting information interpreted in terms of a particular theory. The first report probably would be directed solely to the teacher; the latter would be directed toward a professional audience through possible publication in a scholarly or scientific journal. A teacher-directed report is read and evaluated by the teacher and, perhaps, by members of the author's family. A research report submitted to a journal is read and evaluated by manuscript reviewers for the journal, using criteria appropriate for contributors to that journal. The report may be rejected, may be returned to the author with professional evaluation and suggestions for revision, or may be accepted for publication. If published, the research report is then read and evaluated by subscribers to the journal. The basic difference in the two products is that the first is a "student-type" report whereas the latter is a "professional" type of research product (Renzulli, 1977). Student-type products tend to be contrived and somewhat artificial with a single function—testing whether the student has mastered the objectives of the learning experience. Professional-type products have a real purpose in the life of the individual creator, are aimed toward a particular audience, and are a result of an individual's desire to investigate a phenomenon or to create or develop new ideas or objects. At times, teachers may need to direct students to create certain types of products, or students may need to demonstrate proficiency in a subject area through tests mandated by state or local education agencies. In most cases, however, gifted students should use their abilities and energy to create professional-type products.

The basic guideline for modifying curriculum in the area of products expected from students is that student products approximate, to the extent possible, those developed by professionals in the following ways:

- The proposed product addresses a real problem or concern.
- The product has a real rather than a contrived purpose.
- The intent of the producer is to please, inform, convince, impress, or otherwise have an impact on a real audience.
- The product is a transformation or synthesis rather than a recapitulation or summary of existing information.
- The product will be evaluated by someone, other than the teacher, using criteria appropriate to the field.
- The format has been selected by the producer as appropriate to the proposed audience and to the talents of its creator.

When the content and process modifications recommended in this volume are implemented, teachers cannot assess student progress appropriately if educators accept only a student-type, contrived product. When students are learning abstract, complex ideas or thought systems, their learning requires active investigation in the way that a professional approaches problems. Students should be able to study a few crucial phenomena "in sufficient depth to discover the essential ways of thinking, of discovering appropriate causalities, or handling generalizations, and of establishing conclusions" (Taba, 1962, p. 180). Like professionals, students also should be able to use a variety of materials and processes to create unique products that address real problems in an area appropriate to their talents and interests. The process is carried to its logical conclusion when the resulting products are evaluated by both the producer and experts using criteria appropriate to the field (or by teachers applying the same criteria).

A few authors in this field have discussed in a direct way the modification of products for gifted students (Betts, 1985; J. Feldhusen & Kolloff, 1978; Guilford, 1967; Renzulli & Reis, 1985; Torrance, 1979). Others (cf. chapters on the Parnes, Taba, Taylor, and Treffinger models in Maker & Nielson, 1995) do so indirectly through a discussion of problem finding or problem solving. Van Tassel-Baska et al. (1988) also suggested gradually increasing the complexity of products. Closer attention to the nature of products "would lead educators to a sequential restructuring of product expectations that would require a more complex response on the part of the learner. For example, an assignment to do a written report in seventh grade English on the structural components of a short story might progress to an assignment to do a written critique of a piece of fiction read outside of class in the eighth grade" (p. 79). This approach is appropriate when the purpose of an assignment is the development of particular content and process skills. In the context of independent study, however, students should have the autonomy to choose the nature and format of the resulting product. In the following discussion of product modifications recommended in programs for gifted learners, we follow the same format used in the chapters on content and process.

Addressed to Real Problems

Throughout this chapter, we use the word *problem* as a general term for a variety of possible situations about which an individual must make decisions. For example, an artist transforms internal creative tension into problems. Creative achievement requires the transformation of an intangible conflict into a tangible symbolic problem before a creative solution can be produced (Getzels & Csikszentmihalyi, 1976). Problems should not be viewed as negative situations to be faced; rather they should be viewed as catalysts for creative production.

One of the first strategies a teacher can use to encourage students to focus on real problems is to ask provocative or leading questions such as those suggested by Womack (1966) or Williams (1986; 1990). Students also should be presented a model of the kinds of questions or problems investigated by professionals. In Betts' (1985) *Autonomous Learner Model*, for example, important aspects of the program are student exploration to discover issues of interest and concern followed by an investigation into the issue by a small group of students who share interest in a selected area. After compiling information about the topic, the group invites guests to participate in a seminar in which the information is explored, questions about the issue are raised, and possible alternatives are discussed and evaluated.

A modification (Isaksen & Parnes, 1985) of the *Creative Problem Solving* model is a spotlight on "mess" finding to demonstrate the importance of investigating varied aspects of real problems. Whenever a problem is analyzed in depth, many subproblems and challenges may emerge. In essence, a mess is created. The exploration of the varied facets of a problem may involve brainstorming, concept mapping (J. H. Clarke, 1990), or using an interpretation-of-data strategy (Institute for Staff Development, 1971b) to identify main causes of the problem. Once the main problem is identified, students then can use a problem-solving strategy to devise a solution to the problem.

The real problem may be a major social concern, like the old industrial site near Jackson Elementary School in Salt Lake City that contained thousands of barrels of unidentified products. Barbara Lewis (1991) and her students researched the dangers of hazardous waste and concluded that they had a real problem that endangered the lives of the children who attended the school and their neighbors.

In 1993, four boys in Cymry DeBoucher's 7th grade REACH class at Coronado Middle School in Catalina, Arizona, were concerned over the destruction of saguaro cactus by developers as they prepared sites for home and business construction. The Saguaro Team, as they have become known, identified inadequate laws and lax enforcement of regulations as a problem that presented a serious threat to the Sonoran Desert environment. Their initial purpose was to do research about the subject and to enter their report into a geography contest sponsored by American Express. As they gathered information, their concern grew into a full-fledged campaign to change the laws regarding endangered species (see Exhibit 5.1).

Exhibit 5.1. Letter from Saguaro Team members.

CORONADO K-8 SCHOOL
3401 East Wilds Road
Tucson, Arizona 85737

(602) 292-4400

Gale Lefkowitz   John S. Tindall-Gibson, Ph.D.
Principal   Principal

12/8/94

Dear Dr. Neilson

We are excited that you have chosen to use our Saguaro project as an illustration of community problem solving by students. We have found our project interesting and challenging. This experience has shown us how to cooperate with a team, use problem solving skills, communicate with adults, and learn about the real world.

Some of the things we have done during this project include:
- making presentations to local governing bodies
- writing a bill/ordinance and working to get it passed
- attending meetings /conferences on development and growth
- networking to build support for our project and to gather information
- trips to the local Historical Society to find historic maps and other
      information about the growth of Tucson, the newspaper for more
      research, trips to development sites and relocation sites
- competing in the American Express Geography Competition and placing
      third in the nation
- entering the Arizona Community Problem Solving division of
      Future Problem Solving

We would be honored to have you use our names in your book.

Sincerely,

Adam Krantz

Mike Jaskiewicz

J. D. Pereza

Dustin Agnew

Cymry DeBoucher

These two groups of students involved themselves in serious social problems that affected their environments and, as a result, also took on adult responsibilities while they worked toward a solution to a real-world problem. Other examples of real problems that young people face relate to drug abuse, possession of guns, homelessness, divorce of parents, abusive relationships, illegal immigration, health care, crime, and out-of-control students who disrupt their classrooms.

All real problems are not found in the adult arena, however. Students may identify real problems, for example, in conflicts that arise in their own lives, in goals such as raising money for worthy purposes in ethical and effective ways, in school regulations that result in violation of students' rights, or in a need to improve their classroom environment or relationships with others. The following questions may be rich sources of real problems:

- What are some ideas that would help make my community a better place to live?

- What are some ideas that would improve educational practices in our school?

- What should the government do to help people who are down on their luck? What can people down on their luck do to help themselves?

- In what ways does the proposal to refuse education or health care to children of illegal aliens present moral dilemmas to citizens of the United States?

- How much responsibility do we have for abuses of human rights in other countries?

- In what ways are women discriminated against in careers and in the marketplace?

- If television commercials are the primary way we gain information about persons who run for public office, what are the implications for voters?

- If our state legislature authorizes vouchers for use in any school of a parent's choice, what might happen to our public education systems?

- How does an art form or a communications medium (e.g., painting, music, literature, film, sculpture, architecture, drama, television) reflect or change the culture and customs of a specific time and place?

- How does emphasis on linguistic and logical–mathematical intelligences in education affect the development of individuals whose strengths are in other intelligences?

- What can we do to break down the power of stereotypes in our thinking?

Questions need not be those that have not yet been solved by others; problems that are new to the solver also are real problems to them. For example, the kinds of questions posed to encourage discovery learning are appropriate for gifted students to investigate:

- How can plants grow without soil?
- How can I combine these materials to create an attractive collage?
- What foods would be most appropriate to take on a five-day backpacking expedition?
- What do I need to do to grow crystals in different colors and different shapes?
- How can I create music with drinking glasses and water?

As gifted students begin to think about setting goals and planning research on a problem, they need to consider carefully the form and type of questions they use to guide their work. Two important criteria are open-endedness and focus (Durkin, 1971). Open-ended questions, as discussed in the chapter on process modification, lend themselves to a number of possible answers. Focus pertains to how broad or how narrow a question might be. For example, "What would you like to investigate?" is unlimited in its range, whereas "What do you want to know about the techniques of painting?" is somewhat narrower but still rather vague. A more focused question is "What do you want to know about the painting techniques used by Impressionist artists?" Teachers often need to use increasingly more focused questions with students to help them identify areas to investigate. Teachers also can help students develop focus in their own questions by modeling the use of focused questions in classroom discussions.

One example from the first author's experience may help to clarify this point. The student teacher she was supervising was leading a discussion about solar heaters. The teacher's main purpose was to prompt students to talk about heater design and how the design affected the amount of heat collected. The teacher began by asking, "What did you notice about the experiment you did last week?" Students started talking about how a dog had knocked over one of the heaters and related that students in other classes were envious of them because they were working outside. The first attempt to refocus the students was "What happened in the experiments you did this week?" The answers were more to the point but included such statements as "We had trouble keeping records because there was so much to do in class." The next question was more specific: "What did you notice about the different heaters you made and the temperature changes inside and outside the heaters?" For the young children in the class, this question was too focused. They had no idea how to answer. A bit frustrated by now, the first author decided to intervene to help the student teacher. She brought in two of the children's data charts for two different solar heaters and suggested that the teacher ask, "What do you notice about the changes inside and outside Tommy's heater?" After students had responded, she then asked, "What do you notice about the changes inside and outside Freeland's heater?" After those questions were answered, the teacher could ask, "What do you think caused _____?" about each factor the children had noticed that related to differences in design of the heaters. After discussing these separately, the children finally could answer the question, "What do you think are the major effects of differences in design on the working of a solar heater?" This narration also is an example of successful guided discovery.

Using the methodology of historical investigation, Renzulli (1977) gave examples of questions from a problem-focusing exercise:

- The questions in the first set are *geographical* and center around *where*, for example, Where in the world is the place I want to learn about? In what regions of the world do famines frequently occur?

- The questions in the second set are *biographical* and center around *who*, for example, Whom (person, peoples) do I want to know more about? What individual person had a major impact on the history of South America in the 19th century?

- The questions in the third set are *chronological* and center around *when*, for example, What historical period do I want to study? When were the principles of perspective drawing discovered and how did they change the world of art?

- The questions in the fourth set are *functional* or *occupational*, and center around *what*, for example, What do I want to know about astrophysics? What interests me about economics? How have athletes changed our perception of physical beauty?

Works on the methodology of investigation in specific areas suggest problem-focusing questions specific to that area. Parnes (1967) suggested that educators and students look at "fuzzy situations," or a mess, as sources of real problems for investigation. Through mess finding, students clarify the focus of the problem-solving activity and also identify opportunities or challenges within the fuzzy situation (Isaksen, Dorval, & Treffinger, 1994). Parnes and others (e.g., Isaksen & Treffinger, 1985; Margulies, 1991) suggested the use of organizing tools such as charts, webs, mind maps, or matrices to show what information is known about the situation and what the investigator needs to know. Parnes also suggested restating the problem in several different ways until it is expressed in a creative, solvable form.

Several other authors (e.g. J. Feldhusen, 1985; Nickerson, Perkins, & Smith, 1985; Perkins, 1986) recommended specific techniques useful in problem solving. Coleman (1985), in a summary of literature, identified six essential techniques: (a) produce many ideas; (b) postpone evaluation; (c) use tricks to promote unorthodox combinations of ideas; (d) state the problem clearly; (e) work systematically, yet retain spontaneity; and (f) deliberately reflect on your own thinking. All these scholars emphasized the importance of problem finding. In problem finding, students explore the possibilities, generate their own questions, and select the problem to be investigated.

Problem finding may be one of the most essential elements of the creative process. The process of problem finding includes three major elements: analysis, problem definition, and construction of a clear problem statement.

Elements of Problem Finding

Analysis

Problem finding requires analyzing a fuzzy situation or a mess to clarify what is known about it. Real problems generally are complex situations that lack clarity, organization, and definition. Analysis includes taking the problem apart, sorting its aspects into categories, gathering facts and opinions, comparing the situation with others, researching the issue and developing questions about it, and dissecting it. Young, gifted learners may have difficulty with analysis, and teachers should provide scaffolding to help them with this process (Wood, 1991). The first steps are determining the primary goal for the problem-finding task, helping students identify their goals, and helping them think of possible ways to achieve it. Another important goal of problem finding is encouraging students to claim "ownership" of the problem. Even if novice problem finders initially have only an incomplete understanding of the task, they may understand enough to take task-relevant action. Left to analyze a situation on their own, without some scaffolding support, students are unlikely to recognize whether or not they have analyzed the situation effectively. The teacher may, for example, ask questions to help students identify crucial features of the situation they may have missed and thus help them do a more complete analysis. "Scaffolding functions effectively support and augment learners' limited cognitive resources, enabling them to concentrate upon and master manageable aspects of the task. With experience, such elements of the task become familiar and the child is able to consider further related task elements. Contingent control helps to ensure that the demands placed on the child are likely neither to be too complex, producing defeat, nor too simple, generating boredom or distraction" (Wood, 1991, p. 108).

Bruner (1983) recommended that adults initially structure interactions. "One sets the game, provides a scaffold to assure that the child's ineptitude can be rescued by appropriate intervention, and then removes the scaffold part by part as the reciprocal structure can stand on its own" (p. 60).

Perkins (1986) suggested that teachers begin by presenting situations in which the possibilities have been narrowed somewhat. For example, if students are asked to design a gadget, the teacher first has them *improve* an existing gadget. Novice designers can work to improve designs in many genres such as (a) policies, regulations, and laws; (b) plans; (c) study strategies or problem-solving strategies; (d) definitions for common, nontechnical terms; (e) models for scientific and mathematical terms; (f) explanations of tools; (g) classification systems; (h) techniques of game playing; (i) literary forms; (j) art forms; (k) musical compositions; and dances. As students consider possibilities, teachers can introduce the questions related to purpose, structure, model cases, and evaluation of a design through modeling and can provide scaffolding as needed.

Another useful strategy in problem finding is considering the advantages, limitations, and unique features (Isaksen et al., 1994) of possible problems. In this method, learners brainstorm three sets of ideas. For the first, they list the advantages of focusing on a particular aspect of the mess. For the second, they list limitations in the form of questions (e.g., Do we have the financial resources to investigate this problem?). For the third, unique features of a possible problem are identified. (The same strategy can be applied to evaluation of possible solutions.)

Isaksen et al. (1994) also offered some key ideas to consider during problem finding. They suggested that each possibility be rated (on a scale from 1 to 10) both on its level of importance and on its probability of success. An overall rating is derived by multiplying the rating for level of importance by the rating for probability of success. Then possible problems can be sorted into "promising opportunities" (high in importance and average to high in probability of success), "constructive challenges" (average in importance and average to high on probability of success), "distractions" (low in importance although average to high on probability of success), "submarines" (low in importance and low on probability of success), and "concerns" (average or high in importance but low on probability of success). Students then make an informed decision about the specific problem or opportunity to pursue.

Many other methods for analyzing a mess have been developed. A comprehensive list of strategies suggested by the work of Koberg and Bagnall (1976) is summarized in Table 5.1.

Any of these methods alone or in combination with others provides specific ways to examine any situation, mess, or problem that students or teachers may encounter. Students can be taught to use methods of analysis and encouraged to develop a variety of strategies to use when they need to find or clarify a problem for investigation.

Perkins (1986) recommended that during the process of problem finding and analysis, teachers foster intrinsic motivation in the following ways: "(1) treat the activity as intrinsically interesting, (2) minimize evaluative feedback, (3) maximize informative feedback, (4) allow choices, (5) avoid surveillance, (6) offer tractable problems in a range of difficulties, (7) arrange [for] group work, (8) try to make the activity fun" (p. 123).

Problem Definition

After a student has analyzed a problem, he or she needs to define it. This definition serves two purposes: It provides a focus for research and idea generation, and it serves as a statement of essential elements or the essence of the problem. A definition can be a verbal analogy, the underlying meaning of the issue, an individual's concept or attitude about the problem, or a graphic representation of the essential elements. A problem definition is intended to clarify and focus thinking in a productive direc-

Table 5.1. Methods of Problem Analysis

Method	Description
Questioning	Ask oneself questions about the problem such as, What has been tried already? What is the scope of the problem? Who can help solve it?
Accumulating data	Gather data that have some relationship to the problem. After you have lots of items, stretch imagination and relate each collected item to the problem in some way.
Forcing relationships	Force oneself to make connections between items or ideas that seem to be unrelated. These connections can help in gaining a deeper understanding of the problem.
Finding the source	Trace a problem, or one of the aspects, back to its source. Attempt to identify the genesis of the problem or aspect.
Listing attributes	Make lists of the attributes of different aspects of the problem. The list might involve physical attributes (e.g., color, texture, weight), psychological attributes (e.g., appeal, intensity), and social attributes (e.g., group membership, values, responsibilities). An attribute analysis exposes specific aspects of all parts of the problem.
Recording all you know about it	Write down everything you know about the problem. Record all the ideas and connections you can think of that might have an influence or an effect on the problem.
Review others' work	Critically examine the methods others have used and the results they found.
Building analysis models	Examine a problem by building a model of it. Models can be schematic, three-dimensional, or graphic, and can include charts, prototypes, flow charts, and so on.
Analyzing the structure	List attributes or variables, classify them, and determine the relationships among them by matching an attribute from one list with all others on each of the other lists. A model can be developed to represent the relationship in a visual way.
Creating a matrix	One category of attributes or aspects of the problem is listed across the top of a grid and a second category down the side. The intersection of the attributes on the grid is used to generate ideas about how the attributes are related.
Looking for patterns	Look for subproblems within the larger problem; determine relationships or trends.

Table 5.1. *Continued*

Method	Description
Asking an expert	Actually call in an expert to provide advice, or consult your own beliefs about how an expert might analyze the problem.
Expanding objectives	Continually examine and clarify your objectives related to the problem situation.
Clearing the mind	Gifted students often begin generating ideas long before a problem is defined. These ideas can inhibit thinking by short-circuiting the process of analysis. List the ideas now and put them aside; determine their usefulness after the problem is defined.
Stretching and squeezing	First, stretch out the problem to discover its parts by asking a series of questions beginning with *what*. Next, squeeze the problem by asking a series of questions beginning with *why*.
Using sensory perception	Examine each aspect of the problem through all the senses; see, hear, touch, taste, and smell the problem.
Creating a mind map or an idea web	Create a graphic representation of the components of the problem and the relationships among them. Mind mapping and webbing are less formal than matrix or structural analysis and allow for more complex connections among components.

tion and is aimed toward possible solutions. The most creative artists invest more effort in finding a basic direction for their work than in moving rapidly toward a possible solution (Getzels & Csikszentmihalyi, 1976); they also are more open to opportunities than is a person who is too narrowly focused at the outset of the process.

Some additional strategies for problem definition are presented in Table 5.2.

Problem Statement

After the process of analyzing and defining a problem, teachers and students should take care to state the problem clearly and in solvable form. The purpose of a good problem statement is to open up the range of possible answers. Isaksen et. al (1994) posited that good problem statements (a) invite ideas, possibilities, or actions; (b) identify the *specific* issue that needs to be addressed; (c) are concise and come right to the

Table 5.2. Methods of Problem Definition

Method	Description
Identifying purposes	Extending the stretching and squeezing procedure. Continue through a series of at least 10 *why* questions to distill your purposes in solving this problem.
Finding crucial aspects	Use the matrix developed to select the crucial intersections of attributes and concentrate only on those aspects of the problem.
Exhausting possibilities	Develop as many definitions of the problem as possible. Others can be asked to add to this list.
Finding winners	Match each element or aspect of a problem with each other element to determine which is more important. Develop a hierarchy or rank order with those having the greatest number of "wins" identified as the essential elements.
Identifying *key* words	Develop a long list of various aspects of the problem. Select the key words from the list and put them together into one statement. Key words might be selected from a list of attributes or a list of what others have done, from what a consultant says, or from accumulated data.
Looking for the key	After you have identified the subproblems, pinpoint the crucial one. This subproblem is attacked first because its solution often can provide the solution for the whole situation.
Talking it over	Simply discuss your analysis of the problem with others. Try out definition ideas with your peers or other helpful persons.
Finding consensus	All individuals who ultimately will be affected by the solution collaborate to identify the most important aspects of the problem.

point; (d) identify the owners (person or people) of the problem; and (e) are free of criteria, restrictions, limitations, or qualifications. The structure of a problem statement has (a) an invitational stem (e.g., How to . . . ? How might . . . ? In what ways might . . . ?); (b) an owner or owners who are responsible for the problem statement and have an investment in its outcome; (c) a constructive, positive action verb that specifies the desired action; and (d) an object that identifies the focus of the problem-solving activity. Also, a good problem statement is positive. Negative statements turn thinking off and lead to defeatist attitudes.

Characteristics of Gifted Students

The justification for the emphasis on products that address real problems in programs for gifted learners is based on research by the American College Testing Service, cited by Renzulli (1977), showing that adult accomplishments are unrelated to test scores or grades but are related to comparable nonacademic or extracurricular accomplishments. Renzulli noted that when students participate in nonacademic activities, they have the freedom to choose their own activities. A grading system rarely is imposed, and they have a tangible product at the end of their activities—a performance, a school newspaper, a soccer game, and so on. C. W. Taylor (1967) found little or no correlation between academic success and later career achievement. He pointed out that extracurricular activities require decision making, planning, forecasting, creative thinking, and communication skills—real-world talents that seldom are taught in traditional classrooms. Students who are intensely motivated to do or create, who have passionate interests in a subject or field, and who like to explore or experiment with ideas have a particular need to work on real problems. For students who enjoy the challenge of problem solving and are capable of a high level of reasoning and goal-oriented thought, creating solutions to real problems is a natural outlet for their talents and interests. For example, the Coronado Middle School students mentioned previously found, through their research on the relationship of urban development and destruction of saguaro cacti, a purpose that had academic, social, and personal value. They have needed no external motivation since they began to build their case for county and city ordinances to protect the saguaros in the Sonoran Desert. The boys developed adult skills necessary for successful interaction with adults interested in and opposed to the issue and produced professional-quality research and testimony in their effort to solve this problem. As probable leaders and creators in a chosen field of endeavor, gifted students need continued experience in the development of professional, rather than student, products.

Directing Products Toward Real Audiences

To the greatest extent possible, the products developed by gifted students should be addressed to real audiences (e.g., an academic community, a city council, a local board of education, a state or federal agency, an art gallery, a publisher, a drama critic, schoolmates). Too often, a gifted student uses his or her talents to create unusual products that are seen only by a teacher (or, sometimes, family members). The purpose is to please the teacher and, thus, to earn a high grade. This practice is detrimental for two main reasons:

- Students do not learn the importance of audience analysis in the planning and preparation of products. Also, they have no opportunity to assess the impact of their work on an appropriate audience.

- Students become dependent on external evaluation by a teacher and do not learn the evaluation criteria used by experts in a field. They fail to develop internal criteria to evaluate their own work. The failure to develop internal criteria and dependence on a teacher for rewards lead to learned helplessness.

A product is a form of communication and, as such, involves an interaction among sender (producer), message, medium, and receiver (audience). The producer must ask the following questions:

- What do I want to communicate?

- What is my purpose?

- What are the characteristics of my proposed audience?

- How can I communicate most effectively with that audience?

- What medium (or combination of media) will be best for transmitting my message?

Elements of Communication

Message

When gifted students develop products for presentation to others, each person can use a preferred talent or combination of talents to create a message in some way. C. W. Taylor, Ghiselin, and Yagi (1967) identified four developmental facets of communication—ideational fluency, expressional fluency, associational fluency, and word fluency.

- *Ideational fluency* is the ability to produce a quantity of ideas and share them in meaningful ways. People with this ability may use analogies or examples to help an audience understand ideas.

- *Expressional fluency* is the ability to express ideas in alternative ways and includes skills related to clear, concise, and effective explanations of thoughts and ideas in both verbal and nonverbal modes. Persons with this ability can rephrase or restate ideas in a variety of ways to match the characteristics of varied audiences.

- *Associational fluency* is the ability to produce a large quantity of rich relationships among ideas and to associate ideas metaphorically to create new images and insights. People who are skilled in this ability also can perceive how ideas are related to the experiences or ideas of their audiences, and capitalize on these relationships when they communicate with an audience.

- *Word fluency* is the ability to use a large number and variety of words in communication. In other modes of communication, the related skill would be the ability to produce a variety of images, movements, or sounds. This skill adds color, beauty, or depth to the communication.

Although the research of C. W. Taylor et al. (1967) was focused primarily on communication with language, the definitions above deliberately were not limited to written and spoken messages. The development of messages to be encoded in any medium can be enriched by the use of the four kinds of fluency described.

The sender is responsible for the quality of the message. She or he should check the message for the completeness of its content; for its relevance to the proposed receivers; and for qualities that facilitate understanding, such as clarity, simplicity, organization, and strength of its appeal to the intended audience (Koberg & Bagnall, 1976).

Purpose

Communication is a way to inform or educate others through the sharing of ideas and thoughts, to amuse or entertain others, to evoke emotion, to direct or give orders, to persuade or influence others, and to create a historical record. The producer or producers must decide what to communicate, choose media appropriate to the message and the proposed audience, use the chosen media effectively, and understand the relationship between the communicator and the audience (Atwood, 1974). As any medium can serve as a channel for communication, selection of media appropriate to the message, purpose, and proposed audience is an integral part of planning a presentation for a real audience. One format for analysis presented by Renzulli and Reis (1985) is shown in Exhibit 5.2.

Exhibit 5.2. Communication vehicles and potential audiences.

Type of Professional Activity	How Is It Communicated?	Who Are Some Potential Audiences?
Ecology (Study of pollution in a local stream)	Audiovisual presentation (graphs, tables, photographs, verbal report	—Rotary Club —City council —Local environmental protection agency
	Written report	—Readers of local news —Readers of EPA newsletter —Members of city council or state legislature
	Radio or television report (Local, state, within-school, closed circuit)	—Listeners —Viewers
	Display	—Shopping mall —Town hall —Bank lobby
Creative Writers, Puppeteers (Working together on an adventure story/presentation for young children)	Live puppet show	—Children in primary classrooms —Children in day care center —Children in state home for the handicapped —Children in pediatric wing of hospital —People in senior citizens' center —Parent–teacher association
[Note: With the addition of this dimension, additional areas of interest and talent expression (e.g., cinematography, TV production) can be combined with the work of creative writers and puppeteers.]	Videotape—to be used with —individual groups —closed-circuit TV —educational TV —local TV station	—Any or all of the above —Various groups of viewers in general

Note. From *The Schoolwide Enrichment Model: A Comprehensive Plan for Educational Excellence*, (p. 422), by J. S. Renzulli and S. M. Reis, 1985, Mansfield Center, CT: Creative Learning Press. Copyright 1985 by Creative Learning Press. Adapted with permission.

When one's purpose in communication is persuasion (e.g., to gain acceptance of a proposed solution as in *Creative Problem Solving*), Isaksen et al. (1994) suggest the use of a strategy called "five Ws and an H." In this strategy, the communicator looks for sources of assistance and sources of resistance as shown in Exhibit 5.3.

Media or Channels of Communication

The abilities and interests of students, the kinds of materials, equipment, and mentors that are available to them, the nature of the proposed communication, and the nature of the proposed audience all have an effect on the choice of a medium or channel of communication. A message may be encoded in words, pictures, sounds, movements, or a combination of these.

Exhibit 5.3. Planning for acceptance worksheet.

Promising Options or Tentative Plans		
	Sources of Assistance	*Sources of Resistance*
WHO	Helpful people?	Who may limit the effectiveness of your plan?
WHAT	Helpful things, objects, activities?	Things that may impede your progress?
WHERE	Preferred or useful locations or events?	Locations which may be inappropriate?
WHEN	Appropriate times or situations?	Are there particularly inappropriate times?
WHY	Effective reasons?	Reasons for not accepting your plan?
HOW	Needed actions?	Actions or activities that may be operating against solution(s)?

Note. From *Creative Approaches to Problem Solving* (pp. 364–365), by S. G. Isaksen, K. B. Dorval, and D. J. Treffinger, 1994, Dubuque, IA: Kendall Hunt. Copyright 1994 by Kendall Hunt. Adapted with permission.

The producer of a message needs to consider several factors in the choice of a communication medium. Characteristics listed by Koberg and Bagnall (1976) include (a) appropriateness to message content; (b) appropriateness to sender's skills, knowledge, and attitudes; (c) symbolic characteristics of the message and the medium; (d) the medium's potential for sensory stimulation; (e) the speed of the transmission; (f) whether the medium can transmit messages within the receivers' levels of acceptance; (g) the energy required to produce and transmit a message in that medium; (h) the importance of the message; (i) the size of the potential audience; and (j) the amount of noise (distraction) that the medium may impose between sender and receivers. For students, the expense of using a particular technology, or its availability, also may affect their choice of media.

Audience Characteristics

Students may find real audiences among their classmates, other students in the school, members of the local community, parents, art lovers, music lovers, younger children, senior citizens, and others who gather to see or hear student products. Other audiences may include governing boards or legislative bodies, government agencies, judges of competitions, editors, or sports fans. Sometimes members of an audience will have interests in a particular art form; at other times, the group will be heterogeneous. Sometimes groups will be composed of a single religious or ethnic group; at other times, the group will be mixed. Sometimes, a presentation is made to an audience of one. In each case, the sender (encoder) of a message must make decisions about how to present the chosen ideas.

Each receiver will decode a given message in a unique way. The construction of meaning is only partially a product of the message sent; the age, education, experiences, abilities, interests, awareness, and motivation of a receiver also influence what is understood. A skilled communicator will consider these factors as well as the receiver's expectations, values, needs, and physical state, and potential consequences of the ideas expressed. When communication is one to one, the quality of personal relationships also affects the decoding of a message.

Students who plan to present information to a governing body need to be particularly conscious of the scope of the group's activities, their authority, and their procedures. In what areas do they have influence? What prior knowledge do they have of your area of interest? What are their political and social goals? Students should respect their limited time for receiving delegations and present information clearly and concisely and come right to the point in stating the action desired from that body.

Whether an audience is made up of professional people or preschoolers, presenters must contribute their ideas in a way that shows respect for the receivers and achieves the purpose of informing, entertaining, persuading, or evoking feelings of individual members of the audience.

Characteristics of Gifted Students

Presentations to real audiences are a goal for many talented and gifted students. This principle is particularly necessary for those who have extraordinary ability to convey meaning or emotion through words, actions, symbols, and sounds, either in person or through varied media of communication. It is important also for students who enjoy the challenge of solving real problems and initiating change in one or more facets of the social or physical environment. Students who have extraordinary interpersonal intelligence and are sensitive to experiences and feelings (their own and others') must have opportunities to communicate with others and to develop that intelligence through interactions with real audiences. These young people need the feedback they receive from others to improve their creative products and to refine their abilities to work effectively with a variety of different groups.

Evaluation

Each product developed by a gifted student should be appropriately evaluated. This may include assessment by a teacher using preestablished criteria, self-evaluation by the student, and evaluation by a real audience. When students are creating products that are directed toward a real audience, a single assessment by a teacher does not provide a comprehensive, appropriate evaluation. Renzulli (1977) and Maker (1982a) recommended that gifted students and their teachers use professional end products as standards by which to evaluate student work. Starko (1988) compared the creatively productive activities outside school, career thinking, awareness of personal strengths and weaknesses, and school attitudes of students who had participated in *Enrichment Triad Model* activities with those of students who had not received special services. She found that participation in program activities significantly enhanced student outcomes in all four areas.

Evaluation by Professional Standards

Haensley and Roberts (1983), analyzing the results of questionnaires answered by professionals in different fields, found that professionals considered their intended audience as an integral contributor to the standards they set for their work. As students plan to solve real problems and create original products in any field of endeavor, they need to know the expectations of possible audiences and understand the criteria by which professional work in the same fields would be judged. In Exhibit 5.4, an example of differing evaluation standards for different groups, a fourth column—How Might That Audience Evaluate the Product?—has been added to the chart shown in Exhibit 5.2.

The implication of this example for teachers is that, whenever possible, students should have the opportunity to present their products to real audiences. For example, the Saguaro Team entered its research in a geography competition sponsored by American Express. They made presentations to the County Board of Supervisors, officials of the Environmental Protection Agency, and at a meeting of environmental groups, developers, officials of the Department of the Interior, and interested citizens. In each case, their work was being judged according to standards expected of professionals. As they continue their project, the boys also will submit their project to the Community Problem Solving Competition.

Students should be encouraged to look at a specific product from different viewpoints and think carefully about the criteria that different audiences may use to judge it. These criteria can be used as guides for the product's creators, the teacher, and other classmates to evaluate the product. Gifted students also can learn to use specific criteria in their evaluations of each other's work. Evaluation by (and of) peers is a useful step in the development of internal criteria for excellence.

Although they are not yet professionals, students want to present their best work when they are acting as inquirers and creators. Aesthetic qualities are important. Students should be encouraged to refine their products, to present them to simulated audiences for formative evaluation, and to use appropriate criteria to judge their own work before they

Exhibit 5.4. Analysis of areas of study, potential audiences, and evaluation criteria for products.

Type of Professional Activity	How Is It Communicated?	Who Are Some Potential Audiences?	How Might That Audience Evaluate the Product?
Ecology: Study of pollution in a local stream	Audio-visual presentation (graphs, tables, photographs, and verbal report)	Rotary Club	Does student suggest ways in which Rotary Club or individuals might work to improve conditions? Do photographs clearly show the pollution problem? Does the presentation clearly show the current status of the stream? How clearly, effectively, and efficiently are research results presented?
		City council	Are possible causes of pollution identified? Is the report clear and brief? What actions are recommended? Are suggested actions legal? Are suggested actions within budget limitations? Are suggested actions politically acceptable? How clearly, effectively, and efficiently are research results presented?
		Environmental Protection Agency	How appropriate were data collection methods? Can results of the study be replicated? Do charts and tables show results clearly? Are recommended actions within the mission of EPA? How clearly, effectively, and efficiently are research results presented?

Note. From *The Schoolwide Enrichment Model: A Comprehensive Plan for Educational Excellence* (p. 442), by J. S. Renzulli and S. M. Reis, 1985, Mansfield Center, CT: Creative Learning Press. Copyright 1985 by Creative Learning Press. Adapted with permission.

share the final product in a public setting. Shore et al. (1991) warned that teachers also need to adopt this standard for their own work. "One of the important corollaries of this recommended practice may be that teachers need experience with the process in order to be sensitive to the challenges faced by students" (p. 103)

Self-Evaluation

Practicing professionals in every field need to be able to judge the quality of their own products as an aspect of the refinement process. They must be able to recognize both positive and negative aspects of the product so that changes can be made as needed without complete dismay and total revision. As gifted and creative individuals often are independent and appear to pay little attention to others' criticisms of their products, they must learn methods for assessing their own performances and appreciate the value of self-assessment.

Several of the models recommended for use in programs for gifted students contain guidelines for development of the thinking process of evaluation (e.g., Bloom, 1956; Guilford, 1967). In the *Creative Problem Solving* process (Isaksen et al., 1994; Parnes, 1977), the convergent part of each step includes suggestions for evaluating alternatives, and in the *Multiple Talents* approach (C. W. Taylor, 1968), the evaluative mode of creative thinking and the decision-making process include guidelines for evaluating alternatives and generating criteria.

Essential elements of evaluation include (a) developing criteria for weighing alternatives or making judgments (i.e., What are indicators of quality for a particular product?); (b) developing methods (e.g., checklists, analysis of recorded performance, rating scales) for making assessments; (c) deciding when an evaluation will be done; and (d) applying the criteria as consistently as possible with the methods and materials developed for that purpose. Although the exact processes are not described here,[1] they are invaluable as guides for teaching students to evaluate their own products.

Methods of evaluation can be arranged along a continuum:

　　　　highly objective ⟵————————⟶ highly subjective

---

[1] See Maker and Nielson (1995) for detailed descriptions of the evaluation processes in these models.

In a highly objective evaluation, the criteria are explicit and their application is consistent. At this extreme, few disagreements can arise about the judgments made. In a highly subjective assessment, judgment is based on intuition and may be made without specific criteria stated. Subjective evaluation is based primarily on internalized standards of quality or personal values. As the criteria are not specified, disagreements occur and a satisfactory resolution of the differences may be very difficult to achieve.

Students need to be taught each step of a wide range of evaluation processes and procedures, including both objective and subjective methods. They should have a variety of experiences in making different types of evaluations, including assessment of written products, assessment of performance, assessment of visual products, and assessment of group interactions. One process that has proved useful to us in our graduate classes was developed by the first author to help educators assess their own performance. In turn, many of our students have taught their students the same process. In this process, students are first presented with a listing of the criteria and a form to be used in making the assessment. Then the criteria are discussed as to what they mean and why they are important, and examples of how each criterion can be observed are provided. Students are given opportunities to ask questions, modify the criteria, and generate examples of each criterion.

Another example of the application of criteria for student assessment is a rubric with benchmarks, or quality indicators. The benchmarks for an oral presentation task in Amphitheater School District, shown in Exhibit 5.5, are examples of the application of specific criteria for evaluation.

After the form and the process are clearly understood, the student and the teacher individually apply the criteria to the product or performance. For example, if a performance is on videotape, both evaluators watch the tape at the same time but sit so that their marks on the evaluation form cannot be seen by the other. After a few judgments have been made, the tape is stopped and the two evaluations are compared. If they do not match or if some confusion about the criteria or process exists, the criteria and procedures are discussed and then the tape is replayed at the point of confusion or disagreement. This process is continued, with discussions as needed, until both are satisfied that the process has been learned. (This method is similar to the procedures used in research when interrater reliability is essential to the research process.) After the initial learning period, the teacher randomly selects a tape

Exhibit 5.5. Benchmarks for oral presentation task.

ORAL PRESENTATION TASK

Rationale

Communication through oral language is an essential skill in our society. As adults we are called upon to organize our thoughts and communicate them logically and concisely through the spoken word. Students must be taught these skills and given the opportunity to practice and refine them.

Benchmark	Task Description
1	The student will plan and deliver an individual oral presentation based on research and supported by facts. The presentation may be used to persuade, report, or communicate.
2	The student will plan and deliver an individual oral presentation that is based on research, supports a position, and is supported by facts.
3	The student will give an individual oral presentation before an audience based on research investigating a position on a global issue (e.g., social, environmental, literary, historical).
4	The student will give an individual oral presentation based on scholarly research advocating a position on a global issue. The issue will be clearly defined and will show historical, environmental, literary, social, or personal connections. The presentation will be delivered before an audience of peers and will be videotaped.
5	The student will give an individual oral presentation based on scholarly research advocating a position before an audience or evaluation panel. The issue will be clearly defined and will show historical, environmental, literary, social, or personal connections. Benchmark 5 differs from Benchmark 4 in that the student works independently to select, research, and choose the delivery format for his or her topic. The presentation format should be selected from the range of formats that the individual has been exposed to through his or her education.

Quality Indicators

A quality oral presentation will meet or exceed the following standards:

Benchmark 1	Benchmark 2	Benchmark 3	Benchmark 4	Benchmark 5
Organization that shows a beginning, middle, and end with transitions	Evidence of organization of facts and rehearsal	Evidence of organization, focus, and rehearsal	Evidence of organization, focus, and rehearsal	Evidence of organization, focus, and rehearsal
Speaking with appropriate volume	Use of proper enunciation, volume, inflection, eye contact, tone, body language, speed, and energy	Use of proper enunciation, volume, inflection, eye contact, tone, body language, speed, and energy	Use of proper enunciation, volume, inflection, eye contact, tone, body language, speed, and energy	Use of proper enunciation, volume, inflection, eye contact, tone, body language, speed, and energy
Speaking in a way that does not impede comprehension	Application of standard academic vocabulary and usage	Application of standard academic vocabulary and usage	Application of standard academic vocabulary and usage (specific to the content)	Application of standard academic vocabulary and usage (specific to the content)
Presentation flows smoothly, no help needed to get through the presentation				Selects appropriate format for content and audience
Sense of audience/eye contact	Sense of audience (e.g., topic chosen with audience in mind, monitor and adjust during presentation as necessary)	Sense of audience (e.g., topic chosen with audience in mind, monitor and adjust during presentation as necessary)	Sense of audience (e.g., topic chosen with audience in mind, monitor and adjust during presentation as necessary)	Sense of audience (e.g., topic chosen with audience in mind, monitor and adjust during presentation as necessary)

(continues)

Exhibit 5.5. *Continued*

Benchmark 1	Benchmark 2	Benchmark 3	Benchmark 4	Benchmark 5
Use of visual aids and technology when appropriate	Use of visual aids and technology when appropriate	Use of visual aids and technology when appropriate	Use of visual aids and technology when appropriate	Use of visual aids and technology when appropriate
A question-and-answer period at the end of the presentation	Logical defense of the position as evidenced by response to questions from the audience	Logical defense of the position as evidenced by response to questions from the audience	Logical defense of the position as evidenced by response to questions from the audience	Logical defense of the position as evidenced by response to questions from the evaluators/ audience
	Higher-level thinking (e.g., application, analysis, synthesis, and evaluation of the information presented)	Higher-level thinking (e.g., application, analysis, synthesis, and evaluation of the information presented)	Higher-level thinking (e.g., application, analysis, synthesis, and evaluation of the information presented)	Higher-level thinking (e.g., application, analysis, synthesis, and evaluation of the information presented)
		Evidence of numerical and nonnumerical data analysis	Appropriate and significant use of numerical and nonnumerical data analysis	Appropriate and significant use of numerical and nonnumerical data analysis
			Use and evaluation of a variety of primary and secondary sources	Use and evaluation of a variety of primary and secondary sources

Note. Adapted from *Assessment Program Manual*, by Amphitheater Public Schools, 1994, pp. 25–29. Tucson, AZ: Amphitheater Public Schools. Copyright 1994 by Amphitheater Public Schools. Adapted with permission.

evaluated by a student and analyzes it without first checking the student's analysis (this is done frequently in the early stages of training). If there are differences, the student and the teacher resolve them through discussion. The checking process continues for quality control throughout the semester but is done less frequently as the student learns the procedures.

A next level of self-evaluation is the development of criteria for assessment. For teaching this method, varied examples of criteria should be examined, each analyzed in terms of its appropriateness for a particular situation or a particular product. In the decision-making process of the *Talents Unlimited Model* (Schlichter, 1986), for example, teachers begin by giving two or three criteria for students to use and asking them to supply one or two additional criteria. As students become more experienced, the teacher-generated criteria are gradually replaced by student-generated criteria.

Criteria often are stated in the form of a question that can be answered yes or no or one to which a quantity can be assigned. A better way of considering criteria would be the use of a continuum or a Likert scale ranging from 1 to 5 by which a student can rank how well he or she met each criterion. Students also should examine a variety of evaluation methods so they will have the background required to develop specific methods appropriate to a given situation or product.

An essential element of the learning process is frequent, detailed feedback to each student about his or her progress and about the results of the individual's evaluations. After students have evaluated their own products, using the same forms and criteria as other evaluators, they should compare their evaluation with those of other evaluators and discuss areas of difference. If grades must be assigned, they can reflect both the quality of a student's work as perceived by others and the closeness of the match between the self-evaluation and assessment by others.

Characteristics of Gifted Students

Students who are unusually perceptive and responsive to their own feelings and those of others, who are highly intuitive, who consider implications and alternatives thoughtfully, who have a keen sense of humor, and who are exceptionally imaginative or creative in one or more areas of interest and ability find it necessary to continually evaluate their thinking processes, performances, the products they create, and the effects they have on others. Students who strive toward perfection and those who are highly critical of themselves, and of others, need to be taught appropriate methods for evaluation so they can make more informed judgments. Skill in assessment of their own progress also contributes to a greater degree of self-direction and autonomy.

Gamberg, Kwak, Hutchings, and Altheim (1988) discussed the dangers of inappropriate evaluation of student learning. The "correction" of student mistakes by the teacher has two negative consequences: The teacher focuses only on weaknesses of students; students focus on their grades and do not seek to understand their mistakes. "On both counts, because of the emphasis on end products, such an evaluation system is not effective in helping either the teacher or the children pay attention to strategies for improvement" (p. 219). They also suggested a developmental evaluation procedure suitable for younger learners. "In contrast, if children look over their work with someone who raises questions about it—a partner or the teacher—they learn to be more critical of it themselves and, with practice, improve the quality of the work. It is the children who have to do the learning; no one else can do it for them. Therefore, they have to find their own mistakes and make their own corrections" (p. 219).

Teachers and students do need to be wary of focusing solely on end products. Developing minds is more important, ultimately, than developing products or automatizing skilled performance. The affective characteristics of creative thinking—curiosity, courage to take risks, enjoyment of challenge and complexity, and imagination—must be supported through *appropriate* evaluation. When learners have open-ended tasks, they need to review their work frequently, take measures to improve it as needed, and internalize the criteria for monitoring progress toward their goals. Sternberg (1988) referred to these executive functions of thinking as *metacomponents*, factors of the mind essential to autonomous learning and everyday intelligence. Appropriate evaluation, including self-evaluation, of progress in thinking and learning processes, as well as products, is crucial to the cognitive and affective development of gifted students.

Transformation

A critical principle of curriculum differentiation for gifted students is an expectation that students develop products that are more than mere summaries of the thought and ideas of others. A student who writes a research paper by paraphrasing the information in one or two secondary sources (e.g., encyclopedias) is merely presenting a summary rather than creating a true synthesis or transformation of the information. Students can use reference books as sources of data, but they must subject that data to critical analysis, consider the implications of the analysis, and then synthesize their research to create new knowledge. The student who reports on original research has to collect data, analyze the data in relation to existing theory, synthesize the resulting ideas, and interpret the meaning of the findings. Although doctoral dissertations, for example, require higher levels of thinking and may contain discussions that are synthesized from research results, too often they contain reviews of literature and research that are mere summaries of the thoughts and conclusions of previous investigators rather than a critical analysis and synthesis of those thoughts and conclusions.

Classification systems often provide helpful ways for looking at differences in products. Guilford (1967), for example, classified products into six different types:

- *Units*, the smallest level, are individual items of information—a picture, a letter, a word.

- *Classes* are recognized sets of information grouped by common properties—triangular shapes, words that begin with ant-, musical notes.

- *Relations* are recognized connections between two items of information—logical series, analogies, equations.

- *Systems* are organized or structured collections of information, consisting of interrelated and interconnecting parts—number system, musical notation, alphabet.

- *Transformations* are conversions of known information into new entities—changes in meaning, significance, use, interpretation, mood, sensory qualities, shape.

- *Implications* are anticipated outcomes—expectations, consequences, significance, ramifications, predictions.

In this classification, products that are units, classes, relations, or systems involve only a summary of existing information. Guilford (1975) recommended that activities in programs for gifted children be concentrated on the development of products as transformations and implications. His justification for this emphasis is that creative, productive adults rank these abilities highest in their work.

The use of raw data is one way to encourage gifted students to create transformations. Raw data include an artist's impressions, sensations, and perceptions, or a scientist's quantifiable bits of evidence. Artists and social scientists may collect data through observation and self-awareness. Scientists and pollsters may use interviews, surveys, questionnaires, tests, or rating scales. In short, looking up information just for the purpose of reporting materials gathered, summarized, and interpreted by others is not what investigators and scholars do. Professionals may use others' conclusions and data as additional support for their own position or to compare and contrast the work of several scholars in a discipline in an attempt to create a synthesis of findings related to the same topic. However, this is a small part of the larger task of conducting research.

Elements of Transformation

The concept of transformation contains the following elements: (a) viewing from a different perspective, (b) reinterpreting, (c) elaborating, (d) extending (or going beyond), and (e) combining. When evaluating a product of a gifted student to determine the degree to which the individual has transformed the data, the teacher should include some or all of these elements in the criteria. The same elements can be used as guides to show students varied ways to develop products that are real transformations instead of mere summaries.

Viewing from a Different Perspective

An important aspect of the creative process is looking at things from different points of view or seeing them from different visual or theoretical perspectives. By viewing life in new ways, creative writers construct mental images and communicate their perspectives through drama, poetry, stories, and novels. Creative artists may depict an unusual visual perspective through a sculpture, painting, drawing, collage, or mobile. The element of unusual perspective should include other ways to view both ideas and objects. In a visual perspective, this might include drawing objects from an unusual angle, creating a sculpture to be viewed from above, or photographing objects shown in depth perspective, such as a view of the end of a tunnel as seen from the other end. In philosophy, a different perspective might be the consideration of the nature of learning from two or more different theories; in history, one might view a current event from the perspective of a historical character or an individual from some time in the future. In the sciences or social sciences, a different perspective may involve explaining behavior by means of different theories or by viewing it from the perspective of people from different cultures or environments or looking at an abstract concept, such as environment, as it might be viewed in different disciplines. Very different conclusions will be reached by an individual who is emotionally involved in an issue and one who is not involved and analyzes the conflict through principles of formal logic. Viewpoint is influenced to some degree by one's past experience, values, and the context of a creative act.

Reinterpreting

Reinterpretation might be defined as finding a different focus or a new core of an idea. A musician might take a melody or theme and recreate it in several variations. A philosopher may look at events leading up to a major shift in social patterns and posit a new cause of that shift on the basis of a change in, for example, the primary medium of communication. Reinterpreting also includes redefining a problem, clarifying an idea by translating its meaning, paraphrasing, illustrating, and simplifying the idea or its meaning. Torrance (1979) called this "highlighting the essence," and described reinterpretation as simultaneously synthesizing information, "discarding erroneous or irrelevant information, abandoning unpromising facts or solutions, refining ideas, establishing priorities, and letting a single problem or idea become dominant" (p. 52).

Elaborating

This familiar aspect of transformation is the adding of new details or explanations to enhance the appearance of a visual image or the meaning of an idea. Elaboration can add richness or color, enhance the humor of an image, or develop a plan in detail. It can trigger stronger sensory images in the mind of the receiver of a communication by producing a new auditory, olfactory, tactile, kinesthetic, or taste sensation or visual images. Elaboration is a basic creative process in which an individual adds details to enhance the uniqueness of a product and to intensify its sensory, emotional, or ideological appeal to an audience.

Extending, or "Going Beyond"

Going "beyond the information given" (Bruner, 1973) is interpreting, forecasting, extrapolating, or generalizing, and increasing the scope, range, or application of given knowledge. It may include the extension of present trends and the development of new trends; the new trend may not be consistent with the present information but is a reasoned transformation of the given data. Extrapolating, or going beyond in a way that is consistent with the given information, is an *implication* in the sense of formal logic. Extrapolation requires that an individual infer values of a variable in an unobserved interval (e.g., extend a number series) on the basis of values in previously observed intervals. In extrapolation, one assumes continuity of a series and uses what is known to project or expand known data into an unknown area. Conjectures are made on the basis of assumed continuity or correspondence with what is already known. Extending or going beyond should include the development of new relationships or ways to connect old data with new conclusions. It also includes the application of generalizations to new situations (Taba, 1964).

Combining Simultaneously

Perhaps the essence of the concept of transformation is the element of simultaneous combination of ideas, objects, or images. In the familiar example of review of literature or children's research reports, teachers often find a sequential listing of ideas or conclusions rather than a combination of these ideas into one presentation or conclusion. Often, vocabulary and writing style will be faultless, but the ideas will not be combined into an organized whole.

Simultaneous synthesis also includes the development of conclusions and formation of generalizations. Generalizations were discussed at length in the content chapter, but a few additional suggestions for helping students to develop generalizations are given by Banks (1990). A graphic organizer, like a table or chart, is a useful tool for organizing data from two or more different sources. Once the chart is completed, the following questions guide students in analysis, synthesis, and simultaneous combination of ideas (Banks, 1990, pp. 120–121):

Discrimination of Data	What do you notice about . . . ?
Comparison and Contrast	What similarities do you see? What differences?
Relationships	What things seem to be connected to one another?
Explanation	How do you account for this? What may have caused that?
Inference	What do these data mean? . . . suggest? . . . infer?
Generalization	What can you conclude from all this? What can you say that is generally true, based on these data samples?

The ability to develop products that are transformations rather than summaries of existing information should be a direct result of the growth of higher levels of thinking, the use of a discovery approach, open-endedness of questions, and addressing real problems. Y. Sharan and S. Sharan (1992) pointed out that information presented by a teacher or read from a textbook does not transform into knowledge for students. Instead, students must actively construct their own knowledge from experience. "When people organize pieces of information and use them to build a conception and interpretation of the reality they have experienced, knowledge can then emerge. Knowledge is what people construct out of elements of information, feelings, and experience, not something that exists in chunks in the external world that we imbibe as is, with the requisite amount of repetition" (p. 10).

Characteristics of Gifted Students

This modification is appropriate for all gifted learners but is particularly justified for students who have an unusual capacity to acquire, integrate, and retain information; those who acquire sophisticated understandings with apparent ease; those who reason well and consider implications or alternatives to obvious conclusions; and those who enjoy the challenge of problem solving. Students who communicate very well in their chosen media and those who have an exceptionally keen sense of humor are other individuals for whom this modification is particularly appropriate. These students should be expected to transform existing information rather than merely to accept it as it is and report on it without change. Gifted students who possess the abilities to grasp underlying principles and to make valid generalizations need to synthesize the information they acquire and transform it into new forms. By filtering data through their own conceptual structures, they not only create new knowledge but also deepen and enrich the connections in their own thinking. In essence, transformations are the result of purposefully planning to create unique, new products.

Variety and Self-Selected Format

These principles are discussed together because they are related so closely. They also are related to the process principles of freedom of choice and open-endedness. When teachers plan activities for a unit, students generally are expected to do the same assignments and create similar products. At times, when a particular product, such as an essay, is the content of a learning activity, having all students write an essay is a sensible goal. Having students write an essay every week, however, is not. Communication is not limited to speaking and writing, nor is learning measured well by tests. Gifted students should learn multiple ways of communicating and multiple ways of demonstrating proficiency in a unit. Otherwise, they have little opportunity to use their creativity and may become bored. Teachers should note their own level of enthusiasm when they are evaluating student work. If they become bored, chances are very good that the students also were bored when they did the assignment.

Y. Sharan and S. Sharan (1992) provided several examples of products that a 6th-grade class presented to culminate a study of Ancient Greece. One group explained how Athens was governed and then conducted a mock trial; a second group conducted a quiz show about the Greek gods and made figurines of major Greek gods. One group discussed architecture in Ancient Greece, explained the structure and function of temples, and presented a model of the Parthenon. Another group prepared a learning center with a dictionary of Hebrew words that have

Greek roots and created learning activities related to those words. Still another group investigated theater and presented a dramatization of the battle of Achilles and Hector, and the group that studied sports organized a miniature Olympic games for the class. Other sources also have excellent suggestions for varied products. Polette (1982) designed numerous activities related to reading, writing, and research for gifted students that are filled with open-ended questions to stretch thinking. Books on literature-based learning (e.g., Short & Pierce, 1990) are another source of ideas for activities in which varied products are generated. Finally, a list of many, varied products that can be created by students, used in middle-school classes by the second author, is shown in Table 5.3.

Gifted students need to learn to use a variety of media to communicate the results of their learning. They also should have opportunities to work in a variety of media to find out where their strengths, limitations, and interests are. Another learning value derived from encouraging and rewarding different kinds of products is that students may learn that some major concepts, like analogies, are used in virtually every discipline. In *Art Synectics*, Roukes (1982) discussed this concept:

> Analogies are convenient ways of intuiting or subjectifying knowledge and experience, whether used simply to make comparisons without "trying to prove anything," or in more sophisticated attempts to derive poetic metaphors. Sandburg's famous line, "the fog comes on little cat feet," is an example of analogy used as a poetic device in literature. The painting by Morris Graves, on the other hand, is a visual analogy that equates certain lines and shapes drawn on the canvas with qualities of sound.
>
> (p. 2)

In just a few words, Roukes (1982) clearly showed the relationship between two apparently dissimilar products. He described *nonsymbolic* analogies as "simple comparisons of different things that in some way resemble each other, either on a logical, sensory, or emotional level" (p. 3). *Symbolic* metaphors, like the line from the Sandburg poem, "are *metaphoric* in nature; the properties transferred to each other tend to ignite or spark an insight to a 'larger idea'" (p. 3). Gifted students who have opportunities to learn to create products in many varied media can begin to see the connections among various methods of production. They also can gain greater insight into "larger ideas" as they see how the same abstract concepts are used in different disciplines.

Table 5.3. Possible Products for Gifted Students

ABC book	Flower arrangement	Play
Advertisement	Fugue	Poem
Analytical chart	Game	Poster
Article for journal	Graph	Precision drill plan
Audiotape	Graph, 3-Dimensional	Project cube
Block print	Group presentation	Puppet show
Book	Invention	Puzzle
Brochure	Invitation	Questionnaire
Bulletin board	Journal	Radio show
Cartoon	Learning center	Recipe
Chart	Lesson plan	Recording
Choral reading	Letter to a person	Reflection
Chorale	Letter to the editor	Report
Collage	Magazine	Research report
Collection	Map	Role play
Comic strip	Mask	Satire
Commercial	Mind map	Scavenger hunt
Computer graphic	Mobile	Scenario
Computer program	Model	Scrapbook
Construction	Mosaic	Script
Costume	Movie	Sculpture
Court trial simulation	Mural	Secret code
Cross-number puzzle	Museum display	Seminar
Crossword puzzle	Music video	Silkscreen print
Dance	Musical composition	Simulation
Debate	Musical instrument	Skit
Demonstration	Musical performance	Slide show
Diagram	Musical play	Sociodrama
Diary	News report	Song(s)
Dictionary	Newspaper	Speech
Diorama	Obstacle course	Stitchery
Discussion	Opinion poll	Story
Display	Oral report	Survey
Drawing	Overhead transparencies	Synchronized movement
Editorial	Painting	Synthesis of research
Encyclopedia	Panel discussion	Television show
Experiment	Pantomime	Terrarium
Fabric	Paper	Tesselation
Fact file	Party	Time line
Family tree	Peepshow	Travelogue
Film	Photo essay	Treasure hunt
Filmstrip	Photographs	Wallpaper pattern
Flash cards	Picture	Watercolor
Flip book	Plan	Word search

When students are doing independent studies or doing investigations in small groups, a part of their planning should be the selection of a format for presenting the results of their work. If the students are engaged in a Community Problem Solving project, for example, the format may vary from one presentation to another so that it is appropriate for the intended audience.

Characteristics of Gifted Students

Contrary to conventional wisdom, most gifted students are very talented in some intelligences and have some limitations in other intelligences. Students who are spatially gifted may be "verbally inconvenienced" (Lohman, 1994, p. 251) and vice versa. Students who are very expressive and extraordinarily able to communicate through actions, symbols, or sounds in their chosen areas, those who are imaginative and highly creative in their fields, and those who are excellent problem solvers provide the justification for the modification of variety.

Students who are highly motivated, who have passionate interests, and who prefer to conduct their own inquiries particularly justify the modification of self-selected format. As they have strong feelings about their subjects of study, they also have strong feelings about the best way to present the results. Other students for whom self-selected format is important are those who are unusually open, perceptive, and responsive to experiences and feelings and to other people and those who have extraordinary capacity for ingenious, flexible uses of ideas, processes, or materials. When students have opportunities to choose how they will demonstrate what they have learned, the results often far surpass teachers' expectations.

Summary

The principles of product modification suggested in this chapter build upon the principles of content and process differentiation discussed in previous chapters. If the changes are implemented, students can be expected to develop more sophisticated and more creative products than they would if the changes were not made. We have asserted that the products developed by gifted students should approximate, to the extent possible, those of creative, productive professionals. This means that the product should be the result of a real problem or concern, be directed toward a real audience, be evaluated appropriately, represent a transformation or synthesis of existing information, and be produced in one of many, varied formats chosen by the gifted student.

Part 2

Applications of Curriculum Principles

Introduction to Part 2

After reflecting on the theories and recommendations for making curriculum modifications appropriate for the varied intelligences and interests of gifted students, the teacher must at some point implement the principles in a way that will enhance educational opportunities for specific students. In this section, the "know-how" information so important to implementation is joined with the "know-what" information that characterizes concepts, conclusions, generalizations, and theories.

Learning opportunities for all students will improve when teachers make the recommended modifications in the learning environment. We consider those modifications so basic that they have not been included in the Guide to Selecting Curriculum Modifications Based on a Student's Behaviors (the *Chart*) (see Table 1.5). In fact, we believe that learning environments must be substantially modified before teachers can implement changes in content, process, or product for gifted students. Whereas learning-environment modifications are helpful for all students, they are critical for gifted students. Modifications in content, process, and product are dependent upon the creation of an active, supportive learning community.

In the following chapters, three aspects of implementation are presented for consideration. In these chapters we present examples only;

learning activities, units, and curricula must be specific to the needs of particular gifted children. Teachers should be aware that no one curriculum can ever be suitable for all gifted children. The differences in strengths and interests among students who have exceptional abilities in one or more intelligences are at least as great as the differences between students identified as gifted and those not so identified. Cultural differences also must be honored in the development of any defensible educational plan.

Lannie S. Kanevsky offers a process for developing a *personal learning plan* for gifted students in regular classrooms. Readers will discover a workable, student-sensitive method for differentiating learning experiences for one or more gifted children while still remaining true to the requirements of the core curriculum and the needs of all students.

Judith A. Rogers presents an integrated unit for a 2nd-grade self-contained class of gifted students with activities and suggested resources for helping students learn to value diversity among the peoples of the world. This interdisciplinary unit is unified by a broad theme, "Cultures," and is guided by a generalization related to world peace: Global peace will be attained when people accept, understand, and celebrate the similarities and differences that are found among and between racial, ethnic, and religious groups. Daily and weekly plans, sample lesson plans, and ideas for learning centers are featured in the unit and in the extensive list of resources that teachers may use to implement the 20 content, process, and product modification principles recommended in Chapters 3–5. In addition, the unit has been keyed to the development of multiple intelligences (Gardner, 1983) and designed to develop abilities to solve a range of problem types ranging from highly structured, convergent problems to unstructured real-world messes (Maker, 1992).

Finally, we present a chapter on the development of scope and sequence in curricula for gifted students. In this chapter, multiple intelligences and problem-solving are again featured. Methods are suggested for modifying curriculum in a single discipline or a specific intelligence, but greater emphasis is placed on crossdisciplinary or interdisciplinary planning in which students have opportunities to acquire information or data through a variety of intelligences, to process information through a variety of processes and intelligences, and to present the results of that processing in a variety of ways. Emphasis is placed on the importance of developing (or modifying) curriculum for gifted students in a planned, developmentally appropriate manner. Three important questions are considered: (a) How do the understandings, skills, and values that educators expect students to develop fit together? (b) How do educators assure that a student develops or is provided the opportunity to learn the under-standings, skills, and values that will be important in future personal or career development? (c) How does the student's learning in one setting or at one grade level mesh with his or her learning in a different setting or at a different grade level? In other words, how do educators avoid gaps and repetition in both activities and learning? We believe educators will find many answers and some new questions as they read, adapt, and use the ideas presented here.

Chapter 6

Applying the Principles in an Elementary School Classroom

Lannie S. Kanevsky

Although modifying all lessons in response to the needs of each learner, whether formally identified as gifted or not, would be ideal, the realities of the classroom make this impossible. However, learning activities can be modified as much and as frequently as a teacher desires. The principles described in Chapters 3, 4, and 5 can be used to guide the differentiation of lessons and units of core curriculum for use with highly able students in the regular classroom. The classroom teacher has opportunities to differentiate, as often as possible, for some or for all students. Modifications can be inspired by the characteristics of one student who needs more challenge but then also be offered to other students or to the entire class when the teacher believes the students will benefit from the changes. To use a computer metaphor, when the same input is given to students, a difference will be found in student output due to ability-related differences in the way input is processed. If lessons with higher ceilings and broader horizons are offered to all students, many students will find room to grow.

Often the basic curriculum provides many students with a less-than-optimal level of challenge. A number of the principles for modifying curriculum for gifted students have the potential of expanding the limits on learning without overwhelming students not identified as gifted. Many teachers already have versions of these principles in their professional repertoire of instructional strategies. Rather than necessitating the learning of something completely new, differentiation becomes a matter of teachers' using a variety of instructional strategies more often with those students who need them.

Teachers need not wait for test scores or formal labels to differentiate learning experiences for bright students in the regular classroom. Observing students for evidence of the behavior characteristics in the Guide to Selecting Curriculum Modifications (Table 1.5) is an essential element in this system. Teachers can derive the information they need by watching, not testing, while the student is engaged in a challenging task in an area of interest. Observation offers a window on the qualities of activities that engage students, activities students thrive on, activities they care about.

In schools with part-time programs (e.g., pullout, resource room), the needs of gifted students often are neglected when they return to the regular classroom. The segregated program is assumed to be sufficient to accommodate the students' special needs. However, abilities are not temporary states; they are full-time traits. Activities in both regular and special programs should provide developmentally appropriate challenges. The setting and peer group will change, but the need for an appropriate education will not. If the hours a student spends in his or her homeroom lack academic challenge, she or he may find other types of challenge. Some of these are appreciated by the teacher (e.g., tutoring, organizing and tidying the room) and some are not (e.g., disturbing classmates, planning pranks, acting out). Other bright students, when their abilities are not actively engaged, will respond to a lack of challenge by withdrawing.

The approach to curriculum modification presented here is based on the belief that a gifted student's area of greatest strength is his or her area of greatest need. The frequency and nature of a teacher's response to a student's needs are dependent upon a complex interaction of the teacher's knowledge, commitment, and resources with the student's characteristics and needs. Areas of weakness (deficits or only relative weaknesses) need not be ignored in efforts to accommodate the student; however, they will not be included here for two reasons.

First, the recommended principles are based on research and practice in which differentiation of curricula is addressed in areas of strength, not in areas of weakness. Therefore, use of the principles to remediate a gifted student's weaknesses would be inappropriate. Many teachers who have been trained to work with students who have learning difficulties may feel tempted to address students' weaknesses before addressing their strengths. This is not an either–or situation. With some creative planning, both can be addressed simultaneously. A child's learning difficulties or developmental delays should never be justification for neglecting strengths. If anything, the opposite is preferred: strengths before weaknesses, or weaknesses through strengths. This strategy is a substantial shift for educators who have deficit-oriented training and experience.

Second, the expectation that teachers faced with the diverse needs of students in a regular classroom should be able to address all those needs optimally in every lesson is unrealistic. Each student has a right to an equally appropriate education, but parents and advocates for gifted (or disabled) students must realize that none of them can receive what educational and developmental psychologists might consider an optimal education in the regular classroom. The number and diversity of students and the constraints on teachers' time and school resources preclude optimal education for every child. Compromise is necessary; however, the needs of the gifted student cannot be ignored.

Modifications made to classroom curricula are necessary but seldom sufficient to accommodate all of the special needs of all gifted students. Their abilities may be so intense that they require types or degrees of change that cannot be provided within the regular program time or with the available resources. Examples include a gifted student who is having social difficulties that require intervention by the school counselor or a district psychologist, or a child in first grade who is ready for trigonometry, which her teacher feels unprepared to teach. In situations such as these, a classroom teacher should seek additional support from an expert in the area of the child's need.

For other gifted students, some modifications can be made in learning-environment, content, process, or product dimensions of the classroom curriculum to create, at least partially, a differentiated curriculum for those who need more challenging learning experiences. In the discussion that follows, the use of Table 1.5, A Guide to Selecting Curriculum Modifications Based on a Student's Behaviors (the *Chart*), and the principles of curriculum modification (the *Principles*) are demonstrated as a means for developing a Personal Learning Plan (PLP) for highly able learners.

Differentiating Regular Classroom Curriculum

The process of making large or small adjustments to a regular classroom curriculum begins and ends with observations of the student. These observations include watching, listening, and asking the students about the lessons. The teacher uses the information gained as the basis of the first efforts to differentiate core curriculum activities and as the basis for evaluations of the modified lessons. Although teachers are encouraged to personalize the differentiation process, it is described here as eight sequential steps.

Step One: Using the *Chart* in the Regular Classroom

The *Chart* (Table 1.5) can be used to guide a teacher's observation of any student she or he feels might benefit from more challenging learning opportunities than those provided in the regular program. These "suspects" should be observed while they are engaged in a challenging task in one of the student's areas of interest and strength. All students in the class can be offered the challenging tasks, but all students cannot and should not be observed in one session. A teacher should prioritize his or her observations. Those students suspected of being in the greatest need of differentiated activities should be observed first.

The choice of task is critical. Tasks can be drawn from all areas represented in the theory of multiple intelligences (Gardner, 1983): linguistic, logical–mathematical, spatial, musical, bodily kinesthetic, interpersonal, and intrapersonal. The selection of task also should be guided by a teacher's suspicions regarding the students' areas of passion and strength. Problem-finding and problem-solving activities (e.g., logic problems, mathematical word problems, spatial puzzles), choosing a topic for a story, organizing a group of peers for an activity, composing a melody, writing lyrics for a song, illustrating a story, playing a strategy game (e.g., chess, checkers, Kalah; Martin, McMillan, & Hillam, 1988), resolving a moral dilemma (Casteel, 1978), constructing models, dancing, pantomime, and creating a dramatic or comedy production all are tasks that can be observed to discover a student's strengths and characteristics of giftedness.

The teacher should use a new chart each time she or he observes a student in a different task or content area (or use a different color of ink on the same chart), noting the activity used to elicit the behaviors that were observed. Only one to four students should be observed in a session, and each activity session should be structured to provide a minimum of 20 minutes of observation time. Optimally, more than one charting session is desirable before a teacher begins to modify lessons. Realistically, a lesson can be modified and then the modified activity can provide the context for the next observation if it is sufficiently engaging and challenging.

Step Two: Determining What to Modify

A student's area of strength or passion is the top priority for modification. Other areas can be modified also, but strengths and interests should be the starting point. The basic curriculum is least appropriate and needs the most change in a student's area or areas of passionate interest or strength. These also will be the content areas that inspire the most guilt and feelings of inadequacy in the heart of a teacher. These feelings may be triggered by a teacher's professional intuition, a student's obvious boredom, or a student's disruptive behavior. The degree of need for a differentiated curriculum for any student is equivalent to the extent to which a student's potential to learn differs from the level of challenge provided by the regular curriculum: the greater the difference, the greater the need; the smaller the difference, the smaller the need. Often, teachers may want to round out a gifted student's profile by providing support in his or her area or areas of relative weakness. Because the gifted student may be above average in those areas and only relatively weaker in comparison to his or her strengths, rounding out is not an optimal investment of time and energy.

Units of instruction of any size may be modified: all or part of a lesson, a cluster of lessons, a unit structured around an interdisciplinary theme or topic, a content area, or an in-depth investigation in an area of interest. Regardless of the size or subject of the unit of instruction, a teacher's choice of whether and what to modify should reflect the student's needs, the nature of the activity, and the time and resources available. When modifications can be made that cross or blend disciplines, they should be celebrated because an even greater proportion of the student's educational program is differentiated.

Step Three: Analyzing the Unmodified Lesson

Before changing any part of the curriculum, the teacher must be aware of its objective or desired outcome. The objective is what the average-ability learners will be expected to know or be able to do, and the desired outcome is how well they should be able to know or do the objective at the conclusion of the lesson. In the regular classroom, the objective of the unmodified curriculum must be achieved before or within the modified instruction to ensure that the student has mastered the core content and does not have significant gaps left in her or his understanding of the topic. One way to achieve this is to pretest the class on the core material and allow any students who have mastered the content to proceed with a differentiated activity related to the core material.

If no preinstruction assessment of the objective is conducted, the content of the unmodified lesson should be embedded in the modified version so that a student's mastery can be evaluated. In this way, the modified lesson will enable the student to achieve the objective of the original lesson as well as gain some additional benefit from the modification. The objective, or baseline expectation, may be achieved by having the student complete an abbreviated version of the lesson or by integrating the objective into a differentiated activity. To integrate the core, a teacher must analyze the original lesson in terms of its three modifiable components: content, processes, and products. The *content* of a lesson is the knowledge the student will gain from the activity. The *processes* are the thinking and feeling strategies the student will use to master the content. The *products* are the tangible evidence of student learning. Evaluation criteria and procedures also are aspects of the product component.

With a clear sense of the objective and the three components of the unmodified lesson, a teacher can apply the most recommended modification to the relevant dimension of instruction: content, process, or product. A conscious effort must be made to build the core into the modified lesson or to find a way to ensure that the content is already understood by the student. With this in mind, the educator can ensure that the student has mastered the core content and has gained additional benefits from the changes that result from applying the selected modification.

Few regular classroom teachers have the time, energy, and expertise to create, implement, monitor, and evaluate a completely separate curriculum for the one, two, or three gifted students in their classes. As a result, in the approach described here, the core is embedded in the modified lesson. This embedding ensures that a teacher will be able to collect the information needed to report achievement and growth. Without this link between the core and the differentiated curriculum, equitable evaluation is difficult. Using this system to differentiate curriculum, a teacher is able to obtain evaluation information based on the core curriculum and, also, on the additional learning that arises from the extensions created by implementing the *Principles*. How else could one give the bright student a grade that reflects how he or she ranks among his or her peers if the student has not been assessed on the same skills and knowledge?

Step Four: Modifying Instruction

Through the use of the *Chart*, the teacher will have identified the most appropriate principles to apply to lessons for a student in his or her areas of strength. One or more of the *Principles* can be applied. A focus on one modification often is sufficient because, once one *Principle* is applied, other dimensions of the lesson will change as well. The intentional application of one principle results in incidental changes that produce others. Efforts to apply more than one principle to a lesson are unnecessary and frequently overcomplicate the process. Applying more than one principle often takes too much time and effort, consequences that make it less likely that attempts to modify lessons will be undertaken in the future.

If a series of lessons or a unit of curriculum is to be modified, then the use of more than one *Principle* across lessons and activities is appropriate. Teachers are urged to apply the three to five modifications that were most recommended (i.e., the ones that had the greatest proportion of possible X's highlighted on the student's *Chart*).

The *Principles* can be used in the regular classroom in two ways. One way is finding existing materials that include the desired principle directly in the instruction. These may be commercially developed materials or materials developed by teaching colleagues. An example of the *Prin-*

ciple of open-endedness applied to the reinforcement of single-digit sub-traction skills is found in Figure 6.1, based on *Diffy* (Wills, 1971).

Instead of a worksheet or textbook page cluttered with problems such as $9 - 7 =$ _____, $8 - 3 =$ _____, or $6 -$ _____ $= 0$, the student is given a puzzle-style game. In fact, a whole class can work on *Diffy*. Each student is challenged to find a set of four single-digit numbers to put in the corner positions to start the game. She or he finds the difference between the pairs of corner numbers and writes the result in the circle between the two. These differences create the next set of pairs for which differences are to be found. To win, a student must arrive at the center of the square without getting all zeros in a round. The game continues until the student wins or loses. Students who need subtraction practice will be subtracting while they try to win the game. At the same time, students with a passion for mathematical reasoning will have an opportunity to seek the relationship that must exist between the numbers in the initial four-some that will ensure winning the game (Hint: Both the numbers selected and their positions matter). Regardless of level of math skill, all

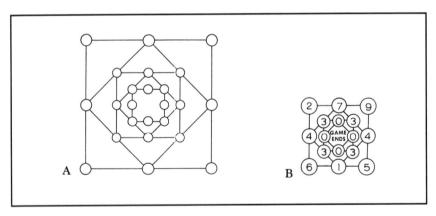

Figure 6.1. An illustration (a) and example (b) of *Diffy*. *Diffy* is a game to be played by one person. The player uses a game board that looks like the illustration in *a* and starts by putting a single-digit number in each corner circle. The smaller number is subtracted from the larger number and the difference entered in the circle between them. The player continues working toward the center in this same manner. To win the game, the player must arrive at the center without having all zeroes. An example of a losing combination is shown in *b*.

Note. From "Diffy," by Herbert Wills, 1971, *The Arithmetic Teacher*, 18(6), pp. 402, 404. Copyright 1971 by National Council of Teachers of Mathematics. Adapted with permission.

students have a chance of finding a winning combination, although they may approach and complete the task very differently.

The second approach to differentiation in the regular classroom is to create new lessons or curriculum that integrates the selected principle with the content of the unmodified instruction. For example, if one of the recommended principles is to introduce the student to methods of inquiry and the content of the curriculum is ancient civilizations, a gifted student could investigate and apply the techniques an archaeologist uses to determine the age and authenticity of artifacts. The breadth and depth of her or his search and the resultant product would be negotiated with the teacher to reflect the student's interest and the time and resources available. During the time the rest of the class is engaged in the regular study of Ancient Egypt, the gifted student is learning about Egypt *and* the methods of an archaeologist.

Step Five: Checking the Defensibility of the Differentiated Instruction

The appropriateness and defensibility of the modified instruction should be checked once the lesson has been modified. The two questions that follow can be used for this purpose:

1. Will the modified lesson take the same amount of time for the bright student to complete as average-ability students need to complete the unmodified activity?

2. Does the modified lesson contain the core content that the rest of the class will be expected to know (or is there some assurance that the core is known and understood) as well as offer an additional challenge and benefit?

The implications of yes and no answers to these questions are described below.

1. Will the modified lesson take the same amount of time for the bright student to complete as the average-ability students need to complete the unmodified activity?

If the answer is yes, the lesson passes the first test of the defensibility of the modification. Bright students often finish before the rest of the class when all students are given an activity that targets the average developmental level of the class. This is due to a lack of developmentally appropriate challenge (i.e., bright students already know the content and processes involved in the task). Gifted students deserve activities that provide them with challenges equivalent to those experienced by their less able peers facing the unmodified task. Once a lesson is modified appropriately, bright students should complete their work at the same time as their classmates who are working on unmodified activities. Like their peers, they even may have homework!

If the answer to Question 1 is no, the lesson may be completed in significantly less or more time. If either occurs, the lesson must be changed. If the lesson takes *less* time, there are two options: The lesson can be left as it is, and the student can move into an independent study for the remaining time; or the instruction can be broadened, deepened, or extended in some other way to provide an appropriate challenge. If the lesson requires *more* time to complete, it should be reduced along the same lines: breadth, depth, or extension. Bright students should not be penalized for their ability by being expected to do more work than their peers do. Changes also can be made to the unmodified instruction to bring the time requirements of both into balance.

2. Does the modified lesson contain the core content that the rest of the class will be expected to know as well as offer an additional challenge and benefit?

If the student has mastered the content of the lesson, the first part of the question becomes irrelevant because the baseline objective (the content of the basic curriculum) has been achieved. If the pretest or assessment results indicate that the student does not know the core content and the answer to Question 2 is yes, the instruction honors the need to ensure that the learner masters the core content *and* the need to offer something beyond the basic curriculum. The able learner will have the opportunity to master the core and to develop a new understanding or a new way of thinking about something new.

If the answer to Question 2 is no, the knowledge and skills that gifted students learn will differ from those learned by the rest of the class. This difference may create some of the gaps in their knowledge bases that are found to be characteristic of bright students who investigate non-core topics at the expense of basic concepts. These students may be at a loss in the future when held responsible for material covered in previous grades that they did not have an opportunity to learn. Gifted students are capable of covering the core *and* of going beyond. There is no need for students to skip the core to go beyond the basic curriculum. A negative answer to Question 2 means that the teacher needs to think of another modified version of the learning activities that will yield a yes to the question of mastery of core concepts and that will also yield a yes on taking a student beyond the basics into more advanced concepts and processes.

Teachers who consider these issues in the process of differentiating curriculum will increase the defensibility of the learning activities that emerge from the process. They will be sensitive to the characteristics of the individual student, will be able to account for the content of the basic curriculum, and will be fair to bright students in terms of the time required to complete the differentiated activities.

Step Six: Implementing Modified Learning Opportunities

Four considerations related to the implementation of differentiated curricula in the regular classroom are discussed in this section: the learning environment, access, cooperative learning, and monitoring.

An Optimal Learning Environment

In this phase of the process, a teacher must consider the critical features of the learning environment discussed in Chapter 2. The extent to which these features are evident in the classroom has a direct relationship to the extent of the benefits a gifted learner will gain from a modified curriculum. In a safe, responsive, learner-centered environment, a student's growth from a differentiated learning experience will be amplified. In a rigid, judgmental, teacher-controlled environment, the benefits will be diminished.

Classrooms with all the features of an optimal environment and no curriculum differentiation offer some gifted students a better education than they would receive in a classroom with an extensively, appropriately differentiated curriculum but with none of the characteristics of an optimal learning environment. When a student feels accepted, taking learning risks is safer, mistakes are learning experiences, and appropriate challenges can be negotiated. Ultimately, the goal is to have both the optimal learning environment *and* an appropriately differentiated curriculum; neither is sufficient on its own.

Access and Exclusivity

Once lessons are modified for the bright student, can one or more of them be offered to the whole class? The teacher's professional judgment will determine who will be offered the modified learning activities. Some activities may be too difficult for any but the gifted student or may be uninteresting to any other students. Some may be appropriate for the bright student and one or more peers for collaborative group work. Some may be appropriate for the entire class. As is the case in any lesson plan, the determination of who participates depends on achieving the best match between the objectives for the activity, the nature of the activity, and the nature of the students. Each decision will always be specific to a particular lesson. Any groupings should be flexible so different groups of students may participate in more challenging curricula on a lesson-by-lesson basis.

If *all* students in the class can achieve the objective of the unmodified lesson by participating in the modified lesson, let them! Withholding participation from students who need and who could benefit from the modified lesson may incite charges of elitism and exclusivity (Kaplan, 1986). There must be educationally relevant and defensible differences between the students who are offered the modified instruction and those who are not; without defensible differences, the charges of elitism are justified. Charges may arise most vehemently when the curriculum offered to gifted students is more fun than that offered to their age peers. As a result, gifted students may become resented by their classmates and alienated from them. For example, if a lesson is modified to make it more open-ended (a process modification according to the *Chart*), it often is appropriate for all students. An activity like *Diffy* (Wills, 1971) can benefit many students. The multiple solutions and solution paths characteristic of an open-ended activity may be recognized only by those students who need them or whose attention is drawn to them. Thus, the teacher can adjust his or her expectations of individual students, although the same lesson is presented to the entire class.

Some modified lessons are not appropriate for the whole class but may provide a suitable challenge for some students. These lessons can be offered to all students who might benefit from the modified lesson as much as or more than from the unmodified lesson. Although one class member provides the inspiration for the changes, others may benefit also from them to a greater extent that they would from the unmodified lesson. These students can be grouped and encouraged to try the more challenging activities. When a modified activity is not suitable for other students and a parent or peer questions the reason for restricting the lesson to the gifted student, the teacher can use the *Chart* as a guide for responding to their questions. Observable behavior characteristics and a defensible process can be described as reasons for a modified program.

When a classmate shows an interest in the differentiated instruction, a teacher has two options. If the student's interest is denied, the gifted student may become more distanced from his or her peers by the teacher's efforts to provide an optimal education. A better option is for the teacher to agree to the request with a condition. The condition is that a class-mate may attempt the modified activities with the understanding that she or he may switch back to the undifferentiated activities if the student or the teacher perceives it as too difficult or otherwise inappropriate. With this atmosphere of trust and risk taking, the threat of alienating the gifted student is greatly reduced.

The application of most of the principles can result in lessons for gifted students that take the same amount of time as the lessons under-taken by other class members. An exception to this statement is the pacing principle. By definition, the pacing principle requires that stu-dents be permitted to learn at a pace commensurate with their ability. This pace will be *FAST*, especially if students are no longer expected to complete redundant work within and across lessons. They will have time to invest in intrinsically motivating learning related to their interests. Further learning can be interest based and need not result in a tangible product. One option under this principle is for the teacher to encourage the student to engage in product-free, independent learning about a topic on a contract basis, using a format something like the *Venture* form (Clark County School District, 1979) reproduced in Figure 6.2. The *Venture* form provides a framework for a student's exploration of a topic. No product is expected, and evaluation is focused on the process, not the outcome, of learning. A *Venture* is about learning in spare moments or during assigned time just for the joy of knowing. The time spent negotiat-ing the contract eliminates the need for preparing "more of the same," and the student has the opportunity to gain good independent-learning skills. This option also can reduce or prevent behavior problems that emerge when some bright students find less productive ways to challenge

VENTURE

A Venture is an open-ended research study. Through the venturing process you will:

1) make decisions
2) organize your study
3) learn in different ways
4) acquire new vocabulary
5) share, and
6) evaluate your efforts

NOW—Create an idea web!

TOPIC:

Have you studied this topic before?
yes ☐   no ☐
If yes, what did you learn?

Who? _____

When? _____

Clark County School District   Las Vegas, Nevada

Figure 6.2. The Venture Independent Study contract form, by Clark County School District, 1979, Las Vegas, NV: Author. Copyright 1978 by Clark County School District. Reprinted with permission.

RESEARCH TOPIC: _____

NEXT. . .

to help you organize your time, write
some things you want to learn or some
questions you want to answer below.

_____

_____

_____

_____

_____

_____

_____

NEW VOCABULARY:

Figure 6.2. *Continued*

I am learning from:

Listening:

_____
_____
_____
_____
_____

Viewing:

_____
_____
_____
_____
_____
_____
_____

Reading:

_____
_____
_____
_____
_____
_____
_____
_____

Investigating:

_____
_____
_____
_____
_____
_____

AND.....
 (check those used)

card catalog
periodicals
encyclopedia
phone book
dictionary
thesaurus
video tapes
records
pictures
graphs
atlas
almanac
field trips
film catalog

Other:

Mentors:

_____
_____
_____
_____
_____

SHARING:

oral
written
visual
other
With whom?

_____
_____

Figure 6.2. *Continued*

STUDENT EVALUATOR: _____ GRADE: __ DATE: _____

1. I chose my own topic. |—+—+—+—+—| Topic was assigned.

2. Topic was intesting. |—+—+—+—+—| Topic was boring.

3. I worked very hard on my venture. |—+—+—+—+—| I did not complete this venture.

4. I used many sources of information. |—+—+—+—+—| I used only one source of information.

5. I did excellent work on this venture. |—+—+—+—+—| My work is just OK.

Comments:

_____

_____

What have you decided to do next?
____ another venture
____ a project
____ an issue

TEACHER EVALUATOR: _____

SCHOOL: _____

Key: √ = objective performed
Ω = needs to improve
X = not expected in this venture

____ worked well independently
____ selected useable information
____ reorganized material in own words
____ communicated main ideas
____ shared adequately

Completed thoroughly |—+—| Not completed

Used time wisely |—+—| Wasted time

Used resources well |—+—| Used resources poorly

Comments:

Figure 6.2. *Continued*

themselves in their spare time. Many benefits can accrue to the student and to the teacher in a product-free activity like the *Venture*, if the student has demonstrated mastery of the core content. Abilities are engaged constructively in student-selected topics that students pursue in their available time.

Cooperative Learning

If the group-interaction principle is recommended, a teacher may choose to offer the whole class an activity that involves cooperative learning or another form of group work that results in a group outcome. The teacher must consider a number of issues when forming student groups and selecting tasks in which gifted students are involved. These considerations are discussed in depth elsewhere (Robinson, 1990, 1991; VanTassel-Baska, Landrum, & Peterson, 1992). Here, the following guidelines are offered for cooperative learning that involves gifted students in the regular classroom:

- Keep group size to three or four students so all students have an opportunity to contribute to the process and to the product of learning. Some students may get "lost" in larger groups.

- Think flexibly about strategies for determining group composition. Groupings can be based on a variety of criteria (e.g., ability, degree of interest, height). If there are not enough highly able learners to fill a group, add students who are extremely interested in the topic. Highly motivated students are more likely to be able to keep up with the pace set by more intellectually able peers. Groups can be made intentionally homogeneous or heterogeneous in terms of any characteristic, teacher-determined or student-selected, rigid or flexible (e.g., students can move in and out of their groups as the work moves on).

- The group task should provide *all* group members with an opportunity to learn something they do not already know.

- The task should be sufficiently complex and challenging to require that all group members work cooperatively to complete the activity.

- When the primary objective of an activity is the students' learning to think in a more sophisticated way about the content of the lesson, group gifted, high-ability, or highly motivated students (or all three) together for collaborative learning activities.

- Provide training and guidelines for good group work and for the roles students are expected to take.

- Provide clear feedback about the qualities of each group's cooperative interaction as well as about the qualities of the outcome of the learning process.

Monitoring the Students During the Activity

Teachers ask themselves hundreds of questions while students are learning. Some are general; some are specific: How is it going? Who seems to be struggling? Is this a good struggle or not? Are any changes necessary now? Who needs encouragement? Who needs feedback? What changes would you make if you were to repeat this lesson or apply the same principle again? Who else would you include? All are relevant when teachers monitor gifted students in differentiated curricula.

Teachers can ask students similar questions during and after learning. These questions might include one or more of the following: How did it go? What would you change? How was the level of difficulty? With whom would you like to work next time we do something like this? In what circumstances would you rather work on your own? How do you feel about the evaluation? What other activities would you like to do like this? Debriefing in this way can strengthen future differentiation efforts.

Step Seven: Evaluating the Outcome

Specific options for the appropriate evaluation of bright students' learning outcomes are suggested in Chapter 5, Product Modifications. Whether or not this *Principle* is one of those recommended for a gifted student, it should be considered for use with all students in the regular classroom. All students can benefit from opportunities to brainstorm, define, select, and apply appropriate evaluation criteria to their own learning and to that of their peers.

As the teacher decides what and how to evaluate in the outcome of a modified lesson, he or she must remember that the core content of the unmodified lesson must be accounted for at some point. If it has not been evaluated before the modified activity was undertaken or during the activity, the core content must be evaluated at the end of the activity. The procedure and criteria should be personalized in response to the needs and characteristics of the learner. Once the core has been evaluated, the next decision is whether to evaluate the additional learning that resulted from the modification. *This is optional.* The student and teacher have fulfilled their commitment to the core curriculum. This is all that is needed to report the student's performance in the material at grade level. After some activities, a teacher may choose not to evaluate the additional benefit and, thus, encourage the student to enjoy learning for understanding rather than learning to satisfy some external evaluation. This option can be used to introduce extremely goal-oriented and competitive gifted students to the experience of intrinsically motivated learning and to demonstrate that the teacher values curiosity and learning as ongoing processes, with or without tangible or graded products.

As mentioned in Chapter 5, bright students have the ability to learn to select and apply evaluation criteria. Self-evaluation can be a powerful tool for those who have a tendency to set high, sometimes unrealistic, standards for their work. Kaplan and Gould (1987) provided a series of lessons intended to train students to select criteria suitable for the evaluation of a variety of products. The student may be involved in the selection of criteria, their application, or both; the roles also can be shared. Figure 6.3 is a sample worksheet drawn from a lesson in which students consider the relative importance of certain criteria in the evaluation of a product.

Many bright students spend a large proportion of their time in the regular classroom trying to figure out what the teacher *really* wants. Among other benefits, inviting them to develop the criteria for the outcomes of the differentiated lesson can remove the mystery in the evaluation process and release the attention focused on the grading game. Attention can be invested instead in developmentally appropriate learning. If a bright student has a tendency to underachieve, a teacher may choose neither to evaluate nor to offer feedback on the quality of the additional benefit of the differentiation. Through this action, the teacher can reduce the threat of the fear of failure or the fear of success that paralyzes many nonproductive students. Encouragement to learn for the sake of knowing, as children do outside the classroom, is all a teacher may want to offer.

Although many or all class members may be able to complete the differentiated task, each child will differ in what and how much he or she is able to learn from it. This fact must be kept in mind when teachers evaluate and compare students' work. The core and the additional learning can be evaluated separately. The core should be evaluated in the same

---

SELF EVALUATION

Student Name _____ Date _____

Describe or illustrate the
product you developed in the
box to the right.

Rate the product by checking
the box below the phrase that
best represents the importance
of that criterion in terms of this
product.

Give a reason for each rating.

Add criteria that should be
used to evaluate this product.

Criteria	Most Important	Important	Undecided	Somewhat Important	Least Important	Reasons
Knowledge	☐	☐	☐	☐	☐	_____
Creativity	☐	☐	☐	☐	☐	_____
Interest	☐	☐	☐	☐	☐	_____
Beauty	☐	☐	☐	☐	☐	_____
Complexity	☐	☐	☐	☐	☐	_____
Accuracy	☐	☐	☐	☐	☐	_____
Neatness	☐	☐	☐	☐	☐	_____
Effort	☐	☐	☐	☐	☐	_____
Expressiveness	☐	☐	☐	☐	☐	_____

Additional criteria: Reason for adding:

_____   _____

_____   _____

_____   _____

Figure 6.3. Example of a self-evaluation form.

manner for all students. This evaluation provides an assessment of the extent to which each child has achieved the baseline objectives for the class curriculum. Students who have aspired higher than the baseline may be given feedback on their achievements. Each student's ability level should be kept in mind during evaluation of the additional learning. Rather than comparing students to each other or rank ordering performance, the teacher can offer students comments with "growing room." In these comments, strengths in the current outcomes are identified, and improvement in future performance is promoted. Students who consistently receive top marks often have the impression that they have learned all there is to know about the topic. Even straight-A students need to know there is more to learn about any topic than is contained in the school curriculum.

Thus, when a teacher is aware of the core and differentiated dimensions of an activity, the evaluation of the lesson may be considered a two-tier endeavor. The core should be evaluated according to the same criteria for all students regardless of ability. The student and teacher can think flexibly when they evaluate the additional benefits that emerge from the differentiated aspects of the lesson.

Step Eight: Monitoring the Modification Process

The effectiveness of this system of differentiating instruction can be monitored by watching for changes in the student. The system is a recursive process in that changes may be seen in the behavior characteristics included in the *Chart* with which the process began. As a result, the teacher should observe the student, using the *Chart*, approximately every 2 months. The behaviors may become more intense, appear more frequently, or last longer, or more of them may appear. If any of these changes do arise, they are likely to affect the specific principles for differentiation that are most recommended. Changes in other important behaviors also may occur. If the modifications have been effective, attitudes toward school, teachers, peers, learning, or task completion, or other feelings may be improving also. This observation is not to suggest that weaknesses were noted in any of these areas before changes were made; however, ways to improve life in the classroom always can be found.

Another strategy for monitoring the process of differentiating curricula is to ask the students for their thoughts and feelings about the lessons and the changes. In fact, students can be invited to assist with a teacher's efforts to complete the *Chart* and apply the *Principles*. Eventually, a student may take responsibility for the selection of activities and the design of a large proportion of his or her own curriculum. Changes are to be negotiated with the teacher, but the students can acquire many of the skills involved in curriculum development. Therefore, even the control over this process may shift gradually from the teacher to the student.

A Personal Learning Plan for Highly Able Learners

Written, individualized educational programs are mandated for gifted students in many states and provinces. With or without a legislative mandate, the process of developing a long-term learning plan can stimulate rich, positive discussions. Team members' commitments to provide resources and to participate in the maintenance of the plan are formalized through the development process. In Figure 6.4, a form is presented to provide a skeleton for developing, implementing, and monitoring a Personal Learning Plan (PLP) for a highly able learner. The form may be used to guide a discussion between the student, the student's classroom teacher, the resource or support teacher, and at least one parent. Others may be invited, but these four team members are essential. The conversations should be highly interactive, with all participants contributing equally. The discussions continue beyond the planning meeting, on a formal or informal basis, as a means of monitoring the plan and its elements. The student's classroom teacher should take responsibility for the written version because she or he will take primary responsibility for implementation on a daily basis. The description of the component parts of the skeleton is followed by a sample plan for an 8-year-old gifted girl.

The PLP Form

Multiple Intelligence (MI) Priorities

The intelligences involved in a student's areas of strength and passion should be circled on the form to indicate a focus for the development of differentiated activities and the selection of appropriate resources.

PERSONAL LEARNING PLAN FOR HIGHLY ABLE LEARNERS

Student _____   Teacher(s) _____

MI Priorities (circle strengths in pen, weaknesses in pencil): Linguistic Logical-Mathematical Spatial Musical Kinesthetic Interpersonal Intrapersonal

Area(s) of Strength or Passion: Language Arts Literature Mathematics Science Social Studies Fine Arts Technology Other _____

Interdisciplinary Themes: _____

Generalizations: _____

Gifted Student's Needs	check	Differentiated Objectives	Differentiated Learning Activities	Monitoring/ Evaluating the Differentiated Learning Activities
Abstractness				
Complexity				
Variety				
Organization				
Study of People				
Study of Methods				

P	*Higher-level Thought*			
R	*Open-endedness*			
O	*Discovery*			
C	*Evidence of Reasoning*			
E	*Freedom of Choice*			
S	*Group Interaction*			
S	*Pacing*			
	Variety			
P	*Real Problems*			
R	*Real Audiences*			
O	*Transformations*			
D	*Variety*			
U				
C	*Self-selected Format*			
T	*Appropriate Evaluation*			

MANAGING THE PLAN

TIME FOR DIFFERENTIATED LEARNING ACTIVITIES (amount and schedule):

TIME FOR MONITORING/EVALUATING DIFFERENTIATED LEARNING ACTIVITIES:

(continues)

Figure 6.4. "Personal Learning Plan Form," by L. Kanevsky, 1995. Copyright 1995 by L. Kanevsky.

RESOURCES NEEDED:
People & Their Roles

Materials

Technology

Location & Transportation

SCHEDULE FOR MONITORING/REVISING THIS PERSONAL LEARNING PLAN (include who, what, when, how):

COMMUNICATION AMONG TEAM MEMBERS (who, how, when, what):

SPECIAL EFFECTS (incentive plan, celebration, vision, other?):

Additional Comments and Information:

Figure 6.4. *Continued.*

Areas of Strength or Passion

This item includes the traditional content disciplines in the basic curriculum. Units and lessons within these disciplines become the specific learning activities to be modified as indicated by the *Principles* most recommended by the *Chart* for the student. The "Other" option allows for additions specific to a particular student.

Interdisciplinary Themes

An interdisciplinary theme is a universal concept or idea that can serve as an organizing element for a curriculum or for a unit of study (San Diego City Schools, 1991). Some examples include

patterns	power	justice
structure	beauty	rhythm
conflict	movement	control
interdependence	communication	systems
adaptation	balance	change
community	economy	time

Generalizations

This element of the PLP is considered at length in Chapter 3 in the discussion of the principle of abstractness in content. Students must be given opportunities to derive generalizations from accumulated information in a systematic way through their learning activities. Some examples of generalizations from San Diego City Schools (1991) are listed here:

The logic of mathematics can be used to describe intellectual inquiry in any field.

The use of complex symbols for communication separates human beings from all other forms of life.

The concept of heroes changes as cultures and cultural values change.

The reflection of human nature in different literary genres increases self-perception.

Every action produces a reaction.

The awareness of prejudice and its underlying elements helps people to understand the value of tolerance for others.

The Needs of Gifted Students

This column contains the 20 *Principles* of curriculum modification. Once the *Chart* (see Table 1.5) is completed for the student, the three to five most recommended *Principles* should be marked (√) in the column headed "check." These are the principles that should be applied to the content, processes, or products in the basic curriculum to develop a differentiated curriculum for the student. If more than one *Chart* has been completed for a student in different areas of strength, the teacher can summarize them on one PLP form by using alternate marks for each strength (e.g., √, †, X, *). Their meaning can be indicated by recording the symbol next to the "Area of Strength or Passion" in the top section of the form.

Differentiated Objectives

The objectives related to the theme and one of the generalizations that the gifted student is expected to achieve within the duration of the PLP are recorded in this column.

Differentiated Learning Activities

The activities are the tasks that the student will undertake to acquire the knowledge and skills required to achieve the differentiated objectives. Each learning activity is composed of three elements: content, process, and product. The learning environment (e.g., location, grouping) for each activity may be specified here or in the section, "Managing the Plan."

Monitoring/Evaluating Differentiated Learning Activities

In this section, the people, criteria, and procedures involved in the monitoring of a student's progress and in the evaluation of each of the activities should be specified. This will ensure that the gifted student's energy can be directed toward learning rather than toward playing the grading game.

Management Plan

The second page of the PLP form concerns the commitment of time, people, and resources to support the student's efforts in achieving the objectives specified on the first page.

TIME FOR DIFFERENTIATED LEARNING ACTIVITIES. The members of the planning team should specify the amount of time per day or per week that will be made available for the student to engage in the differentiated learning activities. It also should be clear when this time is to be found in the regular school day. Times not appropriate are before and after school, during recess, lunch or library periods, or when special activities are planned for the whole class. Differentiated activities are to be a part of this student's regular school day, not an addition to the day planned for other students.

TIMELINE FOR MONITORING/EVALUATING DIFFERENTIATED LEARNING AC-TIVITIES. The planning team members should reserve school time for the student and teacher to meet together to discuss the student's progress and performance in the differentiated activities as often as is deemed necessary.

RESOURCES NEEDED. The nature and extent of resources beyond those available to support the basic curriculum should be outlined so that arrangements can be made to locate them. Responsibility for any costs involved should be negotiated between the school and the parents at this time. Under "People and Their Roles," the individuals to be involved are listed and their activities in support of the student are specified. These individuals may include parents, teachers, mentors, librarians, and con-tacts in the community, high school, colleges, universities, and govern-ment. Under "Materials," the books, art supplies, science supplies, audio-visual equipment and materials, computer software, videotapes and audio media, music, and tools the student will need to complete the differenti-ated activities are specified.

Under "Technology," the team should specify needed computer hard-ware and software, telecommunications equipment and access to local on-line services, and access to support for the equipment and services needed.

Under "Location and Transportation," the team should specify where the student will pursue the differentiated learning activities and how he or she will get to any location that is not on the school grounds. Locations may include space in the classroom, other areas in the school, alternate learning environments in other schools, or sites in the community (e.g., museums, studios, businesses, hospitals, hotels, law courts, laboratories).

SCHEDULE FOR MONITORING/REVISING THIS PERSONAL LEARNING PLAN. Planning team members should discuss who will take responsibility for monitoring and revising each component of the PLP, the schedule and procedures for this review/revision, and when it will occur.

COMMUNICATION AMONG TEAM MEMBERS. Formal and informal arrangements should be made for team members to maintain contact so all are aware of the strengths and struggles in the PLP. Members can exchange ideas for possible revisions through phone calls and written communications in addition to scheduled meetings.

SPECIAL EFFECTS. Some highly able students have very jagged profiles of strengths and weaknesses in their learning. Special efforts must be made to accommodate these peaks and valleys when differentiated learning activities are developed. Although the major concerns of the PLP team members are the student's strengths and passions, ignoring her or his weaknesses may not be appropriate. For example, a student may be a brilliant storyteller, but a "non-producer" (Delisle, 1992), so the stories never make it to the page in creative writing assignments. The planning team may need to build in some sort of "incentive plan" to reward the student for completed writing assignments. Any efforts that will be made to accommodate weaknesses in ways that have not been mentioned elsewhere on the form should be included in this section.

ADDITIONAL COMMENTS AND INFORMATION. Team members can record any additional information about the student that can or should be considered at that time or in the future. This information may be related to successful or frustrating products, learning style preferences, questions for future explorations, favorite characters in a novel, favorite media with which to work, weak study skills, physical or emotional challenges, extracurricular responsibilities, and other information about factors that may affect the student's future learning experiences.

Sandy's Personal Learning Plan

Figure 6.5 offers an example of the process followed in developing a completed PLP form for Sandy. Sandy is an 8-year-old girl with an insatiable appetite for architecture, a natural extension of her passion for mathematical reasoning and her extraordinary ability to sculpt and design models. Sandy is a popular, soft-spoken class member who works willingly and well in groups. She is particularly fond of building weird and wonderful pinata-like creatures out of papier maché for each class celebration. Sandy becomes extremely uncomfortable with the admiration her classmates offer while she works on one of her masterpieces.

Sandy's assignments usually are submitted on time except when she becomes immersed in a topic and cannot let go of it. Her teacher's deadlines come second to her need to know. Recently during a discussion of her geometry homework with her mother (an engineer), Sandy learned how to use perspective to create a sense of three dimensions in her drawings. The homework was never completed, but her enthusiasm stimulated a class discussion related to the use of perspective in occupations like drafting, the arts, architecture, sciences, and mathematics. Sandy reads as well as the majority of her classmates but has a thinly veiled aversion to writing. She says, "It's just not my thing. If you let me shape my stories, they'll speak for themselves." She firmly believes her sculptures say all that needs to be said. Her teacher, Mr. Desmond, is not willing to accept sculptures in lieu of written stories but has found himself embroiled in some challenging discussions with Sandy about alternate media for storytelling. When Sandy does write, her sentences are poorly constructed, and she relies heavily on invented spellings for words that most of her peers can spell correctly. Sandy has shown guarded interest in the classroom computer for word processing, saying "Words written in light have a softer feel than those written in pencil or pen."

Sandy, her father, Mr. Desmond, and the school resource teacher met recently to develop a PLP to integrate and differentiate Sandy's Math and Art curricula from January through the middle of April. All agreed she had strengths in logical–mathematical and spatial intelligences, which emerged in her passions for math and sculpting. When Sandy considered the list of themes Mr. Desmond provided, she settled on "Patterns,"

PERSONAL LEARNING PLAN FOR HIGHLY ABLE LEARNERS

Student ___Sandy___

Teacher(s) ___Desmond___

MI Priorities (circle strengths in pen, weaknesses in pencil); Linguistic (Logical-Mathematical) (Spatial) Musical Kinesthetic Interpersonal Intrapersonal

Area(s) of Strength or Passion: Language Arts Literature (Mathematics) Science Social Studies (Fine Arts) Technology X Other _____

Interdisciplinary Themes: ___Patterns___

Generalizations: ___Patterns are found in all aspects of life.___

Gifted Student's Needs	check	Differentiated Objectives	Differentiated Learning Activities	Monitoring/ Evaluating the Differentiated Learning Activities
Abstractness		Sandy will explore statistics and probability.	Sandy will select activities related to the differentiated objectives from the materials in the attached resource list. They will cover a variety of topics in math.	Mr. Desmond will monitor Sandy's selection and give her feedback to ensure her choices are a broad range of content.
Complexity				
Variety	✓	Sandy will analyze the use of patterns in the works of local and international artists.	Sandy will do one or more Ventures on statistics, probability, and uses of patterns in mathematics, architecture, the arts, and literature.	Sandy and Mr. Desmond will discuss the entries Sandy makes on her Venture form and both will complete their parts of the evaluation form.
Organization				
Study of People				
Study of Methods				

		✔	X	Description		
P	Higher-level Thought			Sandy will explore the use of patterns in mathematics, architecture, the arts, and literature.	Sandy will walk through the school (and neighborhood) to observe patterns that are natural and imposed.	Mr. Desmond will mark the number and accuracy of the natural and imposed patterns.
R	Open-endedness					
O	Discovery			Sandy will use tables, graphs, and statistical measures appropriately to discover and organize knowledge.	Sandy will identify patterns in weather maps in the newspaper over a two week period and report her observations and explanations to her classmates.	Mr. Desmond will mark the accuracy and number of weather patterns as well as the quality of her observations and explanations to the class.
C	Evidence of Reasoning					
E	Freedom of Choice	✔	X			
S	Group Interaction					
S	Pacing	✔		Sandy will learn to select processes and products to use in her efforts to solve well- and poorly defined problems and develop abstract understandings.	Sandy will enter the Tesselation Contest sponsored by Dale Seymour Publications.	Evaluation is up to the Contest Judges.
	Variety					
P	Real Problems					
R	Real Audiences				Sandy will spend one afternoon each week "shadowing" an architect and keep a journal to record her activities and reflections about her experiences. Her entries must each be at least 5 sentences/phrases long, and must be done on the word-processor.	Sandy will share her journal with Mr. Desmond and he will write comments in the margins to answer her questions. Grammar and punctuation are NOT important. Sandy must use the spell-checker to correct spelling.
O	Transformations					
D	Variety		X	Sandy will use illustrations, tables, graphs, oral reports, and a journal to share her ideas and findings.		
U	Self-selected Format					
C	Appropriate Evaluation		X			
T						

(continues)

Figure 6.5. Sandy's Personal Learning Plan. Copyright 1995 by L. Kanevsky.

MANAGING THE PLAN

TIME FOR DIFFERENTIATED LEARNING ACTIVITIES (amount and schedule):

Any time available after Sandy finishes her assignments in any content area can be used for these activities. Sandy will spend Thursday afternoons in Ms. Botteros Architecture offices to shadow her activities.

TIME FOR MONITORING/EVALUATING DIFFERENTIATED LEARNING ACTIVITIES:

Every Monday, Sandy and Mr. Desmond will meet from 10:15 to 10:30 to review the previous week and plan the specifics of the current week's activities.

RESOURCES NEEDED:

People & Their Roles
Architect for Sandy to shadow
Ms. Gagné (resource teacher) will locate architect, reference and other materials for Sandy's PLP, and will bring them to Mr. Desmond.

Materials
List of learning / teaching materials attached

Technology
Macintosh computer and Microsoft Word with Mr. Desmond's help to learn to use the Spell-Checker

Location & Transportation
Regular classroom, school library, and the architect's office. Possibly the public or university library if Sandy wishes to dig deeper.

SCHEDULE FOR MONITORING/REVISING THIS PERSONAL LEARNING PLAN (include who, what, when, how):

Revisions as needed based on ongoing monitoring by Sandy and Mr. Desmond; full team will review PLP first week of April

COMMUNICATION AMONG TEAM MEMBERS (who, how, when, what):

Informal between developing PLP and reviewing in April

SPECIAL EFFECTS (incentive plan, celebration, vision, other?):

Additional Comments and Information:

PRINT MATERIALS (to be located by the Resource Teacher for Sandy's Personal Learning Plan):

Abhau, M., Copeland, R., & Greenburger, G. (1986). *Architecture in education: A resource of imaginative ideas and tested activities.* Philadelphia: Foundation for Architecture.

Ball, D., & Ball, I. (1990). *The spy code handbook: How to make code and cipher machines to outfox your enemies.* North Ryde, Australia: Angus & Robertson Publishers.

Black, H., & Black, S. (1987). *Book 3: Figural lesson plans and teacher's manual: Building thinking skills.* Pacific Grove, CA: Critical Thinking Press and Software.

Black, H., & Black, S. (1990). *Book II: Organizing thinking—Graphic organizers.* Pacific Grove, CA: Critical Thinking Press and Software.

Blizzard, G. S. (1992). *Come look with me: Exploring landscape art with children.* Charlottesville, VA: Thomasson–Grant.

Brooke, M. (1969). *150 puzzles in crypt-arithmetic: Solved by substituting numbers for the letters* (2nd rev. ed.). New York: Dover Publications.

Coburn, T. G. (Ed.) (1993). *Curriculum and evaluation standards for school mathematics addenda series, Grades K-6: Patterns.* Reston, VA: National Council of Teachers of Mathematics.

Downie, D., Slesnick, T., & Stenmark, J. K. (1981). *Math for girls and other problem solvers.* Berkeley, CA: EQUALS in Computer Technology, Lawrence Hall of Science.

Draze, D. (1986). *Blueprints: A guide for 16 independent study projects.* San Louis Obispo, CA: Dandy Lion.

Farrel, M. A. (Ed.). (1988). *Imaginative ideas for the teachers of mathematics grades K-12: Ranucci's Reservoir.* Reston, VA: National Council of Teachers of Mathematics.

Heimann, R. (1990). *Amazing mazes: Mind bending mazes for ages 6–60.* Toronto: Doubleday Canada Ltd.

(continues)

Figure 6.5. *Continued.*

Heimann, R. (1990). *Preposterous puzzles: Brain busting puzzles for ages 6–60*. Toronto: Doubleday Canada Ltd.

Henry, B. (1987). *Experiments with patterns in mathematics*. Palo Alto, CA: Dale Seymour.

Martin, S., McMillan, D., & Hillam, C. (1986). *Brain Boosters*. Palo Alto, CA: Monday Morning Books.

McMillan, D., Martin, S., & Hillam, C. (1988). *More brain boosters*. Palo Alto, CA: Monday Morning Books.

Overholt, J. L. (1978). *Dr. Jim's elementary math prescriptions*. Santa Monica, CA: Goodyear.

Phillips, E. (Ed.). (1991). *Curriculum and evaluation standards for school mathematics addenda series, Grades 5–8: Patterns and functions*. Reston, VA: National Council of Teachers of Mathematics.

Robbins, A. (1989). *3D puzzles to cut & construct and solve*. New York: Dell.

Seymour, D, Laycock, M., Holmberg, V., Larsen, B., & Heller, R. (1975). *Aftermath (Books I–IV)*. Sunnyvale, CA: Creative Publications.

Smith, S. E., & Backman, C. A. (Eds.). (1975). *Games and puzzles for elementary and middle school mathematics: Readings from the Arithmetic Teacher*. Reston, VA: National Council of Teachers of Mathematics.

Stenmark, J. K., Thompson, V., & Cossey, R. (1986). *Family math*. Berkeley, CA: Lawrence Hall of Science.

Welchman-Tischler, R. (1992). *How to use children's literature to teach mathematics*. Reston, VA: The National Council of Teachers of Mathematics.

Wishau, J. (1985). *Investigator: A guide for research projects*. San Luis Obispo, CA: Dandy Lion Publications.

Figure 6.5. *Continued.*

although "Structures" ran a close second. If she becomes bored with "Patterns," she has the option of pursuing "Structures" in her next PLP.

When Mr. Desmond completed *Charts* for Sandy in Math and Art, they yielded recommendations in *variety* of content; *freedom of choice* and *pacing* in mathematics; and *freedom of choice, variety* of product, and *appropriate evaluation* in Art. These principles were applied to the curricula in those content areas. The differentiated objective, learning activities, and evaluation plan all are included in Figure 6.5. The PLP will be monitored informally by Sandy and Mr. Desmond. Any changes will be discussed with her parents and Mr. Gagné, the resource teacher, before they are implemented. Primary responsibility for locating resources will belong to the resource teacher, although Sandy's parents have agreed to provide transportation to the architect's office and any other off-campus locations the team deems necessary. In the first week of April, a new PLP will be developed for the end of April through June. The 2-week overlap will allow time for Mr. Gagné to locate the resources needed to support Sandy's new PLP.

Some of the differentiated learning activities are lesson-sized, and some provide a focus for a unit of study or an independent study of indeterminate length. Cumulatively, they offer Sandy experiences that will enable her to achieve the differentiated objectives if they are evaluated in the manner described in the far right column of the PLP form.

Conclusion

The process described in this chapter takes planning from the initial assessment of the student's behavior, to needs based on strengths, to the differentiation of educational objectives, activities, and the evaluation process. Teachers have the option to use all or part of the process from the *Chart* through the management plan. Some steps will be used on a daily basis; others will be done once or twice a year to determine the most recommended *Principles* to use for differentiated curricula or in the development of a Personal Learning Plan. My purpose in this chapter is to offer educators a systematic, flexible, defensible process for the differentiation of curricula for gifted students that can be implemented in the regular classroom.

Lessons can be modified as often as possible. One differentiated lesson per week is better than none; the more differentiated lessons, the better. However, the needs of all class members must be kept in mind;

modification of every lesson every day in one or more subject areas is an unreasonable expectation. Some lessons may not need to be modified. A teacher's expectations must be kept realistic or the Principles of Curriculum Modification will become yet another burden for conscientious teachers and a source of guilt. In addition, resentment toward the bright students may develop if expectations are set too high. With practice, however, preparing and implementing a Personal Learning Plan for one or more gifted students will pay learning dividends far in excess of its cost in a teacher's time and energy.

hapter 7

Interdisciplinary Units of Study: Scaffolding At Its Best

Judith A. Rogers

The single most powerful statement to come out of brain research in the last twenty-five years is this: We are as different from one another on the inside of our heads as we appear to be different from one another on the outside of our heads. Look around and see the infinite variety of human heads . . . know that on the inside such differences are even greater—what we know, how we learn, how we process information, what we remember and forget, our strategies for functioning and coping. Add to that the understanding that the "world" out "there" is as much a *projection* from inside our heads as it is a *perception*, and pretty soon you are up against the realization that it is a miracle that we communicate at all.

(Fulghum, 1988, pp. 42–43)

Most teachers realize that each individual who enters their classroom brings a unique background—a conglomerate of experiences, ideas, talents, goals, understandings, and connections to the world around her or him. These teachers also must understand that, as eloquently inferred by

219

Fulghum (1988), (a) curricula must be presented in a variety of manners and through a variety of media to accommodate the "infinite variety of human heads" and (b) resultant products must vary from one individual to another in meaningful ways. Finally, all teachers must acknowledge that most, if not all, skills referred to as basic can be introduced to gifted students and subsequently practiced and mastered by them in the context of interdisciplinary units of study.

The concept of scaffolding (Bruner, 1983; Wood, 1991) presented in the content modifications chapter may be a useful construct for teachers to remember when preparing interdisciplinary units for gifted students of all ages. In *Webster's New Collegiate Dictionary* (1973) a scaffold is defined as a "supporting framework" (p. 1029) and a "temporary or moveable platform" (p. 1029). In the context of unit design, this scaffold might be equated to the amount of structure and direction a teacher builds into the unit. The scaffold might encompass also the amount of flexibility that is afforded to students as they progress through the study. A teacher may incorporate a sturdier, more complete scaffold when she or he plans a unit of study to use at the beginning of the year. As she or he begins to recognize the strengths and weaknesses of students through exploration and systematic observation, the teacher can disassemble the scaffold gradually and allow most curricular ideas to emerge from the learners involved. Ultimately the role of a teacher will shift from curriculum planner and implementor to facilitator and fellow learner.

In the discussion that follows a scaffold is presented as an interdisciplinary unit designed for use near the beginning of the year with gifted 2nd- or 3rd-grade children. Although specific activities that span 2 weeks are provided, the study should progress for a longer period of time. In other words, some activities are introduced only; they are not culminated within the given time frame. As with many units of this type, an adept teacher can make adaptations to fit the maturity level of the target population. As written, the unit would enrich any multigrade primary program for gifted students. It may appear completely planned, the scaffold secure; however, upon careful scrutiny, the reader will detect a degree of flexibility that is mandatory in planning learning activities for gifted individuals.

Several layers of description are included for clarity. The unit begins with an overview in which my intent is stated. This is followed by a description of how the general principles of curriculum development for the gifted are implemented. A brief discussion about the inclusion of the

seven intelligences (Gardner, 1983) and the Maker–Schie·
continuum (Maker, 1993) precedes a listing of content, ⌐
product objectives (extracted from the Academically Gifted Curriculum
of the Durham Public Schools, 1992) that are the focus of the unit. A
listing of each major planned product appears with a delineation of
objectives addressed in the development process. Finally, in Exhibit 7.1, a
"Unit Alert" to parents to prepare them for the upcoming study precedes
the "meat" of the unit, that is, the daily and weekly plans, task card
activities, specific lesson plans, evaluation activities and forms for the
students and for the unit, and a bibliography of resources needed.

Understanding and Celebrating
the Peoples of the World

Overview

> In many ways the saying "know thyself" is not well said.
> It were more practical to say "know other people!"
>
> Menander, 343–292 B.C., Greek poet

Peter Spier (1980) aptly incorporated the above reference as an introduction to his delightful book, *People*. The quote, as well as the content of
the book, provide an excellent introduction to a unit designed around
the broad theme of cultures and the following generalization: Global
peace will be attained when people accept, understand, and celebrate the
similarities and differences that are found among and between racial,
ethnic, and religious groups.

The unit is designed to help children begin to appreciate the similarities and differences of all humankind. It is hoped that children will
become more tolerant and less fearful of those from groups different from
their own as they gain knowledge of the ways in which we humans all are
alike and how we are different. With this basic understanding as a framework upon which to build, we hope children will grow into adults who
show compassion for all others who share their home, Mother Earth.

The Academically Gifted Curriculum of the Durham Public Schools
(1992) provides the overall framework for the unit; the Maker–Schiever
problem continuum (Maker, 1993) and Gardner's (1983) theory of multiple intelligences figure prominently in the unit's design. Teaching–

learning models (Maker, 1982b; Maker & Nielson, 1995) used in shaping lessons appropriate for the specified population include Parnes' (1967) *Creative Problem Solving,* Williams' (1972, 1986, 1990) *Teaching Strategies for Thinking and Feeling,* and C. W. Taylor's (1967, 1986) *Multiple Talent Approach.* Williams' model also was used as a framework for designing a series of task cards that provide choices for students to extend their learning. Various techniques, including literature discussions based on text sets and theme sets, total-group lessons, small-group activities, and independent studies are implemented for presenting information to the children in ways that complement their varying intelligences, interests, and entry-level skills.

This unit was designed for highly capable children in 2nd or 3rd grade. Although adaptation for other service delivery models, such as resource room, may be possible, presentation in a self-contained class-room is most desirable. The continuity provided when the theme permeates all activities within a classroom for a given period of time will increase the effectiveness of the unit and the generalizability of the concepts presented. With some modification, as delineated by the class-room teacher, the unit may work for more students in the later primary grades. The learning environment suggested is appropriate for all students but mandatory for the gifted. Important to the success of the study are several key environmental components. A list of these components in-cludes, but is not limited to, an atmosphere of acceptance of individual ideas; an openness to allow student participation in a variety of types of activities simultaneously; an understanding that children's abilities, tal-ents, and interests vary; an acceptance of learning as a social process; and a willingness on the teacher's part to explore along with his or her students and to exhibit the degree of confidence needed to say, "I really do not know an answer for that. How might we work together to find one?"

The basic theme, generalization, and key concepts of the content, although abstract, may be appropriate for most. However, the regular classroom teacher may wish to vary some processes and products to meet the needs of children in a more heterogeneous group.

This unit should be equally effective with highly capable students from all cultures, creeds, and socioeconomic levels. Teachers are encour-aged to view suggested activities and materials in light of cultural and religious affiliation of students with whom they work and to add, delete, and modify activities and materials as needed.

General Principles of Curriculum Development for the Gifted

Maker (1982a) and Maker and Nielson (1995) proposed that educators develop qualitatively different programs through content, process, product, and learning-environment modifications. Further, they delineated several general principles under each construct that complement the characteristics of gifted children. Educators should incorporate these principles when planning units to ensure that the needs of gifted children are met. A summary of how specific principles are incorporated into this unit follows.

The content modifications include abstractness, complexity, variety, organization for learning value, study of people, and study of methods. The unit is based on an abstract theme, *cultures*, and a broad generalization concerning global peace. An element of complexity is added to this abstractness when students compare similarities and differences between or among various ethnic, cultural, and religious groups. A variety of ideas are pursued through each of Gardner's seven intelligences and through problems that are tightly or loosely structured. The material is organized to allow students to build an understanding of the theme and generalization at individual rates, from concrete activities, such as a simulation dig, to more abstract activities, such as researching the Civil Rights and Equal Rights movements, through which students determine similarities and differences in causes and effects of the two social movements. Students will develop their understanding of the theme through a means of their choosing. For example, they may complete tasks as designed, incorporate self-determined variations to these tasks, or determine totally innovative, independent projects. The material is presented economically through large-group, small-group, and independent projects that are shared with others when completed. Thus, all student efforts are optimized when students learn from and with their peers, are encouraged to interact freely, and build content understanding simultaneously with process understanding. Because the data presented in the unit include people from all walks of life, the study of people is a natural component. Finally, methods of various disciplines are practiced, such as formal and informal problem solving, the interview process, and a simulation dig after a session with an archeologist.

All process modifications are included in this unit. Higher-level thinking skills are necessary to complete most activities. For example, in the Discrepancies Task 2, students are asked to reflect on the Golden

Rule ("Do unto others as you would have them do unto you") as they read several newspaper articles and determine how the behavior of the people mentioned in the articles might have changed had they been applying the Golden Rule to their lives. The principle of *open-endedness* permeates the questioning strategies used throughout and is also in the definition of the tasks. That is, some tasks are clearly defined (Problem Types I and II) whereas others are posed as fuzzy situations (Problem Types IV and V) for which students must set their own parameters. For instance, following both the theme set and text set studies, groups must determine the best method for sharing their thoughts about the literature they studied. Students are encouraged to *discover* not only content ideas but also more about themselves as they progress through unit activities. Evidence of reasoning is requested at many junctures along the way. Building on the example just cited, students are asked why they believe that living by the Golden Rule would affect the person's behavior in the way or ways the student described. Students make their own decisions and find their own problems at many levels throughout the unit, requirements thereby encouraging freedom of choice. For example, students will make process choices when they choose Examples of Habit Task 1, in which the selector does an interview, instead of Task 2, in which the selector is required to brainstorm ideas. Student interaction during this study occurs naturally in small and large groups or in pairs. Students also have the option to work independently should that be the most efficient and effective way to achieve their particular goal. The variety of activities found in this unit should be paced according to student needs and interests and should be added to, altered, deleted, or rescheduled when necessary.

Real problems and real audiences, components of product modification, are inherent in this unit. The very subject of the guiding generalization, global peace, which appears so elusive in today's world, poses a very real problem. Frequently students will face the problem of introducing themselves to some unknown person or group as they mature. In this unit they have the opportunity to determine how they might introduce themselves effectively (real problem) to a pen pal (real audience) from another region. As the unit develops in the classroom and as students interact with the content and planned activities or develop side interests to pursue on their own, additional real problems that require real audiences may arise. Throughout, students are invited to transform—both ideas and raw materials—and to evaluate. For example, Tolerance for Ambiguity Task 2 allows students to create something that might be entitled

"People," using their choice of materials, a transformation. Students then determine the types of audiences that might benefit from viewing, reading, or hearing their creation; in what ways this audience might benefit; and the criteria this audience might use to evaluate their product, an exercise with several layers of evaluation. Further, students will complete activity evaluations following pair or small-group activities and an extensive unit evaluation. Finally, students who become absorbed with the activities included in this unit will be rewarded with a clearer understanding of their own intellectual strengths as they reflect on the choices made and the variety of products completed.

The learning-environment modifications are perhaps the most critical changes that must be made for gifted students. All content, process, and product modifications may be made in vain if environmental conditions remain similar to those found in a traditional classroom. Therefore, all learning-environment modifications—learner centered, encourages independence, openness, accepting, complex, high mobility, flexibility, and variety of grouping options—are included.

A learner-centered environment, unlike a teacher-centered or student-centered environment, can include all who participate in the study in any way as learners. In other words, this environment allows the teacher, a master learner, to participate in the learning process and to model appropriate learning behaviors on a variety of levels. As an observer of learner behavior the teacher can model note taking as she or he makes anecdotal records of such items as the interactions that occur, the accomplishments and progress of individuals, skills that may need to be introduced or refined, and the success and or failure of activities. On another level, a teacher may very well discover content that is new to him or her as the unit progresses and share these new understandings and connections with students. Throughout the unit the remaining modifications are encouraged: independence, by providing choices that require learner decision making; openness, by allowing unplanned-for ideas and activities to flow freely; acceptance, through empowering students to express themselves in manners of their choosing and encouraging growth through positive reactions and constructive criticisms; complexity, by insisting that a variety of types of activities should be occurring simultaneously; high mobility, by dispersing students throughout the classroom, school, and community; flexibility, by allowing events to occur as they may; and a variety of grouping options, by listening to the wishes and desires of students.

A Word About Gardner's Intelligences

Gardner (1983) described seven intelligences—linguistic, logical–mathematical, bodily kinesthetic, spatial, musical, interpersonal, and intrapersonal—in his book, *Frames of Mind*, and explained that each of us has the capability to develop, to some extent, expertise in each of the seven. These intelligences play an important role in this unit of study in particular and in the classroom in general. First, the classroom arrangement accommodates seven "learning nooks" to correspond with Gardner's intelligences. In each nook, the "tools" of that intelligence can be found. In the spatial nook, for example, a student can find an odd assortment of "junk" to construct a collage or multidimensional sculpture; a variety of drawing media such as watercolor, markers, drawing pencils, pastels, paints, and charcoal as well as a variety of paper types and an easel; mechanical toys, such as *Capsela* and *Erector* sets; clay and play dough, blocks of all shapes and sizes, and other construction materials. The musical nook might contain a variety of instruments, audio recordings, videos about music making or music makers, books about instrument making, and sheet music.

A conscious effort was made to include all intelligences in the variety of planned activities. Through encouragement to explore through many intelligences, students more readily discover their particular areas of strength and may be in a position to use these strengths to increase capacities in weaker areas.

As is the case in most classrooms for gifted students, linguistic intelligence—specifically the written word—is relied upon heavily in this unit. However, I recognize that many gifted students may be unable to access content and design products effectively through linguistic means. Therefore, teachers must make accommodations for gifted youngsters who, as yet, are unable or unwilling to read or record their thoughts through paper-and-pencil exercises. For instance, prior to unit implementation, many suggested readings and task-card tasks could be audiotaped or videotaped by the teacher, an aide, a parent volunteer, or an older student. Students then have the option to access information in nonreading ways as they simultaneously receive formal reading instruction with content materials. A variety of product-development processes must be accommodated as well. Thus, in addition to the tools of each intelligence, several audiotape players with a supply of blank cassettes, computers and discs, video recorders and tapes, and manual and electric typewriters should be available for student use at all times. Further, students must be aware of their options. Students should know that a list or a journal entry might include words that they write or dictate to someone else to write, illustrations that they draw, or pictures that they cut from magazines.

Because the study is based on literature and the language arts, children will "read," "reflect," "discuss," "edit," and "rewrite" as they progress through the study, but these activities may be accomplished in nontraditional ways such as audio recording, illustrating, working with a writing partner, using a computer, or videotaping movement or pantomime.

Children will use their logical–mathematical intelligence when they examine money systems in various cultures, when they write as many problems as possible that have the answer of 13, and when thinking at higher levels. In many tasks, students are asked to draw conclusions, clarify and support their inferences, and make comparisons, all tasks which require logical thought.

Several tasks incorporate music, such as Examples of Change Task 1, in which students vary the tempo of a recorded song to discover the effects of variation. It is hoped that through this activity children with musical intelligence will visualize the connections between their strength and the content presented, processes used, and products developed during the unit of study. Children can share their spatial abilities with the class frequently throughout this study. For instance, each student will design a poster or other representation relating four of his or her most frequent feelings following the Williams (1972) lesson. They also have the opportunity to explore various media to find materials with which they feel most comfortable for their expressions.

Because the unit is designed to allow free movement within the classroom and school, students have opportunities to exercise their bodily kinesthetic intelligence, albeit in a limited manner. Other activities that encourage the use of this intelligence include creating dances to respond to music from various cultures and learning dances that representatives of these groups might teach.

Finally, the children will have many opportunities to express and refine their interpersonal and intrapersonal intelligences. Varied activities that require working with a partner, in a small group, or in a large group will require certain skills. If not inherent within the children, these skills can be practiced as the students progress through their study. Evaluating personal and partner contributions will help children identify their own strengths and those of others. Reading about, discussing, and responding in some way to the lives of others may help a student recognize parallels between his or her own life and experiences and those of some noteworthy individual.

A Word About Problem Types

Maker and Schiever (Maker, 1992) proposed a continuum of five problem types that vary in the degree of learner input allowed and the type of thinking required. For instance, in a Type I problem, the learner must think convergently to determine the one right answer selected by the problem presenter. On the opposite end of the continuum in a Type V problem, an open situation is presented in which the learner must think divergently, shape the parameters of his or her own problem, and then progress to solve this problem (see Maker, Nielson, & Rogers, 1994, for a complete description). Gifted students must have the opportunity to select from this array of problem types across multiple intelligences to facilitate their personal growth. In this unit a variety of problem types are presented, but no clear type indication is made for activities.

Objectives

Designing a curriculum unit requires that an educator identify cognitive and affective goals and objectives to be met by students during the unit. The objectives for this unit were selected from several content, process, and product objectives developed by educators of the gifted in Durham, North Carolina (Durham Public Schools, 1992).

Content Objective 1

Present content related to broadbased issues, themes, or problems that may be used either in individual disciplines or in an interdisciplinary format.

Theme	Cultures
Generalization	Global peace will be attained when people accept, understand, and celebrate the similarities and differences that are found among and between racial, ethnic, and religious groups.

Concepts	global peace ethnicitiy celebration similarities respect differences acceptance cultures understanding
Data	Books, videotapes, audiotapes, magazines depicting people from a variety of cultures—organized around subthemes of families, friends, biographies, grandparents, and feelings
	Student ideas about similarities and differences in people
	Music, foods, dances, and art from a variety of cultures
	Student ideas about respect
	Student ideas about global peace
	Student ideas about acceptance, understanding, and celebration

Process

Please note that some process goals are not specifically reflected in the activities that follow. Rather, the atmosphere of the classroom is modified to encourage advancement toward these goals at all times.

Cognitive Process Goal 4

The student will develop independence and self-direction.

Cognitive Process Objective 4.1	The student will make informed choices.
Cognitive Process Objective 4.2	The student will develop and implement a plan of action for

	individual and small-group projects.
Cognitive Process Objective 4.3	The student will use a record-keeping system to track progress toward individual goals.

Cognitive Process Goal 5

The student will develop critical and higher-level thinking skills in both cognitive and affective areas.

Cognitive Process Objective 5.1	The student will validate information based on credibility, accuracy, and logic.
Cognitive Process Objective 5.2	The student will draw tentative conclusions and make predictions about cause-and-effect relationships.

Cognitive Process Goal 6

The student will develop affective behaviors involved in the creative process, including risk taking, curiosity, imagination, and complexity.

Cognitive Process Objective 6.1	The student will have opportunities to express ideas and to create spontaneously without regard for orthodoxy, practicality, or relevance.
Cognitive Process Objective 6.2	The student will have opportunities to admit a mistake.
Cognitive Process Objective 6.3	The student will have opportunities to generate new ideas.
Cognitive Process Objective 6.4	The student will have opportunities to visualize realistic and fantastic images and situations.

Cognitive Process Goal 7

The student will develop the convergent and divergent abilities involved in the creative process.

Cognitive Process Objective 7.1	The student will develop convergent thinking skills such as inductive and deductive reasoning.
Cognitive Process Objective 7.2	The student will develop divergent thinking skills such as fluency, flexibility, originality, and elaboration.

Affective Process Goal 9

The student will be encouraged to develop self-actualization, including self-respect, self-understanding, self-confidence, and internal motivation.

Affective Process Objective 9.1	The student will trust his or her perceptions even when different from those of others and have confidence in his or her own creative thinking.
Affective Process Objective 9.2	The student will ask questions and explore ideas that arise spontaneously.
Affective Process Objective 9.3	The student will use the mind's eye to travel through time and space, to probe structures, to manipulate ideas, and to create change.
Affective Process Objective 9.4	The student will become a contributing group member by incorporating her or his own ideas with those of another person to produce a different, more complete, and interesting idea or product.

Affective Process Goal 10

The student will be encouraged to develop sound relationships, including tolerance of human differences, respect for the needs and rights of others, recognition of the contribution of others, and interaction with intellectual peers.

Affective Process Objective 10.1	The student will learn how and why cultural traditions affect family values and how and why cultural traditions affect students' feelings about themselves.
Affective Process Objective 10.2	The student will understand how and why social, political, economic, and technological changes affect their lives.

Product

Product Goal 11

The student will develop products that refine or challenge existing ideas; that incorporate innovative ideas; and that utilize techniques, materials, forms, and a body of knowledge in a unique way.

Product Objective 11.1	Student products will reflect application of a variety of techniques and materials in creative ways.
Product Objective 11.2	Student products will communicate ideas creatively and clearly in an appropriate form to a real or simulated audience for a response.
Product Objective 11.3	Student products will be based on self-, group-, and teacher-developed criteria.
Product Objective 11.4	Student products will incorporate and reflect the language arts system—including the ideas of communication, symbol, writing,

interpretive language, or oral
language.

Product Objective 11.5   Student products will reflect the
appreciation of the concept of
aesthetics.

Product Listing

1. Prior to beginning this unit, students will complete two thirds of a
K–W–L strategy sheet (Ogle, 1986). Students will list what they know
about the similarities of people from various cultures. They will also list
what they might like to learn about the similarities of peoples. The third
portion of the sheet will be completed during the culminating activity.
On this section, children will list what they have learned through the
study.
Objectives: Content and 5.1, 5.2, 7.1, 7.2, 9.1, 9.2, 10.1, 10.2, 11.4

2. The student, with a small group of peers, will make a presentation
to the class in an effort to "sell" the theme story they read. The presentation possibilities are limited only by student imagination and available
materials.
Objectives: Content and 4.1, 4.2, 5.2, 6.1, 6.3, 6.4, 7.1, 7.2, 9.1, 9.2, 9.4,
       11.1, 11.2, 11.3, 11.4, 11.5

3. The student, with a small group of peers, will present their text
set to their classmates. Presentation possibilities include but are not
limited to an original skit, a videotaped presentation, or a multimedia
presentation.
Objectives: Content and 4.1, 4.2, 4.3, 5.1, 5.2, 6.1, 6.3, 6.4, 7.1, 7.2, 9.1,
       9.2, 9.4, 10.1, 10.2, 11.1, 11.2, 11.3, 11.4, 11.5

4. The student, with a peer, will produce a list of their similarities.
Objectives: Content and 5.1, 5.2, 7.1, 7.2, 10.1

5. The student will present himself or herself to a pen pal of the same
age from a different culture. Presentation possibilities include but are not
limited to a letter, an original drawing or painting, a videotape, an audiotape, or an original publication.
Objectives: Content and 4.1, 4.2, 6.1, 7.2, 10.1, 10.2, 11.1, 11.2, 11.4,
       11.5)

6. The student will design a "My Feelings Poster" that will relate four
of his or her most frequent feelings. The student will select the most
appropriate medium to complete this activity.

Objectives: Content and 4.1, 4.2, 5.2, 6.1, 6.4, 7.2, 9.1, 10.1, 10.2, 11.1,
       11.2, 11.4, 11.5

7. The student will keep a unit journal, adding a daily reflection on either a teacher- or self-chosen topic. Some task-card work may also be included in the journal.

Objectives: Content and 4.1, 4.3, 5.2, 6.1, 6.3, 7.1, 7.2, 9.1, 9.2, 10.1,
       10.2, 11.4

Weekly and Daily Plans

This multiweek unit was designed to allow for flexibility in accordance with student interest and the availability of materials and resources. Much "planning to plan" must take place on a teacher's part within the weeks preceding the unit. For instance, materials should be collected; guest speakers, field trips, and special events scheduled; and task cards designed. Two weeks prior to beginning, the teacher should send the "Unit Alert" (see Exhibit 7.1) home with students to inform parents and to request their help. To encourage student input into the study, learners can share ideas and thoughts during class meetings several weeks prior to beginning the study.

During the introductory week, students will complete the first two columns of the K–W–L strategy sheet (Ogle, 1986) shown in Exhibit 7.2. In the first column, students list what they know about the similarities of peoples from various cultures. Students list what they might like to learn about the similarities of peoples in the second column. The final column will be completed at the end of the unit as a culminating activity. That is, students will list what they learned during the study and will have the opportunity to compare what they learned with what they had hoped to learn.

Daily lesson plans for 2 weeks follow. Most activities will extend beyond these 2 weeks and others may be added as learners progress through the planning stages in the weeks before the unit begins and during the study.

Children also will work on task-card activities throughout the unit to accumulate a total of 30 points. Children should be encouraged to design their own tasks, to share task ideas with their teacher, and to negotiate point value. Together the two can decide if the idea addresses content, process, and product goals. Ideally, at least 25% of the children should

Exhibit 7.1. Unit Alert.

Dear Parents,

Soon we will begin an exciting new unit and, as always, we hope you will be able to help. The theme we plan to build on through our interdisciplinary study is CULTURES. The generalization we hope to develop is "Global peace will be attained when people accept, understand, and celebrate the similarities and differences that are found among and between racial, ethnic, and religious groups." Our key concepts are global peace, similarities, differences, cultures, ethnicity, respect, acceptance, understanding, and celebration. Through the planned activities, and others that children will help develop, we hope to establish a basic understanding of others that will provide a framework for your child. Our goal is that with this foundation and your cooperation, the children will grow into adults who show compassion for others who share our home, Mother Earth.

During this unit we will take several field trips. We greatly appreciate any help you can give with transportation or supervision. Also, we have an exciting guest speaker agenda. If you have some information, experience, or interest in this topic, please call to discuss the possibilities. We hope to bring in an archaeologist, a sociologist, and representatives from various cultures, ethnic groups, and religious affiliations. Your children will brush up on their interview skills before our speakers' visits, so do not be surprised if you find yourself being interviewed!

Please plan to visit our classroom sometime during this study. Many exciting activities will be taking place simultaneously as we learn all we can about the peoples who inhabit our earth.

develop independent projects during this beginning-of-the-year unit. It is hoped that this percentage will reach 100 as the year progresses and students take more responsibility for their own learning.

Week 1

Monday

1. As an introduction to the unit, children should work with partners to develop a list of all the ways the two of them are alike. The lists can be written on large sheets of butcher paper and, after being shared with the group, the lists will be posted on the wall to remain throughout the course of the unit. Encourage students to add to the lists as they determine new ways that they are like their original partner.

Exhibit 7.2. K–W–L strategy sheet.

K-W-L Strategy Sheet		
K—What we know	W—What we want to find out	L—What we learned and still need to learn

Categories of information we expect to use:

A.   E.
B.   F.
C.   G.
D.

Note. From "K–W–L: A Teaching Model that Develops Active Reading of Expository Text," by D. M. Ogle, 1986, *The Reading Teacher, 39*(5), p. 565. Copyright 1986 by International Reading Association. Reprinted with permission.

2. Read Spier's (1980) book, *People*, to the class. Point out the statistics on the first page and the copyright date. Allow children to discuss the accuracy of the statistics in light of the copyright. What conditions exist that might make these estimates too high? What conditions exist that might make these estimates too low? How might the students find more accurate statistics? Allow interested students time to check out their ideas in the school resource center. If no student shows interest, this is an excellent opportunity for the entire group to visit the resource center to be introduced to the types of sources they might use to check their predictions.

3. Journal entry topic for today—Thoughts on the unit the class began. Students include ideas concerning what they may like to learn, how this could be learned, field trips the class might take, and guest speakers the class might invite.

Tuesday

1. Each child will select a pen pal from the identified group. The class should decide exactly how to accomplish this task. Independently each student can determine how she or he might like to introduce herself or himself to a new friend. After individuals have made notes about the plan, each will share ideas with a friend. Together, pairs or trios will list the possible negative and positive points of each plan and determine what must be done to alleviate negative factors. Also, groups will list the materials needed and possible sources of these materials so that plans can be implemented by the end of the week. The students are gathered as a group to discuss findings and materials.

2. Introduce theme sets of the books, *At This Very Minute* (Bowers, 1983), *The How: Making the Best of a Mistake* (Boyd, 1981), *The Keeping Quilt* (Polacco, 1988), *All in a Day* (Anno et al., 1986), and *Coyote Dreams* (Nunes & Himler, 1988). Encourage children to browse through the books and to select one that interests them to begin theme set study the following day. Allow students to sign up on sheets posted in the room; specify the maximum number allowed per group.

3. Discuss the multiple-copy culminating activity. Relate that each group will prepare a presentation that they believe will sell this book to the remainder of the class. Establish that presentation possibilities are limited only by student imagination. Determine, as a group, the criteria by which presentations could be evaluated.

4. Children who pursued the statistics discussed yesterday are allowed time for their reports.

5. Read the story *The Old Hogan* by Margaret Kahn Garaway (1989) as the introduction to the task cards designed for the unit.

6. Journal writing topic for today—I want to read and discuss the story _____ because _____. I hope to learn _____.

Wednesday

1. Begin theme set studies. Allow time for students to read, listen to, or view their selection.

2. As a group, do the lesson presented in Table 7.1 based on the Williams' (1972) model. Following the lesson, each child designs a poster or other expressive product showing himself or herself displaying at least four of the feelings they frequently have and what usually causes each

Table 7.1. Williams' Teaching Strategies for Thinking and Feeling Lesson Plan

Theme: Cultures

Generalization: Global peace will be attained when people accept, understand, and celebrate the similarities and differences that are found among and between racial, ethnic, and religious groups.

Key Concepts: global peace, similarities, differences, cultures, ethnic groups, respect, acceptance, understanding, celebration

Objectives	Focusing Questions	Support Procedures
1a. Students will *listen creatively* to the stimulus story.	1. What are the many different feelings Michael had while sitting on his mother's lap?	Read the story *On Mother's Lap* by Ann H. Scott.
1b. Students will relate all the many possible feelings Michael may have felt through the story.		Encourage all students to respond.
2. Students will cite *examples* of change in Michael's feelings through the progression of the story.	2. How did Michael's feeling change as the story progressed?	Encourage all students to respond.
3a. Students will participate in a *visualization* experience.	3. What feelings did you experience while you were sitting in your loved one's lap? Why did you feel this way?	Read visualization script. Encourage all students to respond.
3b. Students will discuss how they felt while visualizing.		
4a. Students will *evaluate* the similarities and differences between their feelings and Michael's feelings.	4a. How are your feelings different from Michael's? 4b. How are your feelings like Michael's?	Encourage all students to respond.

Visualization Experience—William's Lesson

Please stretch out quietly on the floor. Close your eyes gently if you like. I want you to think about yourself cuddling in the lap of someone you love. You are in your favorite rocking chair, rocking slowly. The chair is positioned right next to a fire that is crackling in the fireplace. How do you feel? Lay your head against the chest of your loved one. You can hear a heartbeat. Your loved one is speaking to you gently. How does the voice sound when you have your ear against that person's chest? Take a slow, deep breath through your nose. Your nostrils fill with the fragrance of your special person. How does this fragrance make you feel? You feel very sleepy but you want to stay awake and remember every special moment. How can you keep yourself awake? Your idea didn't work—you wake up under a warm blanket in your very own bed! When you are ready, slowly open your eyes and sit up.

feeling. Supply a variety of materials (papers, markers, paints, colors, material scraps, etc.) and encourage free expression!

3. As a group, share thoughts compiled from Monday's journal entry. Brainstorm ideas; allow a student volunteer to list all new suggestions on the board. Be sure to include ideas on what students would like to learn, how they might like to learn this, resources available, and so on. (A student volunteer may act as secretary to note on paper what is placed on the board.)

4. Introduce more task cards.

5. Journal writing topic for today—Student choice.

Thursday

1. Continue theme set study with students reading their selections in pairs and sharing some initial thoughts. Encourage students to ask each other questions that may show another's comprehension of the text, interpretation of the data, feelings about the ideas presented in the story, and so on.

2. As a group, discuss the interview process—the reasons for interviews, the steps in the process, gaining access to the interviewee, methods of recording and reporting the data, and factors that might contribute to an effective interview process.

3. Model the interview process with the school librarian. (Be sure to prearrange the date and time!) Ask questions of the librarian that relate to the unit of study, how she or he might help individual students with the topic, and what resources are available in the media center or from other accessible sources (e.g., through interlibrary loan).

4. Conduct the Taylor lesson based on C. W. Taylor's (1967) model shown in Table 7.2. Following the discussion, refer to the interview process by asking students, "What questions might you like to ask Jenny were she to visit our class?" Allow a student volunteer to list all questions on the board.

5. Journal writing topic for today—List in your journal the many, varied, unusual adjectives that you might use to describe yourself.

Friday

1. Theme set groups will meet together today to discuss their book. Each group will select a chairperson to monitor the discussion and to

Table 7.2. Taylor's Multiple Talents Lesson Plan

Theme: Cultures

Generalization: Global peace will be attained when people accept, understand, and celebrate the similarities and differences that are found among and between racial, ethnic, and religious groups.

Key Concepts: global peace, similarities, differences, cultures, ethnic groups, respect, acceptance, understanding, celebration

Objectives	Focusing Questions	Support Procedures
Communication: 1. Children will provide adjectives to describe Jenny.	1a. What word would you use to describe Jenny? 1b. Why would you describe Jenny in that way?	Read the story *Jenny* by Beth Wilson. Encourage all students to respond. Write descriptive words on the chalkboard.
Communication: 2. Children will provide adjectives to describe themselves.	2a. Choose three words you would use to describe yourself. 2b. Why would you describe yourself in this way?	Encourage all students to respond. Write descriptive words on the chalkboard, next to the "Jenny" words.
Forecasting: 3. Children will predict how Jenny might view their school	3a. Based on what we know about Jenny from reading her story, what do you predict she would say about your school if she were a "student for a day" here? 3b. Why do you think she would say this? 3c. What would have to happen for Jenny to say . . . ? Why? 3d. Which of these would Jenny most likely say? Why?	Encourage all students to respond.

ensure that all students have an equal opportunity to voice opinions. Move from one group to the next to listen to the discussions. Groups will determine the best method of selling their selection to the other members of the class and use the time today to prepare to present on Tuesday.

2. Begin the pen pal project. Allow adequate time for students to prepare the first draft of their projects.

3. Interview Simulation—Students work in pairs for this activity. Each person will plan his or her interview questions, conduct the interview, and analyze the process with his or her partner. Take time to discuss findings and feelings about the process in a large-group setting.

4. Guest Speaker—An archaeologist will visit the class to discuss his or her method of finding out about other cultures. Students should be prepared to ask questions.

5. Journal writing topic for today—Student choice.

Week 2

Monday

1. Theme set groups will have the opportunity to finalize their book "sale" plans. Students also can use this time to practice a planned presentation.

2. Begin the editing process for the pen pal project.

3. Simulation Dig in the playground sandbox—Partition off the box into four areas. In each area, carefully hide a collection of small items that could come from the same culture. Students work in teams to search the area, uncover the items, speculate on the type of culture they have discovered, and report to the larger group. (Before going out, revisit the reasons for caution when involved in a "dig," as discussed by the visiting archeologist.)

4. Introduce more task cards.

5. Journal writing topic for today—The characteristics of an archaeologist and why I would or would not make a good one.

Tuesday

1. Theme set groups will make their presentations today.

As a group, the class evaluates the effectiveness of each presentation, using the criteria established by the class and by discussing "Why I would or would not read _____, based on the presentation." The discussion should continue by pointing out the positive aspects of each presentation and making suggestions as to what might have been done to improve each presentation. (If this has not been done in the past, the children learn the process and understand the serious nature of this type of evaluation.)

2. Conduct the lesson based on Parnes's (1967) *Creative Problem Solving* model shown in Table 7.3. Following the lesson, read the remainder of *Daddy's a Monster . . . Sometimes* (Steptoe, 1980). Ask students to pantomime situations that may cause their mom or dad to turn into a "monster." Finally, allow the group to present situations that bring out the monster in them.

3. Allow time for students to work on task cards, after introducing all tasks that remain. This time could be used also for self-selected student projects.

4. If available, show a videotape of dancers from other cultures or ethnic groups to the entire class. View a dance or series of dances through one time. Then speed up the tape to view the dance. Discuss how the increased speed affected the dance. Next, slow down the tape and view again. Discuss how the decreased speed affected the dance. Finally, start the tape, count to five, and stop the tape. Continue this process until you have viewed the entire dance. Discuss how starting and stopping the tape affected the dance. Encourage the students to discuss their feelings as they viewed the dance in four different ways. Follow this activity with movement time. Turn on a recorded or taped song and allow the group to listen first. Play the song again, encouraging students to display the mood of the music through movement. Follow the strategies described to alter the speed of the music while allowing children to respond through movement. Discuss how students' movements changed with music changes and why these changes occurred.

5. Journal writing topic for today—Student choice.

Wednesday

1. Introduce the text sets. Encourage students to browse through sets and select the set they want to study in depth by the following afternoon. Post sign-up sheets that specify the maximum number of students allowed in each group.

2. Prepare final copies for pen pal project.

Table 7.3. Parnes' Creative Problem Solving Lesson

Theme: Cultures

Generalization: Global peace will be attained when people accept, understand, and celebrate the similarities and differences that are found among and between racial, ethnic, and religious groups.

Key Concepts: global peace, similarities, differences, cultures, ethnic groups, respect, acceptance, understanding, celebration

Objectives	Focusing Questions	Support Procedures
Step 1: Fact Finding		
Students will explore the facts of the situation.	1a. What are some of the important things we know about this situation?	Form the group into a semicircle.
	1b. What are some of the things we need to know about this situation?	Read John Steptoe's *Daddy Is a Monster Sometimes* to the middle of page 7. ("Then she said . . . you're enjoying yours").
	1c. How could we go about finding out these unknowns?	Request that students speak clearly and one at a time.
		Make a fact grid on a chart and write responses.
Step 2: Problem Finding	2a. What part of this situation contains the main problem?	List all statements.
2a. Students will narrow down the major problem.	2b. Restate this problem in this form—"In what ways might we . . . ?"	Encourage students to reach consensus on the best statement.
2b. Students will restate the problem in a solvable form.	2c. Select the best statement of the problem.	

2c. Students will select the most appropriate statement of the problem.	2d. Why do you think this is the best statement?	

Step 3: Idea Finding

3. Students will produce as many ways as possible to solve the problem as defined in Step 2.	3. In what ways might we solve this problem?	Review rules of brainstorming. List ideas on chart.

Step 4: Solution Finding

Students will choose the alternatives with the greatest potential for solving the problem by developing and applying criteria to the solutions and evaluation.	4a. What are some ways to judge these ideas? 4b. Which of these possible ways to judge the ideas would be the best or most important? 4c. Using a 1–3 scale, 1 for "yuk" and 3 for "great," rate the solutions on the criteria we have developed.	Develop solution grid.

Step 5: Acceptance Finding

5a. Students will consider audiences who must accept the solutions. 5b. Students will develop a plan of action for carrying out the solution.	5a. Who are some of the people who must accept our solution? 5b. What are some steps we might take to implement our solution?	Pass out and develop acceptance grid.

3. Field Trip—Visit a neighboring ethnic restaurant today. Treat everyone to a snack and interview the owner to find out more about his or her culture and the ins and outs of owning and operating a restaurant.

4. Task cards and independent projects during choice time today.

5. Journal writing topic for today—Field trip reflections.

Thursday

1. Read *The Patchwork Quilt* (Flournoy, 1985). Reflect on the many ways people throughout the ages have kept warm. Discuss how people in various cultures acquire the things they have used to keep warm. Encourage children to bring special quilts or blankets to school and share their "warm" stories. If a quilter or weaver is available, make arrangements to have her or him visit today. Children should have the opportunity to ask questions and, possibly, to get involved in the craft.

2. Discuss the art of weaving and begin an individual weaving project with paper or yarn.

3. Discuss the possibility of making a class quilt. If students are interested, they can work in committees to determine the size and design, the materials needed, and the price of the total project; and to shop for the materials with the help of a parent. This would be a student project with cooperation from interested parents.

4. Several students will take the pen pal projects to the post office with a parent volunteer. While there, they will determine the cost of mailing the package based on the cost per ounce. They also will discuss the care of the package and the mail process with the postmaster.

5. Allow time for report from the post office group.

6. Task cards or independent projects.

7. Journal writing topic for today—Keeping warm.

Friday

1. Begin text set studies today. All students should have signed up for a set by this time. If they have not, they must do so now. Groups meet together to determine how they will conduct their study.

2. Guest speaker—A sociologist will visit to discuss his or her profession, including methods employed by the profession.

3. Task cards—independent projects.

4. Meet with individuals to see how they are progressing with the projects. Should individuals need help to organize time, work together to develop a plan.

5. Share music from other cultures. Allow students to demonstrate moods the music portrays through facial expressions, body movements, dance, or any other method they choose.

6. Spend some time evaluating the study with the large group. Seek suggestions for extension, elaboration, or revision.

7. Journal writing topic for today—Student choice.

Culminating Activity

After completing this unit, students will complete the K–W–L strategy sheet (Ogle, 1986) they began on the first day. Allow as much time as needed for students to fill in the final column, listing all they learned from this unit of study. As students share ideas, write them on the chalkboard; the ideas expressed may spur new ideas for others. When the list is well established, pose the question, "Based on the ideas you have presented, what general statements might we make about people from various cultures?" Students may respond in writing first. Once again, list ideas on the board.

This is the time that students also should complete the student evaluation of unit (presented in Exhibit 7.3). Encourage students to respond individually, but allow time to share responses with the group. In this way, all will get a better idea of what worked and what did not work, what was enjoyed and what was not. By sharing in this manner, students also have the opportunity to hear about activities they did not select.

Other Possibilities

Field Trips

archaeological dig	ethnic restaurants
art gallery	culture-centered radio or TV station
museum	
varied neighborhoods in the local community	Native American reservation

Exhibit 7.3. Form for student evaluation of the unit.

STUDENT EVALUATION OF THE UNIT

Name: _____

Unit: _____

While working on this unit I learned:

I learned the most from:

    because:

I learned the least from:

    because:

The best part of this unit was:

    because:

I did not care for:

    because:

I would change the unit by:

Overall I rate the unit: 5   4   3   2   1

                                      Great   Poor

    because:

Guest Speakers

quilter	dancer
sociologist	weaver (basket or blanket)
archaeologist	culturally different senior citizens
parents	high-profile representatives of
artist	different cultures (e.g., newscaster, athlete, politician, religious figure)
author	

Other Ideas

incorporate cooking activities	learn and create dances
learn and create songs	learn and create rhythms
play music from various cultures softly during work periods	

Task-Card Activities Based on Williams' Teaching Strategies for Thinking and Feeling

Paradoxes

Task 1 (5 points)   Design a visual representation for one or both of these sayings: "You are what you eat." "No man is an island." Think about how your representation might change if you were a child from the culture of your pen pal.
Objectives: Content and 5.2, 6.1, 6.4, 7.1, 7.2, 10.1, 11.4, 11.5

Task 2 (10 points)   Superstitions exist in most cultures throughout the world. For instance, some people believe breaking a mirror will result in 7 years of bad luck! If you are interested in learning about superstitions of people from various cultures, this is the task for you. Use any means available to discover how people come to believe what they do and what superstitions exist in different cultures. Think about how you perceive these superstitions as being alike and different.

Design a product that will relate what you learned
to the audience of your choice.
Objectives: Content and 4.1, 4.2, 5.1, 5.2, 6.1, 7.1,
7.2, 9.2, 10.1, 11.1, 11.2, 11.4, 11.5

Attributes

Task 1 (5 points)   An attribute is a characteristic or quality. If we were
to list the attributes of our class, we might say that
it consists of people, is housed in a room, and has
an atmosphere that is warm, friendly, and respectful.
Now test your attribute-listing skills. Select one of
the cultural artifacts we have in the room. List all
the attributes that you can think of for that item.
Share your list with a friend. Add to your list any
other attributes that you and your friend can
determine together.
Objectives: Content and 7.2, 7.4

Task 2 (5 points)   Work with a partner to list the attributes of the
community in which you live. How might these
attributes differ from those of the community in
which your pen pals live? What conclusions might
you draw about the attributes of communities?
Objectives: Content and 5.2, 7.1, 7.2, 9.1, 10.2

Analogies

Task 1 (5 points)   List all the attributes that you can for a horse. Then
list all the attributes you can for a car. What
attributes did you list for both? Think of all the
ways that a horse and a car are alike and list these
ways in your journal.
Objectives: Content and 5.1, 5.2, 6.3, 7.1, 7.2, 9.1

Task 2 (15 points)   Maybe you have heard the saying "Laughter is the
best medicine." If you choose this task, you may
decide that the saying is appropriate! First record, in
some way, all the situations that you can think of
that make you laugh. Then record all the situations
that you can think of that make you cry. Which
situations did you record for both? In what ways do
you think the two emotions are similar and

different? Share your discoveries with at least two friends. In what ways did they agree or disagree with your thoughts? Now the fun *really* begins! Use the class camera for the next week to record instances of people of all ages laughing and crying. (You may want to check out the camera to use in other locations.) If possible, ask your photographic subject to relate reasons for the tears and laughter. Assemble you photos in some way that will "tell the story of laughing and crying" to all who view your finished product.

Objectives: Content and 4.1, 4.2, 4.3, 5.1, 5.2, 6.1, 6.2, 6.3, 6.4, 7.1, 7.2, 9.2, 9.3, 10.1, 11.1, 11.2, 11.4, 11.5

Discrepancies

Task 1 (5 points)   Select some culture other than your own. List all the things you do not know about children from this culture. List ways you might find this information.
Objectives: Content and 7.1, 7.2, 9.2

Task 2 (10 points)   This task should be done with a group of three people. We all know the Golden Rule, "Do unto others as you would have others do unto you." Think about this rule as you read the attached newspaper articles. Discuss the articles in light of the Golden Rule. How might the behavior of the people in the articles have changed had they been applying the Golden Rule to their lives? Why do you believe this? What might we do to encourage others to live by the rule? Spend a few minutes with your teacher relating the important ideas of your discussion.
Objectives: Content and 5.1, 5.2, 6.3, 6.4, 7.1, 7.2, 11.2

Examples of Change

Task 1 (5 points)   Select one of the cassette tapes provided. Listen to the entire song one time. Now speed up the tape to

listen to the song. In what ways did increased speed affect the song? Next, slow down the tape and listen again. In what ways did decreased speed affect the song? Finally, start the tape, count to 5 and stop the tape for a minute. Continue this process until you have listened to the entire tape. In what ways did starting and stopping the tape affect the song? What conclusions might you draw about the tempo of a song and the mood it creates?
Objectives: Content and 5.2, 9.3

Task 2 (5 points) Study your picture on our "How We've Changed" bulletin board. Make a list of the changes that have occurred in you since your youngest picture was taken. Determine why each change took place. Post your list on the bulletin board after you have shared it with your parents.
Objectives: Content and 5.1, 5.2, 7.1, 7.2, 10.2, 11.2

Examples of Habit

Task 1 (10 points) Interview a senior citizen to find out about his or her habits now and when she or he was younger. In what ways have this person's habits changed over the years? What factors contributed to the changes? Arrange a time to share the results of the interview with your class.
Objectives: Content and 4.1, 4.2, 4.3, 9.2, 10.2, 11.2

Task 2 (10 points) Discuss these queries with a friend. What might happen if we ate dinnertime foods in the morning for breakfast? What might happen if we advance at red lights instead of stop? What might happen if we slept during the day instead of during the night? What might happen if we started school at 50 years of age instead of 5? How might you go about finding out how these habits originated? What generalizations might you make about cultures and the habits of the people within them? Report your findings to the class.

Objectives: Content and 5.6, 6.1, 6.4, 7.1, 7.2, 9.1,
9.3, 10.1, 10.2, 11.2

Provocative Questions

Task 1 (5 points)   What would your world be like if you had been
born in the culture of your choosing? Share your
thoughts in any way you like.
Objectives: Content and 6.1, 6.4, 7.1, 7.2, 9.1, 10.1,
10.2, 11.1, 11.4

Task 2 (5 points)   What would the world be like if all children were
taken from their parents at birth and raised with all
other children until age 10? Reflect on this question
in your journal.
Objectives: Content and 6.4, 7.1, 7.2, 9.1, 9.2, 9.3,
10.1, 10.2, 11.2, 11.4

Organized Random Search

Task 1 (5 points)   The number 13 in some cultures is considered an
unlucky number. Write as many mathematical
equations as you can think of that have this unlucky
number for an answer.
Objectives: Content and 7.1, 7.2

Task 2 (5 points)   Use 15 new vocabulary words that you have learned
during this unit of study for this task. Develop a
crossword puzzle, word search, or jumbled word
puzzle to challenge a friend. Respond to these
questions after your friend has an opportunity to
solve the puzzle: In what ways can you change your
puzzle to make it harder or easier? What steps did
you take to design your puzzle?
Objectives: Content and 4.1, 4.2, 6.1, 6.3, 7.1, 7.2,
9.1, 11.1, 11.2, 11.3, 11.4

Skills of Search

Task 1 (15 points)   This task will require extensive library research but
should prove a most satisfying task for those up to
the challenge. Historically, many individuals or

groups of individuals, some racial, some ethnic, some religious, have been repressed. List as many of these people or groups of people as you can. In what ways were these people repressed? In what ways was the repression of one group similar to the repression of another? What conclusions might you draw about repressed peoples? Report your findings to the class.
Objectives: Content and 5.1, 5.2, 6.4, 7.1, 7.2, 9.3, 10.1, 10.2, 11.2

Task 2 (15 points)   People in various cultures celebrate special occasions in many ways. This search is designed to allow you the opportunity to explore celebrations. Select two or three celebrated occasions in which you and your family participate. Describe your method of celebration. (You may choose to write, illustrate, and so on.) Use whatever resources you need to find out how people from other cultures celebrate these occasions if, indeed, they do. Record your findings. Based on your findings, what generalizations might you make about people and their celebrations?
Objectives: Content and 5.2, 6.4, 7.1, 9.1, 10.1, 10.2, 11.4

Tolerance for Ambiguity

Task 1 (10 points)   Read the story *Very Last First Time* (Andrews, 1986), stopping on the page that begins with "The tide!" Write and illustrate an ending for the story. Now finish reading the story. In what way is your ending similar to the ending of the author's, Jan Andrews? Share your version of the story with your kindergarten buddy.
Objectives: Content and 5.2, 6.1, 6.3, 6.4, 7.1, 7.2, 9.1, 9.3, 11.1, 11.2, 11.4, 11.5

Task 2 (10 points)   Use any materials that we have in the classroom or other materials that you bring from home to create something that you could entitle "People." Determine the types of audiences that might benefit from seeing or hearing your creation. Why would these be good audiences? Arrange to share your project as you see fit.

Objectives: Content and 4.2, 6.1, 6.3, 6.4, 7.1, 7.2,
9.1, 9.2, 11.1, 11.2, 11.5

Intuitive Expression

Task 1 (10 points)   Natural disasters occur in all parts of the world.
Choose a specific natural disaster, such as the 1989
tornado that killed more than 20 people in
Huntsville, Alabama, and research the topic in the
media center. Pretend you are a victim of the
devastation. Prepare a newspaper article, telecast, or
broadcast about the experience. Now pretend you
are the mayor of the city and do the same. How are
the two alike? How do they differ? How and why
might the perceptions of the two individuals differ?
Objectives: Content and 5.1, 5.2, 6.1, 6.4, 7.1, 7.1,
9.1, 10.1, 11.4

Task 2 (5 points)   Study our "People" bulletin board. Select 5 people
pictures. Write a sentence or two or draw an
illustration for each picture to explain what might
have occurred to make the person's facial expression
as it is.
Objectives: Content and 5.2, 6.4, 7.1, 7.2, 9.1

Adjustment–Development

Task 1 (15 points)   Do some research in the library on the Civil Rights
Movement and the Equal Rights Movement. How
are the two movements similar? How are they
different? What changes have the movements made
in our society? How might the lives of the persons
directly involved in the movement been affected by
their involvement?
Objectives: Content and 4.2, 5.2, 6.4, 7.1, 10.1, 10.2

Task 2 (10 points)   Imagine that one of the following happened to you
in the near future:
your family moved to a new community
your mother had a baby
you were given a large amount of money
your best friend moved in with your family

> your grandmother or grandfather came to live
> with you
> your parents got a divorce
> Make a list in your journal of all the ways your life
> might change under that condition. Be sure to
> include both positive and negative changes. Now
> select another condition and make a second list.
> Discuss with a partner why you think these changes
> would occur and how the life adjustments under
> the two conditions are alike and how they are
> different.
> Objectives: Content and 5.1, 5.2, 6.4, 7.1, 7.2, 9.3,
> 10.1, 10.2

Creative People—Creative Process

Task 1 (15 points)   Read the stories or listen to the audiotaped versions of *A Weed Is a Flower: The Life of George Washington Carver* (Aliki, 1965) and *The Country Artist: A Story About Beatrix Potter* (Collins, 1989). How were George Washington Carver and Beatrix Potter similar? How were they different? What characteristics do you share with each? Which person are you most like? Why? Set a time with your teacher to report your findings, in any manner you like, to the class.
Objectives: Content and 4.2, 5.2, 6.4, 7.1, 7.2, 10.2, 11.2, 11.4

Task 2 (10 points)   At some point in our lives, all people create something. Interview your parents to find out how they go about the process of creating, be it a meal in the kitchen, a construction in the garage, or a report for school or work. Think about the process you go through yourself. How is your process similar to that of your parent? How does it differ?
Objectives: Content and 7.1, 9.2, 10.2

Evaluate Situations

Task 1 (5 points)   Predict what the world might be like if all people on earth lived by the Golden Rule, "Do unto others

as you would have others do unto you."
Objectives: Content and 5.2, 6.1, 6.3, 6.4, 7.1, 7.2, 9.1

Task 2 (15 points)   You may use any means available to study the money systems used in three countries of your choice. Briefly summarize your findings in your journal. You should include types and value of coins and paper money and examples of what each might buy in the given country, along with other information you found of interest. Now the fun begins! Compare the money systems to determine which you believe is more efficient. Why do you believe this? Which is least efficient? Why? How do those you studied compare with the money system in the United States? What changes might you make to any or all of the systems? Share your findings with your teacher first and arrange a time to present your findings to the entire class.
Objectives: Content and 4.1, 4.2, 4.3, 5.1, 5.2, 6.3, 7.1, 9.1, 9.2, 10.2, 11.2

Creative Reading

Task 1 (5 points)   Select a story from our library corner. Read the story silently or listen to the audiotaped version. Retell the story, pretending that you are the main character. You may choose to tape your new version or relate it to a friend.
Objectives: Content and 6.1, 6.4, 11.2

Task 2 (5 points)   Find an article in a newspaper or magazine that tells about someone from another culture. List two facts about the article and two opinions that you formed after reading the article. Do this written work in your journal.
Objectives: Content and 5.2, 7.1

Creative Listening

Task 1 (5 points)   Carefully listen to your pen pal's taped biographical sketch. Fold one piece of journal paper in half

lengthwise. On the first half, write facts that you know about your pen pal from listening to the tape. On the other half, write guesses about what you believe your pen pal is like. Copy your list and send it to your pen pal in your next letter. Ask him or her to let you know how close you came with your guesses.
Objectives: Content and 5.2, 7.1, 7.2

Task 2 (10 points)   Select a cassette from our music collection. Listen to the tape to select the song you would like to work with during this activity. Listen to this song at least two more times. Now you are ready to begin. Choose a crayon, marker, or pastel that seems to "fit" the music. Get a large sheet of manilla paper from the supply area. Close your eyes, turn on the music, place the crayon, marker, or pastel anywhere on the paper and let the mood of the music move your hand across the paper. You must keep the instrument moving on the paper continuously during the entire song. Now study your product carefully. Share your product and discuss the following with your teacher. What thoughts went through your head as you were involved in this activity? What picture or pictures did you see in your mind? What did you say to yourself as you were working? How do you feel about your product? How did you feel about doing the activity? Why do you think you felt that way?
Objectives: Content and 4.1, 5.2, 6.1, 6.4, 9.3, 11.1, 11.2

Creative Writing

Task 1 (5 points)   Complete a paragraph on the following topic in your journal: "If I could have been born into another culture or at another period of time, I would have liked to have been born _____ because _____."
Objectives: Content and 5.1, 5.2, 6.1, 6.4, 7.1, 9.1, 11.4

Task 2 (5 points)   Complete a paragraph on the following topic in your journal. "All children _____."

Objectives: Content and 5.2, 6.1, 6.2, 6.4, 7.1, 7.2, 9.1, 9.2, 11.4

Visualization

Task 1 (5 points)   Use the cassette tapes provided. Select one tape and listen to the entire song once. Decide which medium would best help you portray the emotions of the song. Use this medium to design an abstract creation as you listen to the tape again. Display your finished product.
Objectives: Content and 4.1, 4.2, 6.1, 6.4, 7.1, 7.2, 9.1, 11.1, 11.2, 11.5

Task 2 (20 points)   You are an internationally known artist who has illustrated several children's books. You have been invited to contribute to a book that has been published but will be reprinted in an expanded form. Read the story, *All in A Day*. Select a country not included in the book. Use whatever resources are necessary to determine what a child might be doing in your selected country at the times stated in the book. Draw an illustration that can be included on each page of the reprinted book. You should have eight illustrations when you are finished. Include a sentence or two of explanation with each picture. Share your finished product with your class. You may decide to submit your product to one of the original artists to let him or her know how much you enjoyed the book.
Objectives: Content and 4.1, 4.2, 5.1, 6.4, 7.1, 7.2, 9.1, 9.4, 10.1, 10.1, 11.1, 11.2, 11.4, 11.5

Evaluation

Evaluation of Students

The evaluation of students for this unit may include several components as shown in Exhibit 7.4. First, one might evaluate their performance based on the criteria decided on by the class. These criteria might in-

Exhibit 7.4. Components for the evaluation of students.

EVALUATION OF STUDENTS

Objective	Criteria	Method
Content I	• number of similarities listed • types of similarities listed • involvement in/with unit ideas • enthusiasm in/with unit activities	observation discussion written work products
Cognitive Process		
4.1	• follows through on self-selected and self-designed activities	observation written work products journal
4.2	• participates in theme set and text set group presentations • completes tasks worth 30 points • follows plan to present self to pen pal	presentation observation written work pen pal introduction
4.3	• completes tasks worth 30 points	observation written work journal products
5.1	• logically supports ideas • selection of resource materials	discussion written work products
5.2	• number of predictions • quality of predictions • provides concise clarification and extension	discussion written work
6.1	• participates in discussions • views situations from different perspectives • expresses ideas clearly	discussion
6.2	• shows ability to learn from mistakes • recognizes when a mistake is made • takes mistakes in stride	observation
6.3	• generates many ideas • generates quality ideas	discussion observation written work products
6.4	• relates ideas about visualizations	discussion written work products

Exhibit 7.4. *Continued*

Objective	Criteria	Method
7.1	• determines appropriate audiences for finished products	observation
7.2	• number of ideas expressed • expresses original ideas • able to elaborate on ideas of others	observation discussion written work products
Affective Process		
9.1	• relates freely perceptions of literature read • relates freely perceptions that are different from those of others	discussion written work journal products
9.2	• generates new questions • expresses questions clearly to others	observation discussion
9.3	• puts self in the shoes of those from other cultures	observations discussion
9.4	• works cooperatively with partners • works cooperatively with multiple-copy group • works cooperatively in text set group	observation products presentations
10.1	• tells how values affect family • tells why values affect family • tells how cultural traditions affect their feelings • tells why cultural traditions affect their feelings	discussion written work products
10.2	• relates changes that affect their life	discussion written work products
Product		
11.1	• uses a variety of materials • uses a variety of techniques • produces original products	products
11.2	• shares finished products with audience	observation of final product presentation
11.3	• evaluates partners appropriately • evaluates partners fairly • evaluates presentations accurately	activity evaluation

Exhibit 7.4. *Continued*

Objective	Criteria	Method
11.4	• expresses self in many ways • expresses self in varied ways • expresses self in original ways	observation
11.5	• produces aesthetically appealing finished products	observation

clude, but are not limited to, cooperation during the unit studies, participation or involvement with the unit, fluency (written, verbal, in creative endeavors), and so on.

A second evaluation component could come from the peers with whom each child worked during the unit activities. The evaluation form included as Exhibit 7.5 might be used in the classroom following selected partner activities. The form provides peer evaluation information as well as a portion of the third component, a child's self-evaluation. The remainder of the self-evaluation—students' final reflections on the unit, their feelings about what they accomplished during this time, what they learned and what they still might want to know, and how this information might help them in the future—will be discussed during an exit interview that teacher and student share. Together the two examine and evaluate student accomplishments.

Evaluation Of Unit

Evaluation of the unit can occur on several levels. First, effectiveness of the unit can be gauged by the involvement and enthusiasm of the students. Quantitative and qualitative information can be recorded throughout the study to provide data for the following questions:

How involved did students remain in activities?

How many students generated their own ideas for projects?

What was the quality of products?

In what ways and with whom were students involved outside of the classroom in activities related to this unit?

Exhibit 7.5. Form for activity evaluation by peers.

ACTIVITY EVALUATION BY PEERS

Name: _____

Partner's name: _____

Activity: _____

During this activity I helped by:

During this activity I hindered our effort by:

My participation was:
5	4	3	2	1
Great				Poor

   because:

During this activity my partner helped by:

During this activity my partner hindered our efforts by:

My partner's participation was:
5	4	3	2	1
Great				Poor

   because:

Second, students can respond to the unit evaluation form shown in Exhibit 7.3.

Third, each person who has contact with the group during this unit (for example, the librarian, the guest speakers, parents who accompanied the class on field trips) can be asked to comment briefly on the effort. These comments should be recorded. Finally, parents should be encouraged to share their perspective of the effectiveness of the study.

Bibliography

Biographies

Aliki. (1977). *The many lives of Benjamin Franklin*. New York: Simon & Schuster.

Aliki. (1965). *A weed is a flower: The life of George Washington Carver*. New York: Simon & Schuster.

Blackwood, A. (1987). *Beethoven*. New York: Bookwright Press.

Clarke, B. (1988). *Children of history: Charles Darwin*. New York: Marshall Cavendish.

Clarke, B. (1988). *Children of history: Gandhi*. New York: Marshall Cavendish.

Collins, D. R. (1989). *The country artist: A story about Beatrix Potter*. Minneapolis, MN: Carolrhoda Books.

Gleiter, J., & Thompson, K. (1985). *Daniel Boone*. Milwaukee, WI: Raintree Childrens Books.

Jakes, J. (1986). *Susanna of the Alamo: A true story*. San Diego, CA: Gulliver Books.

Keeler, S. (1986). *Louis Braille*. New York: Bookwright Press.

Leder, J. M. (1985). *Marcus Allen*. Mankato, MN: Crestwood House.

Lepscky, I. (1984). *Pablo Picasso*. New York: Barron's.

Montgomery, M. (1990). *Marie Curie: What made them great*. Englewood Cliffs, NJ: Silver Burdett Press.

Newman, M. (1986). *Larry Bird*. Mankato, MN: Crestwood House.

Newman, M. (1986). *Mary Decker Slaney*. Mankato, MN: Crestwood House.

Sabin, F. (1983). *Amelia Earhart: Adventure in the sky*. Mahwah, NJ: Troll Associates.

Say, A. (1990). *El Chino*. Boston: Houghton Mifflin.

Stanley, D., & Vennema, P. (1988). *Shaka: King of the Zulus*. New York: Morrow Junior Books.

Wheeler, J. C. (1989). *Forest diplomat: The story of Hiawatha*. Bloomington, MN: Abdo & Daughters.

Wheeler, J. C. (1989). *Forest warrior: The story of Pontiac*. Bloomington, MN: Abdo & Daughters.

Wheeler, J. C. (1989). *Wolf of the desert: The story of Geronimo*. Bloomington, MN: Abdo & Daughters.

Woodson, J. (1990). *Martin Luther King, Jr. and his birthday*. Englewood Cliffs, NJ: Silver Burdett Press.

Families

Aleichem, S. (1978). *Hanukah money*. New York: Greenwillow Books.

Alexander, M. (1975). *I'll be the horse if you'll play with me*. New York: Dial Press.

Alexander, M. (1988). *Even that moose won't listen to me*. New York: Dial Books for Young Readers.

Alexander, M. (1979). *When the new baby comes, I'm moving out*. New York: Dial Press.

Anderson, L. (1974). *The day the hurricane happened*. New York: Scribner's.

Birdseye, T. (1988). *Airmail to the moon*. New York: Holiday House.

Blaine, M. (1975). *The terrible thing that happened at our house*. New York: Scholastic.

Brandenberg, F. (1984). *Aunt Nina's visit*. New York: Greenwillow Books.

Bunting, E. (1991). *Fly away home*. New York: Clarion Books.

Bunting, E. (1989). *No nap*. New York: Clarion Books.

Clifton, L. (1977). *Amifika*. New York: Dutton.

Cooney, B. (1990). *Hattie and the wild waves*. New York: Viking Press.

dePaola, T. (1989). *The art lesson*. New York: Putnam.

dePaola, T. (1983). *Marianna May and nursey*. New York: Holiday House.

Edelman, E. (1984). *I love my baby sister (most of the time)*. New York: Puffin Books.

Goble, P. (1988). *Her seven brothers*. New York: Bradbury Press.

Greenfield, E. (1974). *She come bringing me that little baby girl*. New York: Lippincott.

Johnston, T. (1985). *The quilt story*. New York: Putnam.

Lattimore, D. N. (1990). *The dragon's robe*. New York: Harper & Row.

Lindgren, A., & Wikland, I. (1963). *Christmas in noisy village*. New York: Viking Press.

Loh, M. (1987). *Tucking mommy in*. New York: Orchard Books.

Martel, C. (1987). *Yagua days*. New York: Dial Books for Young Readers.

Mendez, P. (1989). *The black snowman*. New York: Scholastic.

Seeger, P. (1963). *Abiyoyo*. New York: Macmillan.

Shelby, S. (1990). *We keep a store*. New York: Orchard Books.

Steptoe, J. (1980). *Daddy is a monster . . . sometimes*. New York: Lippincott.

Steptoe, J. (1987). *Mufaro's beautiful daughters*. New York: Lothrop, Lee & Shepard Books.

Udry, J. M. (1966). *What Mary Jo shared*. New York: Scholastic.

Waber, B. (1972). *Ira sleeps over*. Boston: Houghton Mifflin.

Walter, M.P. (1983). *My mama needs me*. New York: Lothrop, Lee & Shepard Books.

Williams, V. B. (1986). *Cherries and cherry pits*. New York: Scholastic.

Yolen, J. (1987). *Owl moon*. New York: Philomel Books.

Zemach, M. (1976). *It could always be worse*. New York: Scholastic.

Feelings

Aardema, V. (1981). *Bringing the rain to Kapiti Plain*. New York: Dutton.

Alexander, L. (1971). *The king's fountain*. New York: Dutton.

Aliki (1984). *Feelings*. New York: Greenwillow Books.

Anderson, E. A. (1973). *Carlos goes to school*. New York: Frederick Warne.

Andrews, J. (1986). *Very last first time*. New York: Atheneum.

Baker, L. (1990). *Morning beach*. Boston: Little, Brown and Company.

Baylor, B. (1977). *The way to start a day*. New York: Scribner's.

Blos, J. W. (1987). *Old Henry*. New York: William Morrow.

Brown, T. (1984). *Someone special, just like you*. New York: Holt, Rinehart & Winston.

Browne, A. (1989). *The tunnel*. New York: Knopf.

Clifton, L. (1983). *Everett Anderson's goodbye*. New York: Henry Holt.

Cohen, C. L. (1988). *The mud pony*. New York: Scholastic.

Craven. C. (1987). *What the mailman brought*. New York: Putman.

dePaola, T. (1983). *The legend of the blue bonnet*. New York: Putnam.

dePaola, T. (1979). *Oliver Button is a sissy*. New York: Harcourt Brace Jovanovich.

Dragonwagon, C. (1986). *Half a moon and one whole star*. New York: Macmillan Publishing.

Goble, P. (1990). *Dream wolf*. New York: Bradbury Press.

Hamilton, V. (1985). *The people could fly*. New York: Knopf.

Nunes, S., & Himler, R. (1988). *Coyote dreams*. New York: Atheneum.

Scott, A. H. (1972). *On mother's lap*. New York: McGraw–Hill.

Serfozo, M. (1990). *Rain talk*. New York: McElderry Books.

Sharmat, M. W. (1977). *I don't care*. New York: Macmillan.

Taylor, A. (1987). *Lights off, lights on*. New York: Oxford University Press.

Viorst, J. (1972). *Alexander and the terrible, horrible, no good, very bad day*. New York: Atheneum.

Wilson, B. P. (1990). *Jenny*. New York: Macmillan.

Wondriska, W. (1972). *The stop*. New York: Holt, Rinehart & Winston.

Yashima, T. (1955). *Crow Boy*. New York: Viking Press.

Yashima, T. (1958). *Umbrella*. New York: Viking Press.

Grandparents

Ackerman, K. (1988). *Song and dance man*. New York: Knopf.
Addy, S. H. (1989). *A visit with great grandma*. Niles, IL: Albert Whitman.
Aliki (1979). *The two of them*. New York: Greenwillow Books.
Baylor, B. (1972). *Coyote cry*. New York: Lothrop, Lee & Shepard.
Blos, J. W. (1989). *The grandpa days*. New York: Simon & Schuster.
Bryant, J. (1963). *The burning rice fields*. New York: Holt, Rinehart & Winston.
Bunting, E. (1989). *The Wednesday surprise*. New York: Clarion Books.
Bunting, E. (1990). *The wall*. New York: Clarion Books.
Burningham, J. (1984). *Grandpa*. New York: Crown.
Carlstrom, N. W. (1990). *Grandpappy*. Boston: Little, Brown.
dePaola, T. (1974). *Watch out for chicken feet in your soup*. Englewood Cliffs, NJ: Prentice–Hall.
dePaola, T. (1973). *Nana upstairs, nana downstairs*. New York: Putnam.
dePaola, T. (1981). *Now one foot, now the other*. New York: Putnam.
Garaway, M. G. (1989). *Ashkii and his grandfather*. Tucson, AZ: Treasure Chest.
Gray, N. (1988). *A balloon for granddad*. New York: Orchard Books.
Greenfield, E. (1980). *Grandmama's joy*. New York: Philomel Books.
Greenfield, E. (1988). *Grandpa's face*. New York: Philomel Books.
Hayes, J. (1987). *The terrible Tragedables*. Santa Fe, NM: Trails West.
Henkes, K. (1986). *Grandpa & Bo*. New York: Greenwillow Books.
Isaac, M. G. (1988). *The tourist in Navajoland*. Cortez, CO: Mesa Verde Press.
Le Tord, B. (1987). *My grandma Leonie*. New York: Bradbury Press.
Luenn, N. (1990). *Nessa's fish*. New York: Atheneum.
MacLachlan, P. (1980). *Through grandpa's eyes*. New York: Harper & Row.
Passen, L. (1990). *Grammy & Sammy*. New York: Henry Holt.

Friends

Alexander, M. (1989). *My outrageous friend Charlie*. New York: Dial Books for Young Readers.
Aliki (1978). *The twelve months*. New York: Greenwillow Books.
Aliki (1987). *We are best friends*. New York: Greenwillow Books.
Appiah (1988). *Amoko & Efua bear*. New York: Macmillan.
Bauer, C. F. (1987). *The midnight snowman*. New York: Macmillan.
Baylor, B. (1963). *Amigo*. New York: Macmillan.
Baylor, B. (1977). *Guess who my favorite person is*. New York: Scribner.
Bonsall, C. (1973). *Mine's the best*. New York: Harper & Row.
Bornstein, R. L. (1980). *Of course a goat*. New York: Harper & Row.
Brisson, P. (1989). *Your best friend, Kate*. New York: Bradbury Press.

Butler, D. (1988). *My brown bear Barney*. New York: Greenwillow Books.
Clark, A. N. (1941). *In my mother's house*. New York: Viking Press.
Havill, J. (1986). *Jamaica's find*. New York: Scholastic.
Kellogg, S. (1986). *Best friends*. New York: Dial Books for Young Readers.
Kimmel, E. A. (1987). *The Chanukkah tree*. New York: Holiday House.
McKissack, P. C. (1988). *Mirandy and brother wind*. New York: Knopf.
Perrine, M. (1970). *Nannabah's friend*. Boston: Houghton Mifflin.
Walter, M. P. (1980). *Ty's one-man band*. New York: Scholastic.

Teacher Materials

Professional Readings

Fulghum, R. (1988). *It was on fire when I lay down on it*. New York: Villard Books.
Gardner, H. (1983). *Frames of mind*. New York: Basic Books.
Maker, C. J. (1982). *Curriculum development for the gifted*. Austin, TX: PRO-ED.
Maker, C. J., & Nielson, A. B. (1995) *Teaching models in education of the gifted*, (2nd ed.). Austin, TX: PRO-ED.
Peterson, R., & Eeds, M. (1990). *Grand conversations*. New York: Scholastic.
Short, K. G. (1991) Making connections across literature and life. In K. E. Holland, R. A. Hungerford, & S. B. Ernst (Eds.), *Journeys: Children responding to literature* (pp. 284–301). Portsmouth, NH: Heineman Press.
Valett, R. E. (1983). *100 + peace strategies for conflict resolution and the prevention of nuclear war*. Fresno, CA: Panorama West.
Webster's new collegiate dictionary. (1973). Springfield, MA: Merriam.

Literature Cited in Unit

Aliki. (1965). *A weed is a flower: The life of George Washington Carver*. New York: Simon & Schuster.
Andrews, J. (1986). *Very last first time*. New York: Atheneum.
Anno, M., Briggs, R., Brooks, R., Carle, E., Calvi, G., Chengliang, Z., Dillon, L., Dillon, D., Hayashi, A., & Popov, N. (1986). *All in a day*. New York: Philomel Books.
Bowers, K. R. (1983). *At this very minute*. Boston: Little, Brown.
Boyd, S. (1981). *The how: Making the best of a mistake*. New York: Human Sciences Press.
Collins, D. R. (1989). *The country artist: A story about Beatrix Potter*. Minneapolis, MN: Carolrhoda Books.
Flournoy, V. (1985). *The patchwork quilt*. New York: Dial Books for Young Readers.

Garaway, M. K. (1989). *The old hogan.* Cortez, CO: June Eck.

Nunes, S., & Himler, R. (1988). *Coyote dreams.* New York: Atheneum.

Polacco, P. (1988). *The keeping quilt.* New York: Simon & Schuster.

Spier, P. (1980). *People.* New York: Doubleday.

Steptoe, J. (1980). *Daddy is a monster . . . sometimes.* New York: Lippincott.

Chapter 8

Developing Scope and Sequence in Curriculum for Gifted Students

One of our most difficult tasks as educators is to view students as growing, changing individuals who spend approximately 13 years in elementary, middle, and high schools. All too often, students are viewed in segments—as first graders, second graders, sixth graders—and each year's teacher plans learning experiences to deliver that year's curriculum. Due to the segmentation of teachers and curriculum, students are not viewed as developing individuals whose experiences need to build upon and extend previous experiences.

Because students are not segmented, educators must address important questions: (a) How do the understandings, skills, and values we expect students to develop fit together? (b) How do we assure that a student develops or is provided the opportunity to learn the understandings, skills, and values that will be important in future personal or career development? (c) How does the student's learning in one setting or at one grade level mesh with his or her learning in a different setting or at a different grade level? In other words, how do educators avoid gaps and repetition in both activities and learning?

These questions are not answered easily and, in many schools, are not addressed. When programs for the gifted existed in only one or two schools, or at only a few grade levels within a school district, such questions were not even considered! However, the field has progressed in the past few years, and, to continue this progress, educators of the gifted must find effective and defensible answers for these and other curriculum questions. The criticism of other educators regarding our lack of articulation, clear goal setting, and coordination with other programs in the educational setting must be addressed.

One important way to respond to some of our critics and to the questions just outlined is through the development of scope and sequence for the curriculum for gifted and talented students. In this chapter, we describe the elements needed in a scope and sequence for a program for gifted students, suggest a general process for developing a scope and sequence, and present some examples of different curricula.

An in-depth discussion of all the issues and processes involved in the development of a scope and sequence would take volumes. Only some of the most important ideas can be presented, and only a few examples can be provided. The processes described are a result of the authors' personal experiences in assisting individual teachers, school districts, and a state department of education in the development of a scope and sequence for curricula. Initially, the ideas and processes were used by the first author with individual teachers in one school district program during the development of a curriculum framework. The processes and four examples of products were presented in *Curriculum Development for the Gifted* (Maker, 1982a). After publication of the book, the process described for use with individuals was modified by the first author based on attempts to follow it with larger groups in different settings (Maker, 1986). In our recent work (Maker, Nielson, & Rogers, 1994), we emphasized that curriculum for gifted students must be sensitive to all students who are highly competent, notwithstanding differences in specific areas of intelligence, culture, or language.

The DISCOVER projects[1] were designed to *D*iscover *I*ntellectual *S*trengths and *C*apabilities through *O*bservation while allowing for *V*aried *E*thnic *R*esponses (Maker, Nielson, & Rogers, 1994). Through the DISCOVER network, a number of individuals from several sites have cooperated in the development of curricula using common formats to reach mutual goals. In this chapter we present an introduction to the

[1] Research and development of the DISCOVER projects at the University of Arizona are supported in part by the Javits Gifted and Talented Students Education Program (Grant No. R206A30138) and the Office of Bilingual Education and Minority Languages Affairs (Grant No. TOO3L30034).

development of scope and sequence in curriculum for gifted students and a summary of the basic ideas and processes based on these experiences.

Necessary Elements of a Scope and Sequence

For our purposes in this chapter, *scope* is very simply defined as the *extent* of what is taught—the understandings, skills, and values that are goals of the program. *Sequence* is the *order* in which the understandings, skills, and values are addressed. A scope and sequence for a program for the gifted differs in some important ways from the scope and sequence often developed for other educational programs. Some of these differences follow:

- A scope and sequence must be flexible, to permit both students and teachers to pursue their individual interests.
- Abstract principles and concepts rather than specific facts or topics are the focus.
- Process skills, such as higher levels of thinking, decision making, and problem solving, are included as separate elements to be integrated with the development of content understanding.
- Development of sophisticated products resulting from integration of the content and process are emphasized.
- Students' opportunities to pursue accelerated content, processes, or products are not restricted.
- Input from scholars and researchers in academic areas is solicited in evaluating the importance of proposed principles, concepts, skills, and values.
- Opportunities for exposure to a variety of content areas, skills, values, and types of content are provided.
- The focus of learning is on concepts that are important in several academic areas, with the goal of integrating rather than separating what is learned.
- For efficiency and articulation in learning, the scope and sequence builds upon and extends the regular curriculum but does not duplicate it.
- A variety of professionals experienced in curriculum development and those experienced in education of the gifted are included in the development process.

To facilitate the development of a curriculum scope and sequence that meets these criteria, the following general process is suggested. At each step, ideas for implementation of the process are presented along with examples of possible products.

Choose Key Individuals and Define Their Roles and Tasks

The persons primarily responsible for the development of curriculum scope and sequence should be teachers and educators directly involved in the program for gifted students. However, other educators, parents, and concerned individuals should be involved in some way. For example, in one school district, the teachers selected a content area of interest and worked with representatives from other grade levels to develop student outcome objectives. Parents (of gifted students) who possessed expertise in academic areas helped in the writing process. Curriculum specialists helped by reviewing the products and identifying ways the program for the gifted could extend the regular curriculum. They also suggested ways to prevent overlap or redundancy with this curriculum.

Generally, all educators involved with education of gifted students should participate in the development of the scope and sequence for gifted students. If regular classroom teachers are the primary providers of learning experiences for gifted students, they also should participate in the process.

Develop Curriculum Goals To Address Differentiated Content, Process, and Product Expectations for Gifted Students

Connections with the educational goals of the district and the differences in expectations for gifted students should be reflected in curriculum goals for gifted students. Goals can be stated in general terms, but they must be clear enough to guide the development of student outcome objectives in the next phase. In the Tucson Unified School District (TUSD, 1993), goals were written in the areas of content, process, product, and affective development. Following are examples of goals in each area:

- Present content that is related to broadbased issues, themes, or problems in an interdisciplinary format. (content)

- Develop critical-thinking and higher-level thinking skills in both cognitive and affective areas. (process)

- Develop products that redefine or challenge existing ideas; incorporate new and innovative ideas; and utilize techniques, materials, forms, and a body of knowledge in an innovative way. (product)

- Encourage the development of sound relationships, including tolerance of human differences, respect for the needs and rights of others, and recognition of the contributions of others. (affective)

Goals of the DISCOVER network are similar, but a clear emphasis is placed on multiple forms of giftedness, integration of cultural and linguistic components of the community, and problem solving:

- Present content that is related to the interdisciplinary themes, returning to these themes as students grow and change. (content)

- Develop problem-solving skills in seven intelligences. (process)

- Develop products using self-selected formats that are relevant in a particular cultural context. (product)

- Provide exploratory learning centers or stations in which the tools of each intelligence are readily available. (learning environment)

Educators involved in the program for gifted students should assume the major responsibility for writing curriculum goals but should arrange for extensive input from others, especially parents. One way the educators can gather ideas from others is to develop tentative statements of goals and to send these to parents, classroom teachers, administrators, other concerned educators, and gifted students, asking them to indicate the extent of their agreement or disagreement with each. These people should be asked to list additional goals they believe are important but which are not included on the list. Revisions, additions, and deletions can be made on the basis of the ideas gathered. Another way to solicit input from others is to hold meetings of parents, classroom teachers, administrators, other concerned educators, and gifted students; then groups are asked to assign a priority to these goals. The writing team, consisting mainly of educators of the gifted, then must take these ideas and formulate them into clear goal statements to guide the development of student outcome objectives.

Analyze Teaching–Learning Models for Appropriateness in Meeting Curriculum Goals

Too often, the chosen model or combination of models determines the goals of a program for gifted students rather than the goals determining the models used. Setting clear goals must come first! After goals are developed and clarified, decisions can be made about the models to be used. The importance of models should not be minimized, however. Creators of models have provided a thoughtful framework and guidelines for development of objectives and teaching activities that have been tested in educational settings. Many models have been based on extensive research and development activities, and others have a research base showing their effectiveness in reaching certain goals (Maker & Nielson, 1995). This information, as well as any practical and theoretical aspects of models, should be considered before their adoption.

Scope and Sequence for a School District

In the Tucson Unified School District, for example, teachers familiar with the various teaching–learning models often used in programs for the gifted listed models that could be useful in meeting each goal (TUSD, 1993). For example, for the content goal, "Present content that is related to broadbased issues, themes, or problems . . ." the teachers listed Bruner's (1960) *Structure of a Discipline* and Taba's *Teaching Strategies Program* (Institute for Staff Development, 1971a, 1971b). Several models useful in meeting the process goal, "Develop critical and higher-level thinking skills . . ." were identified: Guilford's (1967) *Structure of Intellect*, Kohlberg's (1966) *Discussions of Moral Dilemmas*, Parnes's *Creative Problem Solving* (Parnes, 1967), Williams's (1972, 1986, 1990) *Strategies for Thinking and Feeling*, Bloom's *Taxonomy of Cognitive Objectives* (Bloom et al., 1956), Taba's *Teaching Strategies Program*, C. W. Taylor's (1967) *Multiple Talent* approach, Krathwohl's *Taxonomy of Affective Objectives* (Krathwohl et al., 1962), and Ennis's (1964) *Critical Thinking Behaviors*. For the product goal, they recommended Guilford's *Structure of Intellect*, Parnes's *Creative Problem Solving* process, Renzulli's (1977) *Enrichment Triad Model*, Treffinger's (1975) *Self-Directed Learning* guidelines, and C. W. Taylor's *Multiple Talent* approach. The models listed as useful in meeting the affective goal, "Encourage the development of sound relationships, including tolerance of human differences, respect for the needs and rights of others . . ." were Kohlberg's *Discussions of Moral Dilemmas*, Taba's *Teaching Strategies Program*, and Krathwohl's *Taxonomy of Affective Objectives*.

Next, the teachers analyzed the models to determine their usefulness in providing guidelines for developing student outcome objectives that were clear, specific, and observable. Criteria for selecting the models for this task included (a) the clarity of objectives in the model, (b) the extent to which the model is oriented toward observable student outcomes, (c) the comprehensiveness of the model in meeting a goal, and (d) the ease with which the model could be combined with others to provide a comprehensive listing of student outcomes related to a particular objective. With respect to the previously stated goals, Taba's model, with influences from Bruner (1960), was used for development of content objectives, and Taba's model also formed the basis for the process objectives related to higher levels of thinking. Ennis's (1964) list of critical-thinking skills was used to define student outcome objectives for the critical-thinking aspect of the process goal stated previously. For the product goal identified, Renzulli's (1977) *Enrichment Triad Model* was the primary model used in developing objectives, with ideas integrated from three other sources: Torrance's (1972, 1979) writings, Guilford's (1967) *Structure of Intellect* and Treffinger's (1975) *Self-Directed Learning* approach. For the affective goal identified, a synthesis of several models was used. After useful models have been identified for each goal, student outcome objectives can be written for each goal.

Scope and Sequence for a Network of Schools

In the DISCOVER network, Gardner's (1983) theory of multiple intelligences was chosen as the overall framework to guide all aspects of program development, including identification of students. This theory was chosen because of the extensive research leading to its development, its usefulness as a guide for all components of a program, its sensitivity to varied cultural contexts, and the results of research on its validity (Maker, 1993). Within this overall framework, other models have been incorporated. Problem-Based Learning (Stepien, Gallagher, & Workman, 1993) has been used to help teachers develop real-life problems to pose to students at the beginning of units of study. The problem continuum developed by Schiever (1991) and Maker (1993) has helped teachers design problem types ranging from well structured to unstructured. Gardner's theory and the seven intelligences provided the framework for development of products, with emphasis on student selection of formats and relevance to the cultural context. Gardner's theory, combined with the principles in Chapter 2, guided educators in structuring a learning environment in which centers play a key role.

Develop Specific Objectives (Stated as Student Outcomes) for Every Program Goal

Content

Content objectives are most appropriately stated as generalizations or principles to be discovered, as key concepts to be learned, or as themes. Abstract ideas and principles provide direction in the selection of specific information to be taught while allowing flexibility to both the teacher and student in the selection of specific examples or areas of study. Stating content goals in one of the three ways listed also provides a framework for supplementing without duplicating the content from the regular curriculum.

In the Tucson Unified School District (TUSD, 1993), teachers selected 10 themes: aesthetics, causality, change, communication, conflict, ethics, interdependence, power, socialization, and systems. For each theme, they developed key conceptual issues for the theme, which spanned all grade levels and program types. They also developed a focusing question and sample disciplinary problems for grades K through 5, 6 through 8, and 9 through 12 in the content areas of math, science, social studies, and language arts. Finally, for each theme, a focusing question was written for interdisciplinary studies, and sample interdisciplinary units were provided for elementary-school, middle-school, and high-school levels. Thus, for each theme, the curriculum framework was similar to the example presented in Table 8.1. In Table 8.1, the theme of change is shown as an example.

In the DISCOVER network, 16 themes were chosen:

cycles	change
interaction	culture
harmony	invention
patterns	systems
cooperation	communication
relationships	beauty

interdependence   exploration

environment   ethics

Teachers selected themes for each year based on their potential value in the integration of the content from both the local district's regular curriculum and the essential skills prescribed by their state's department of education. For example, teachers of prekindergarten and grades K through 2 selected patterns as an important theme because it provides a foundation for concepts they needed to teach in math and science, and environments because of its importance in integrating language arts skills with social studies and in connecting learning activities to the local community. Relationships was chosen as the third theme because, for many of the students, this is their first experience in school or in working with children not from their own families. These themes were to be revisited at later grade levels (e.g., 3 through 5 and 9 through 12) when the students have a greater range and complexity of experiences to relate to the theme.

Using the problem-based learning approach, teachers (and students) selected relevant, local problems related to the theme as a focus for their studies. One problem for a group of prekindergarten children, as they studied the theme of environment, was "What changes are being made in our environment because of the new high school on campus?" At grades 3 through 5, students were interested in the destruction of nearby forests resulting from the cutting of trees; and at grades 9 through 12, students at one school decided to investigate the possible effects of strip mining on their local environment. This choice was made in response to a proposal under consideration by the town council.

Benefits of a Scope and Sequence

In Tucson and DISCOVER documents, the content scope and sequence permits flexibility while providing direction and coordination for the curriculum. For instance, if the service delivery model at a particular grade level or school in TUSD is a resource room or pullout program, the teacher may wish to select an interdisciplinary unit for all of her or his elementary students and change themes periodically. A regular classroom teacher serving students who are gifted in math, for instance, may feel more comfortable providing enriched experiences within the discipline of math rather than restructuring the entire curriculum based on inter-

Table 8.1. Example of Development of a Theme Within and Across Disciplines

Goal 2: The student will develop an understanding of broadbased issues, themes, or problems with interdisciplinary and multicultural contexts.

Theme: Change

Key Conceptual Issues for Themes: Any in-depth study of this theme will cover some if not all of these questions, either overtly or covertly: Who/what initiates change? What is the process of change? How is change measured in time or magnitude? How is change institutionalized? What are the patterns (random, systematic) in change? What are intermediate and long-term changes? How do changes occur in attitudes and beliefs about other people? How do these changes become institutionalized? What is the relationship between diversity and change?

Focusing Question 1: What roles do equilibrium, cause, and effect play in change?

Sample Disciplinary Problems

Subject	K–5	6–8	9–12
Math	Observe and graph physiological changes such as respiration and pulse rate and discuss possible causes. Examine changes in population patterns.	Design a computer program to understand manipulation of variables.	Compare trigonometric identities that are equal through algebraic manipulation but appear to be different.
Science	Experiment with various chemicals to observe the cause and effects of change (e.g., kitchen chemistry).	Explore changes that are required to achieve equilibrium, such as shifting tectonic plates and earthquakes, salt water, and osmosis.	Explore implications and effects of changes in form of various kinds of energy, such as fluorocarbons, carbons, and ozone.

	K–5	6–8	9–12
Social Studies	Discuss the effects of changes in the nuclear family on family members and on the community. Look at changes in demographics.	Examine cultural, economic, and technologic changes associated with the coming of the railroad to Tucson.	Explore effects of economic change on government and of government on economy.
Language Arts	Examine how various types of literature change over time in style, content, and form.	Examine dynamic role of variables in change (e.g., Ray Bradbury's "The Sound of Thunder")	Examine causes and effects of changing forms of personal expression (e.g., video, rap).

Sample Interdisciplinary Problems

	K–5	6–8	9–12
Unit Focus:	**Patterns**	**Cycles**	**Patterns**
	Examine predictable results of controlled change (e.g., angle change in tessellations; level of language usage in communicating effectively). Examine cultural patterns (e.g., linear vs. circular views of time, life, tessellation, pattern in historical and contemporary Southwestern pottery).	Examine components and patterns of cyclical change (e.g., water, culture, carbon). Examine world view of Native American cultures (e.g., emphasis on the number 4 as in seasons, life cycle, the round shape in nature, etc.).	Explore implications of chaos theory in such areas as ecology.

Note: Adapted from GATE *Curriculum Scope and Sequence* (p. 14), by Tucson Unified School District, 1993, Tucson, AZ: Author. Copyright 1993 by Tucson Unified School District. Reprinted with permission.

disciplinary themes. In a self-contained, full-time program for the gifted, however, teachers may be expected to restructure the curriculum, using interdisciplinary themes for the entire curriculum and for all the students in the class.

At middle- and high-school levels, similar flexibility is built into the framework. In some schools, for example, students are selected because of their overall achievement and giftedness in more than one academic area. In such schools, interdisciplinary problems and units are appropriate; in schools in which students are selected because of high achievement in one content area, discipline-based problems and questions better fit the structure.

In the DISCOVER network, teachers are provided with a framework that can be used to integrate local issues, concerns, and required curricula with state mandates for skill and content development. A wide range of themes is provided, and teachers work within their schools and classroom settings to develop several themes each year. They are encouraged to make plans to return to these themes at least twice during a student's school career.

Process

Statements of student outcomes for process skills may be similar to statements of student outcomes written for the regular curriculum. However, an important difference that causes difficulties in writing specific, observable objectives is that the goals for gifted students often involve long-term use and refinement of skills rather than simple acquisition of skills. Usually, this difference results in more complex goals for which development of clear student outcomes that can be measured or observed is difficult. In other words, no time comes when one can say, for example, that problem-solving skills have been developed; rather, continual improvement and refinement are observed. Thus, success in meeting objectives often must be measured by degree of improvement.

The objectives for processes more appropriately are stated separately from content because most can and should be developed through all content areas. However, stating these objectives separately should not lead to separation of the teaching of processes from the teaching of content and the development of products. Integration of the three areas should come in the development of units of study and teaching activities.

Some examples of process objectives developed in Tucson (TUSD, 1993) for the goal of higher levels of thinking and critical thinking are the following:

Higher Levels of Thinking

- The student will apply and extend rules and concepts within and across content areas.
- The student will apply principles and generalizations within and across content areas.
- The student will analyze and apply laws and theories within and across content areas.
- The student will analyze and apply elements of the whole within and across content areas.
- The student will analyze and apply relationships within and across content areas.
- The student will analyze the structure and organization of elements within and across content areas.

Critical Thinking

- The student will distinguish between fact and opinion.
- The student will distinguish relevant from irrelevant information.
- The student will determine the accuracy of a statement.
- The student will determine the credibility of a source.
- The student will recognize ambiguities.
- The student will identify underlying assumptions.
- The student will identify external and internal bias.
- The student will recognize valid and fallacious arguments.

To make the implementation of these objectives easier and to provide assistance to teachers in connecting process objectives with content, the developers included sample learning experiences in the framework for each of several levels (K–2, 3–5, 6–8, and 9–12). One cognitive and one affective experience was written for each student outcome. In Table 8.2, two examples are given for critical thinking, and two are given for higher levels of thinking.

Table 8.2. Examples of Development of Four Process Objectives

Goal 4: The student will develop critical-thinking and higher-level thinking skills in both cognitive (C) and affective (A) areas.

4.1: CRITICAL THINKING

Objective	K–2	3–5	6–8	9–12
The student will have the opportunities to				
4.1.1 Distinguish between fact and opinion.	C Solve estimation problems and learn the difference between fact and opinion. A From stories and real-life situations, identify statements about feelings that are factual (e.g., "I" statements—"I feel ___ when you ___"). Practice using such statments through role play.	C Analyze commercials, identifying factual and nonfactual statements (e.g., cigarette commercials and news releases). A Use conflict-management techniques to settle playground or class-room disputes.	C Research periodicals and newspapers to compare and contrast fact and opinion on a given topic. C Look for examples in school texts and discuss whether inclusion of opinion is appropriate. A Debate opposing opinions regarding topics of concern to adolescents, (e.g., drug use, sex, and laws concerning minors).	C Examine historical development of scientific theory, emphasizing time periods and lives of individuals in which fact and opinion were of importance (e.g., Galileo). A Identify and evaluate the impact of facts, emotions, and opinions in conflict situations (e.g., teens and parents regarding money, freedom, trust, etc.).

4.1.2 Distinguish relevant from irrelevant information	C Identify irrelevant statements within given reading selections.

C Identify irrelevant responses during collection and analysis of opinion survey responses.

A Eliminate irrelevant data found in games and activities such as *Magic Circle* and *Project Pride* | C Identify irrelevant information directed toward consumers in mass media advertising.

C Determine relevant and irrelevant information and solve mathematical word problems.

A In resolving disputes, determine which items of information are relevant to the solution of the problem. | C Identify relevance of numerous variables in scientific experiments.

A Participate in classroom discussions using structured strategies, (e.g., Taba Resolution of Conflict). | C Read or view published mysteries (e.g., *Murder on the Orient Express* (Christie, 1934), *And Then There Were None* (Christie, 1939), distinguishing relevant clues from "red herrings."

A Discuss moral dilemmas such as those developed by Kohlberg (1966), distinguishing relevant information from irrelevant information and issues. |

The student will have opportunities to

4.2.1 Apply and extend rules and concepts within and across content areas.	C Apply math and language concepts to complete activities in computer-assisted instruction programs.

A Determine which classroom rules could be applied or extended to other environments or situations (e.g., home, concerts, the mall). | C Learn and apply rules for creative problem solving.

C Use analogies to describe scientific situations or results.

A Participate in simulation games (e.g., prey–predator, parent–child) and analyze the results. | C Apply graphing skill concepts to a social, political, economic, or geographic topic.

A Adapt rules of a physical game, such as kickball, to include students with special needs. | C Use analogies to describe and develop characterizations for creative writing.

A Evaluate methods by which groups reach agreement. |

(*continues*)

Table 8.2. *Continued*

Objective	K–2	3–5	6–8	9–12
4.2.2 Apply principles and generalizations within and across content areas.	C Apply principles of cause and effect to predict results in a science experiment. A Discuss how feelings are affected by change (e.g., family structure, environment, physical and mental growth).	C Look for patterns and permutations across and within content areas. A Develop criteria for positive group dynamics (e.g., Will a "good partner" in one area be a "good partner" in other areas?). A Analyze generalizations about social issues to clarify values.	C Apply scientific principles to the study of diverse cultures and civilizations A Clarify values related to war, street gangs, vandalism, human rights, illiteracy, etc.	C Discuss principles of "objectivity." Examine writing on scientific subjects to determine whether the principles of objectivity have been applied by the author(s). A Extend, modify, or reject the following generalization: An individual's attitude toward a subject influences the degree of success she or he has when researching and conveying knowledge to an audience.

Note. Adapted from *GATE Curriculum Scope and Sequence* (pp. 38, 51, 52), by Tucson Unified School District, 1993, Tucson, AZ: Author. Copyright 1993 by Tucson Unified School District. Reprinted with permission.

In the DISCOVER network, teachers designed learning objectives and experiences using two different formats. To insure that all seven intelligences were included in planning for development of the themes, teachers first used a "lesson palette" (see Figure 8.1 and Tables 8.3, 8.4, 8.5, and 8.6.).

Using the palette, teachers wrote at least one sample learning activity for each intelligence and at least one activity that connects the school experience with either the home or the community. A similar palette was

Text continues on page 292

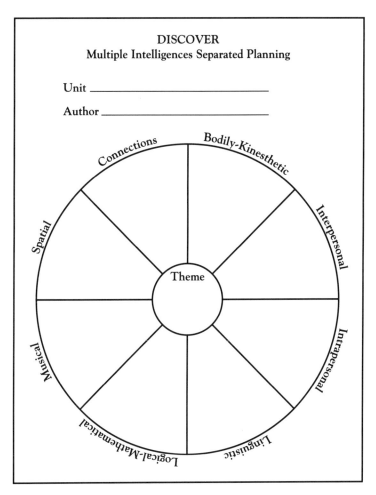

Figure 8.1. Multiple intelligences separated planning.

Table 8.3. Example of DISCOVER Multiple Intelligences Separated Planning

Unit: Social Studies (K–2)

Theme: Patterns

Author: Maker

Intelligence	Sample Activities
Bodily Kinesthetic	Using your body, make a high shape, a low shape, a small shape, a large shape. Move fast, slow, up, down.
Interpersonal	Talk to other children. Find out their daily patterns. Compare your family patterns to theirs.
Intrapersonal	Listen to your heartbeat or feel your pulse. Run or jump for a minute. Then feel your pulse again. How did it change? Why?
Linguistic	Find the rhyming words in a story or poem. What are some other words that rhyme with these words?
Logical– Mathematical	Use unifix cubes, attribute blocks, or pattern blocks to reproduce patterns and to create new ones.
Musical	Clap the syllables of the names of children in the class. Notice which ones are alike.
Spatial	Use finger painting to create different kinds of patterns.
Connections	Take a walk around the neighborhood. Look for patterns in the environment and anywhere you can find them.

Table 8.4. Example of DISCOVER Multiple Intelligences Separated Planning

Unit: Social Studies (3–5)

Theme: Change

Author: Maker

Intelligence	Sample Activities
Bodily Kinesthetic	Show with your body how a caterpillar changes into a butterfly.
Interpersonal	Compare your pictures or drawings of how you have changed with the pictures or drawings of others in your class.
Intrapersonal	Make a collection of pictures or drawings showing how you have changed since you were born.
Linguistic	Tell about the life of a piece of paper. Tell how it was made, where it came from, what it was used for, where it went.
Logical– Mathematical	Observe an insect, an animal, or a plant, and show or tell how it changes. Tell why you think these changes have happened.
Musical	Listen to a familiar piece of music and one that is unfamiliar. What are some ways they change? Using an instrument, play the parts that change.
Spatial	Choose two objects and make a series of drawings showing how one changes into the other.
Connections	Ask someone older than you to tell you some stories about how the world has changed since they were your age.

Table 8.5. Example of DISCOVER Multiple Intelligences Separated Planning

Unit: (6–8)

Theme: Cycles

Author: Maker

Intelligence	Sample Activities
Bodily Kinesthetic	Show with your body how a plant or animal goes through the seasons of the year.
Interpersonal	Talk to someone else about what they do every day, and how they feel about it. Compare your activities and feelings with theirs.
Intrapersonal	Think about what you do in your daily or weekly cycle. What do you do every day, and how do you feel about it?
Linguistic	Brainstorm or look in a thesaurus to find words that mean the same as *cycles*. Create a poem or a description of cycles.
Logical–Mathematical	Make a diagram of different phases of some cycles.
Musical	Play or create music for each of the seasons of the year. Make up a song that has two cycles in it.
Spatial	Draw pictures of some part of nature as it goes through a cycle.
Connections	Talk with an elder—your parents, grandparents, or anyone older than you—and ask them what important cycles they have experienced in their lives.

Table 8.6. Example of DISCOVER Multiple Intelligences Separated Planning

Unit: Social Studies (9–12)

Theme: Patterns

Author: Maker

Intelligence	Sample Activities
Bodily Kinesthetic	Learn the dances of different historical periods. What are their distinctive patterns?
Interpersonal	How are the musical, dance, visual arts, and language (e.g., poetry) patterns from each historical period related? Why?
Intrapersonal	Imagine that you are a particular historical figure. Write a journal of your feelings.
Linguistic	Write a short story or poem from the point of view of an Englishman (or Englishwoman) during the American Revolution.
Logical–Mathematical	Analyze one of the maps of women in the world. Show the patterns of change for women in two different societies.
Musical	Listen to music from various historical periods. What are their distinctive patterns?
Spatial	Create a color-coded map showing the patterns of movement of troops during the American War Between the States.
Connections	How does the geography of your city (state, or nation) influence living patterns there?

used for recording activities in which two or more intelligences are integrated (see Table 8.7).

After this initial planning, a matrix is used to assess the learning activities and to make certain that a wide range of problem types has been incorporated into the instructional plan. The matrix may be used to determine both whether and where additional problems are needed. In Tables 8.8, 8.9, and 8.10, examples are provided for several problem types and all intelligences. A teacher or students may select problems from these examples as needed, and would not be required to complete all of them. Problems from the matrix also could be selected as options on student learning contracts or as activities in learning centers.

Product

Product objectives can be developed in several ways, depending on the needs of students and orientation of the program. First, the objectives can be written as criteria that will be used to judge all student products regardless of their format or purpose. For example, the Tucson teachers separated the product goal into three parts and wrote student outcome objectives for each part. Some examples are shown in Table 8.11.

The teachers then took each objective and developed specific examples of ways the objective could be met at each grade level (K–2, 3–5, 6–8, and 9–12). In Table 8.12, examples are given for three different objectives.

In the DISCOVER network, students often have the opportunity to select the format of their products and the symbol system used to convey their ideas. However, students also need opportunities to explore and learn how to use different media and symbol systems. Thus, teachers organized some optional and some required product development experiences using examples such as the following.

Linguistic

essay

poem

fresh combination of words

original figures of speech

speech

debate

short story

news report

textbook

novel

letter

Spatial

painting

holographic image

architecture

map

geometrical image

photograph

pottery

wood carving

diagram

form

sculpture

furniture

beadwork

weaving

transformation of visual image

re-creation of visual image

Logical–Mathematical

mathematical proofs

solutions to problems

explanations of observed phenomena

equations

analogies

mathematical theories

charts

graphs

Musical

original compositions

melodies

lyrics for tunes

performance of compositions of others

reproduction of tones and tonal patterns

reproduction of rhythms and rhythmic patterns

Bodily-Kinesthetic

dance

sports and games

crafts

choreography

play

mechanical drawing

mime

inventions

needlework

Interpersonal

leadership role

collaboration

demonstration of empathy

active listening

discussion

conflict resolution

Intrapersonal

career goals

description of feelings or motivations

personal philosophy of life

self-analysis

mental health

reflection journal

Table 8.7. Example of DISCOVER Multiple Intelligences Integrated Planning

Unit: (6–8)

Theme: Change

Author: Maker

Intelligences	Sample Activities
Musical Intrapersonal Linguistic	Play tapes of several different kinds of music (e.g., country western, classical, powwow, rap, Native American flute, mariachi) and talk about how each one makes you feel. How does music change your mood?
Spatial Logical– Mathematical	Make a color wheel using watercolors or tempera paints. How can you change blue to purple? Yellow to orange? Yellow to green? How can you make colors lighter?
	Paint a watercolor scene using only the primary colors; then paint the same scene using secondary colors. How does this change the picture?
Logical– Mathematical Spatial	Using tangram puzzles, show how you can change a square to a triangle, a triangle to a parallelogram, and a parallelogram to a rectangle.
	How can you create a figure that is double the size of any of the shapes?
Linguistic Interpersonal Spatial Musical	Make a book or a videotape about how your local community (or your school) has changed. Interview people who have lived there, collect pictures and drawings, listen to music, and read newspaper articles or books about it.

Table 8.8. Example of DISCOVER Matrix of Problem Types for Gardner's (1983) Seven Intelligences

Theme: Relationships

Unit: (K–2)

Authors: Maker, Nielson, Rogers

			Problem Types		
Intelligence	Type I	Type II	Type III	Type IV	Type V
Linguistic	Label the plants and animals in the mural (use both languages).	Do descriptive sentences about the mural (created).	Generate descriptive words about animals and plants in a particular environment.	Create a drama about the mural, with dialogue.	Create a word picture of your own desert creatures.
	Match words (in both languages) to pictures.	Given a stem (e.g., "The cat is as white as"), complete similes.	Contrast the animals and plants in two different environments by generating words.	Tell a story about the mural.	Tell about something in the environment.
	Develop vocabulary in both languages to represent different sizes.	Generate attributes of two different objects. How are they alike and how are they different?	Write descriptive words about the relationship between plants and where they grow.	Make up a story about your creature.	
			Do a word expansion.		

Logical–Mathematical				
Sequence objects according to size.	Look at various plants in an environment (desert). Predict why a plant grows in certain ways.	Make a recording of environmental sounds.	Tell what might happen to the desert if it rained every day.	Do an experiment to find out something you want to know.
Plant a seed and observe it; chart how long it takes to grow.	Take photos of an environment and collect photos, models, and real things from other environments.	Compare recorded sounds with what your ear hears.	Choose two things and tell how they are related.	
Which sandwich has more ingredients and which has fewer?	Compare and contrast evaporation and absorption in flat desert and in a wash.	Compare results of drying on figures sculpted from different soils.		
Clap syllables of names.	Examine the cohesion properties of different soils.			
Using groups of things, examine concepts of more and less, bigger and smaller.				

(continues)

Table 8.8. Continued

			Problem Types		
Intelligence	Type I	Type II	Type III	Type IV	Type V
Spatial	Find different shapes in the alphabet.	Make letters, numbers, figures with Cleversticks.	Create a mural of habitats to hang on the wall. After a field trip, draw pictures of some things that you saw. Sculpt models of flat desert and washes. Use pastel or watercolor techniques to represent plants in environment	Put pictures together in a relationship. Use varied art techniques to create a desert picture. Use various kinds of soil to sculpt different objects in environment.	Create a work of art with some or all objects found (after a walk). Create your own desert creature.
Musical	Listen to different kinds of music and watch different dances. Then match dances to the music	Explain the relationships of parts of the day to types of music. Explain the relationship of activities to types of music.	Select music to accompany a story, poem, or creature personality.	Create a musical intro to play (e.g., about mural). Create music to go with a book. Create the music to go with a dance.	Create (select) music to communicate or represent some of your ideas and feelings.

Bodily Kinesthetic	Mirror movements from the four quadrants. Mirror movements of teacher. Play "Mother, May I."	Use your body to show how a specific animal moves. Spin around rapidly and tell how head and body feel. Create movement of animals seen on video.	Create a dance to go with a piece of music. Create your own movements to go with music.	Create a dance to represent movements of plants and animals in the mural.	Create a dance or body movement that lasts at least a minute.
Interpersonal	Name the people in your family.	Watch a videotape of selves in group. What did you notice? Show what happens when you go to doctor, to policemen, etc.	Make a family tree with photos or pictures. Interview members of your family.	Look at a photo of group. Who would you like to be your friend? How can you become friends with him or her?	Find and learn a family story. Share it in some way.
Intrapersonal			Listen to various types of music. Tell or show how each makes you feel. Listen to Tomi de Paola's (1989) The Art Lesson. Show how it made you feel.	View photo of classroom. Show where you spend the most time and tell why. Tell or show how different colors make you feel.	Draw yourself doing something you like to do. Show in some way something you like to do with a friend.

Table 8.9. DISCOVER Matrix of Problem Types for Gardner's (1983) Seven Intelligences

Theme: Systems

Unit: (3–5)

Authors: Ruiz, Rogers, Maker

			Problem Type		
Intelligence	Type I	Type II	Type III	Type IV	Type V
Linguistic	Choose two or more books about the system you chose to study. Read them to yourself or someone else.	Find out the meanings of words about systems that you do not know.	Make a word worth chart using words from the books you read.	Make a puppet show, a play, or a news report about the system you chose to study.	Create something using words that tells what you have learned about systems.
Logical–Mathematical	Using the books about your systems, find out distances, sizes, and other numbers that describe the system you chose to study.	Make a chart or a graph showing the information you learned about the parts of that system.	Imagine that one part of the system you chose to study became three times its size and other parts stayed the same. Show what might happen.	Create a scale model of the system you chose to study. Use materials in the math center.	Using the materials in the math center, create something that shows what you have learned about systems.
Spatial	Look at the pictures of the system you chose to study. Identify the parts of the system.	Choose one of the pictures and make what is in it using any of the materials at the center.	Imagine that you are inside one of the parts of the system. Show what it looks like.	Think about how the parts of the system you chose to study are related. Make a model of these relationships.	Using the materials at the spatial center, create something that shows what you have learned about systems.

Musical	Listen to the tapes at the center. Identify sounds that are like parts of the system you chose to study.	Listen to the tapes. Think about how the instruments create a system.	Using instruments of your choice, create sounds for the parts of your system.	Create a melody or musical work with no words, using the sounds of your system.	Make up some music to show what you have learned about systems.
Bodily Kinesthetic	Using your body, imitate some of the parts of the system you chose to study	Watch the video. Study how the body acts as a system. Try some of the movements. See how they feel.	Choose one part of the system you chose to study. Demonstrate how it works using only your body.	Make a mime (no words) showing how the system you chose to study works.	Create a performance using only your body to show what you learned about systems.
Interpersonal	Read or look at the pictures in books about the system you chose to study. Identify how people are involved in it.	Discuss the system and the books about it with another person.	Write two or three questions to ask people about the system. Ask five or six people these questions.	Create a way to show how people answered the questions. Involve everyone in your group	Working with your group, design a way to show how people often interact with the system you chose to study.
Intrapersonal			Imagine you are a part of the system you chose to study. Show or tell how you feel.	Imagine you have become ruler of your system. Show or tell what changes you would make. Explain or show why.	Using the materials in any of the centers, create something that shows how you are related to the system you chose to study.

Table 8.10. DISCOVER Matrix of Problem Types for Gardner's (1983) Seven Intelligences

Theme: Exploration

Unit: (6–8)

Authors: Maker

Intelligence	Type I	Type II	Problem Types Type III	Type IV	Type V
Linguistic	Choose one era of exploration of different environments. Read several accounts of that era from different time periods and points of view.	Prepare a debate about why we should or should not continue space exploration.	Imagine you were living during the first expedition to the moon. Write a front page news report about the event.	Write a fictional short story based on one event during the era of exploration you chose.	Using words, create something to demonstrate what you have learned about exploration.
Logical–Mathematical	Identify famous mathematical explorers from different time periods. Compare and contrast their inventions.	Show how algebra and geometry are used to calculate unknown distances.	Create budgets for the Lewis and Clark expedition and for the first expedition to the moon. How and why are they different?	How can probability and statistics be used to predict what will happen on an expedition?	Use your imagination to show in some way how computer networks might facilitate future explorations.
Spatial	Trace the routes of exploration in the era you have chosen to investigate.	Create a color-coded map showing regions of the world and the time period of greatest exploration.	Choose a work of art that is innovative for the time period in which it was created. Modify it, but retain the artist's style.	What connections do you see between the art and science of the era you have chosen to study? Create a construction to show these connections.	Create a work of art about exploration.

Musical	Listen to music about various explorations.	Notice the differences and similarities in music related to the Gold Rush and space exploration.	Choose musical instruments and improvise with different forms and types of music.	Choose a book or poem about the westward movement. Create a musical score to accompany it.	Create a musical piece about exploration.
Bodily Kinesthetic	Learn dances from the era of exploration you have chosen to study.	Explore how each part of your body can move: head, shoulders, trunk, arms, hips, legs, feet.	Show with your body how explorers move differently in outer space and in the ocean.	Choose a book or a poem about an expedition that interests you. Create a mime about the expedition.	What are your body's boundaries? Show how you can explore them alone or with others.
Interpersonal	Watch "To the Moon and Beyond" (National Academy of Sciences, 1991). Discuss space exploration with someone else.	Choose one leader of an expedition. How did he or she recruit followers?	In your opinion, who are the 10 most famous explorers? Why do you think they are famous?	Imagine you are organizing an expedition to Nepal. Who would you want to take with you? How would you convince them to go?	What kinds of conflicts would you expect on an expedition to unknown territory? How should they be resolved?
Intrapersonal			Choose an event during the era of exploration you chose to study. What role would you play in that event and why?	Choose a new idea, place, or event to explore. Write, tell, or show your feelings.	What are the boundaries of your mind? How can you explore them?

Table 8.11. Examples of Product Objectives

7.1 *Products that refine or challenge existing ideas*

7.1.1 The student's product will reflect the exploration of a variety of appropriate and sophisticated sources, including primary and secondary sources.

7.1.2 The student's product will reflect effective application of a variety of questioning techniques.

7.1.3 The student's product will reflect the application of new solutions to an already existing problem.

7.1.4 The student's product will reflect the ability to evaluate the work of others, with an appreciation of human differences.

7.1.5 The student's product will reflect the appreciation of the concept of aesthetics.

7.2 *Products that incorporate concepts*

7.2.1 The student's product will incorporate and reflect basic math concepts (e.g., ideas of number, time, classification, and money).

7.2.2 The student's product will incorporate and reflect the language arts system, including the ideas of communication, symbol, writing, interpretive language, or oral language.

7.2.3 The student's product will incorporate and reflect the basic science processes and concepts (e.g., interdependence, change, cycles, living things, environment, and classification).

7.2.4 The student's product will incorporate and reflect basic social studies concepts, including religious belief, culture, politics, values, economics, and history.

7.3 *Products that use techniques, materials, forms, and knowledge in innovative ways.*

7.3.1 The student's product will reflect how questioning leads to problem definition and resolution.

7.3.2 The student's product will reflect the application of a variety of techniques and materials in innovative ways.

7.3.3 The student's product will reflect the application of a variety of forms in creative ways.

7.3.4 The student's product will reflect the use of acquired knowledge in innovative ways.

7.3.5 The student's product will reflect the application of solutions to ethical problems.

Note. Adapted from G.A.T.E. *Curriculum Scope and Sequence* (pp. 99–101), by Tucson Unified School District, 1993, Tucson, AZ: Author. Copyright 1993 by Tucson Unified School District. Adapted with permission.

Table 8.12. Examples of Ways to Develop Product Objectives

Goal 7: The student will develop products that refine or challenge existing ideas; incorporate concepts; and use techniques, materials, forms, and knowledge in innovative ways.

7.1: PRODUCTS THAT REFINE OR CHALLENGE:

The student will have opportunities to

Objective	K–2	3–5	6–8	9–12
7.1.1 Reflect the exploration of a variety of appropriate and sophisticated sources, including primary and secondary sources.	Use card catalog and library resources. Employ family and friends as sources.	Interview teachers, peers, staff, and experts. Use local media as a source. Utilize a variety of reference sources (e.g., *Reader's Guide to Periodical Literature*, thesaurus, dictionary, synonym finder, encyclopedia).	Interpret primary and secondary sources. Petition (e.g., school board). Attend seminars. Research through use of microfiche.	Utilize interlibrary loan network. Make presentations to governing boards (product videotapes, slide shows). Search on-line computer databases.

7.2 PRODUCTS THAT INCORPORATE CONCEPTS:

The student will have opportunities to

Objective	K–2	3–5	6–8	9–12
7.2.1 Incorporate and reflect basic math	Write the parts of a story problem in a logical number sentence.	Compare number systems (e.g., Roman, Egyptian, Arabic).	Show the application of dendrochronology.	Calculate probabilities. Do a statistical analysis.

(continues)

Table 8.12. *Continued*

Objective	K–2	3–5	6–8	9–12
concepts (e.g., ideas of number, time, classification, and money).	Put the parts of a story in logical sequence. Use manipulatives to show correlation between numbers of objects. Develop a number line. Draw a picture graph. Categorize, using attribute blocks. Learn to tell time with digital and analog clocks.	Develop and use an original barter system. Develop a timeline and use it to illustrate social studies content. Distinguish similarities and differences of any given set.	Make a chart comparing quantities in varied number bases. Write computer programs. Create a geodome.	Apply physics principles to an item or system of your choice.

7.3 PRODUCTS THAT USE TECHNIQUES, MATERIALS, FORMS, AND KNOWLEDGE IN INNOVATIVE WAYS:

Objective	K–2	3–5	6–8	9–12
The student will have opportunities to				
7.3.1 Reflect how questioning leads to problem definition and resolution.	Do sink and float experiments. Mix colors. Have paper airplane flight contests. Do Transformations. Play Twenty Questions.	Create a science fair project using the scientific method. Write a "What if . . ." scenario.	Evaluate math theorems. Conduct opinion polls. Prepare research paper.	Do physics experiments. Select a controversial issue, define an inherent problem, collect and evaluate data, then recommend a solution.

Note. From GATE *Curriculum Scope and Sequence* (pp. 102, 107, 116), by Tucson Unified School District, 1993, Tucson, AZ: Author. Copyright 1993 by Tucson Unified School District. Reprinted with permission.

The goals, objectives, and sequence of skills for achieving these objectives in the three areas of content, process, and product constitute the major part of the scope and sequence. However, the use of goals, objectives, and sequences of skills in an appropriate and individualized manner is facilitated by the incorporation of three additional steps into the process of developing a scope and sequence.

Assess the "Match" Between the Regular Curriculum and the Differentiated Curriculum

Many teachers of gifted students are held accountable for teaching basic skills as well as for differentiating the curriculum to meet the special needs of gifted students. Only when the program for the gifted is considered an "enrichment" or an "add-on" curriculum is this requirement not true. When the curriculum is delivered in a regular classroom setting, in classes substituted for required courses (usually at middle- or high-school levels), or in self-contained (full-time) classes for the gifted, assurance that required skills have been learned is particularly important.

Educators must keep in mind, however, that being accountable for basic skills does *not* mean all these skills have to be *taught* to the gifted students in their classes. Rather, these skills must be *learned* by the students. In many cases, students have mastered many of the required basic skills already, especially in their areas of giftedness, and need to be allowed to engage in challenging extensions of their abilities.

The match between the regular and special curriculum can be assessed in many ways, depending on the format of the regular curriculum. As an example of how this assessment can be done, we developed a tool based on the Arizona Essential Skills for K through 5 and demonstrate how it can be used to assess the extent to which the content, process, and product objectives of the TUSD curriculum includes the Arizona Essential Skills (see Table 8.13). Only the essential skills in one math subject area and one language arts were analyzed, but others could be analyzed in a similar way.

By using a process such as this, educators can discover areas in which assessments or additional activities need to be planned to determine a student's levels of skill development or acquisition. A similar chart can be developed for each student and included in her or his portfolio or cumulative folder. To do this, simply substitute either dates or names of

Table 8.13. Analysis of TUSD GATE Curriculum Center

Arizona Essential Skills (K–5)	Content		Process					Products		
	Change	Communication	Apply and extend rules and concepts	Apply principles and generalizations	Distinguish between fact and opinion	Distinguish relevant from irrelevant information	Reflect the exploration of a variety of sources	Reflect application of varied questioning techniques	Incorporate and reflect basic math concepts	Incorporate and reflect the language arts system
Math: Numbers										
1. Understand place value of whole and decimal numbers.	X		X							
2. Read and write whole numbers, fractions, decimals.			X						X	
3. Use appropriate symbols and order relations.			X						X	
4. Identify and use number properties: commutative, etc.	X			X					X	

GATE Curriculum Objectives

5. Recognize greatest common factor, least common multiple.		X			X		X
6. Find equivalent fractions.		X			X		X
7. Recall $+$, $-$, $\times$, $\div$, with reasonable speed.		X					X
8. Use basic operations with whole numbers, fractions, decimals.		X			X		X
9. Use mental arithmetic.	X	X			X	X	X
10. Estimate to predict answers. Check answers for reasonableness.				X	X	X	X
11. Know how to use a calculator.		X					X
12. Interpret story problems, choose method of calculation, and solve.					X		X
13. Solve money problems.	X	X			X	X	X
14. Round off numbers to a specific place value.	X	X				X	X
15. Use ratios and proportions to solve problems.			X			X	X
16. Convert among percent, fractional, and decimal equivalents.		X					X

(continues)

Table 8.13. Continued

Arizona Essential Skills (K–5)	GATE Curriculum Objectives									
	Content		Process					Products		
	Change	Communication	Apply and extend rules and concepts	Apply principles and generalizations	Distinguish between fact and opinion	Distinguish relevant from irrelevant information	Reflect the exploration of a variety of sources	Reflect application of varied questioning techniques	Incorporate and reflect basic math concepts	Incorporate and reflect the language arts system
Writing										
1. Participate in some aspect of writing process daily.						X		X		X
2. Participate in a rewriting activity.						X		X		X
3. Identify purpose for writing.				X		X		X		X
4. Identify audience for writing.				X				X		X

						Item	
5.	Decide organization for writing task.					X	X
6.	Narrow topic or subject.		X	X			X
7.	Draws or free write first or rough draft.						X
8.	Monitor own writing.						X
9.	Revise for ideas.		X	X	X		X
10.	Revise for sentence structure.	X		X			X
11.	Revise for paragraph structure.	X					X
12.	Revise for word choice.	X					X
13.	Edit for usage.	X					X
14.	Edit for spelling, capitalization, punctuation.	X					X
15.	Rewrite paper.		X			X	X
16.	Proofread final draft.					X	X
17.	Share or publish final draft.					X	X
18.	Write a personal experience narrative.			X		X	X

(continues)

Table 8.13. *Continued*

| | GATE Curriculum Objectives | | | | | | | | | |
| | Content | | Process | | | | | Products | | |
Arizona Essential Skills (K–5)	Change	Communication	Apply and extend rules and concepts	Apply principles and generalizations	Distinguish between fact and opinion	Distinguish relevant from irrelevant information	Reflect the exploration of a variety of sources	Reflect application of varied questioning techniques	Incorporate and reflect basic math concepts	Incorporate and reflect the language arts system
Writing										
19. Write an imaginative story.	X							X		X
20. Write a report based on personal observation.	X			X			X	X		X
21. Write a communication.	X	X		X				X		X
22. Write a poem.	X			X						X
23. Write a dialogue.				X						X
24. Write a play.				X						X
25. Write a summary.	X	X				X	X			X

activities or products for the content, process, and product objectives at the top of the chart and make a check in the appropriate column (or record a date) when the skill was observed.

Select or Develop Instruments or Procedures for Needs Assessment and Evaluation in Areas Addressed by Program Goals and Objectives

A scope and sequence for gifted students must never be used in a lock-step manner. The scope and sequence should facilitate rather than inhibit learning. Thus, teachers should not assume that just because a student is in the 4th grade, he or she has mastered certain skills. Conversely, one should not assume that the student has *not* mastered certain skills. If used appropriately, the scope and sequence will provide checkpoints for skill and content development rather than dictating exactly when these can be learned.

Both informal and formal procedures should be developed (or selected) by teachers to evaluate student needs with respect to the curriculum goals and objectives. These procedures must yield specific information that can be used in instructional planning for individual students and must be tied directly to the student outcome objectives. Needs assessment procedures also can be used (as posttests) to evaluate student progress and the success of the curriculum.

Unfortunately, tests that measure objectives common to programs for gifted students and that provide information useful in instructional planning are not published or readily available. Thus, informal checklists and tests must be developed, and selected parts of existing instruments must be used.

Increased use of portfolios as a method of authentic assessment is a trend we believe will and should continue. Actual work samples demonstrate a student's use of needed skills in a realistic context and provide specific, practical information to guide teachers in creating challenging learning experiences that will build upon existing skills.

Many people indicate that they have difficulty selecting instruments for assessment of processes but that finding instruments for content assessment is much easier because of the availability of achievement tests. However, few achievement tests measure conceptual understanding of the kind usually viewed as important in a program for the gifted. Standardized achievement tests rarely yield data useful in instructional planning because only general scores are reported to teachers without an analysis of these scores and their relationship to learning objectives.

Develop Sample Units and Lesson Plans

Sample units and lesson plans should accompany the scope and sequence to demonstrate how the objectives and skills in the three areas of content, process, and product can be integrated. Too often, the teaching of process is separated from the teaching of content, and existence of a separate scope and sequence for these areas could create the impression that they should be taught separately.

Providing opportunities to develop supplementary materials can be a way to recognize the creativity of certain teachers. Units and lesson plans can be developed by individuals working alone, and existing units or plans can be included. If materials follow a standard format and they all include certain types of information, the units and lessons will be used more easily by those not involved in their development. The format and exact information to be included in units or lesson plans should be provided to teachers interested in writing them. Meetings to explain the format and to answer questions should precede the actual writing process. Sample units and lesson plans using the required format would be useful as models. Finally, each unit or lesson plan should have a cover sheet summarizing what is contained within it, especially listing which content, process, and product objectives are addressed.

Implementation

The final task of the team involved in development of a scope and sequence is to hold meetings and workshops in which the product is presented and explained. Simply sending it to administrators, teachers, or curriculum specialists is not enough. Those involved in the writing should be available to answer questions and to provide assistance in implementation. Depending on the experience and sophistication of the teachers involved in the program, workshops and other inservice education may need to be planned.

Summary

The development of a curriculum scope and sequence can provide effective answers to the three major questions presented at the beginning of this chapter. As educators, we can show how the learning of a variety of understandings, skills, and values fits together; we can assure that students are given opportunities to learn what will be useful to them in the future; and we can avoid gaps and repetition in learning. The process described in this chapter has been useful in a variety of settings and has resulted in the development of scope and sequence documents that meet the requirements outlined. Although variations and modifications will be needed because of the differences in settings, the examples are provided because of their potential to be helpful in designing an articulated curriculum useful in each reader's situation.

References

Ackerman, D. B. (1989). Intellectual and practical criteria for successful curriculum integration. In H. H. Jacobs, (Ed.), *Interdisciplinary curriculum: Design and implementation* (pp. 25–37). Alexandria, VA: Association for Supervision & Curriculum Development.

Adams, H. B., & Wallace, B. (1991). A model for curriculum development. *Gifted Education International, 7,* 105–113.

Adams, H. B., & Wallace, B. (1988). The assessment and development of potential of high school pupils in the third world context of Kwa-Zulu/Natal. *Gifted Child International, 5,* 132–137.

Artabasy, J. (1991). A curmudgeon's guide to the classroom. *Illinois Council for the Gifted Journal, 10,* 14–15.

Banks, J. A. (1990). *Teaching strategies for the social studies: Inquiry, valuing, and decision-making* (4th ed.), with contributions by A. A. Clegg, Jr. New York: Longman.

Baron, J., & Sternberg, R. J. (Eds.). (1987). *Teaching thinking skills: Theory and research.* New York: Freeman & Sons.

Betts, G. (1985). *The autonomous learner model for the gifted and talented.* Greeley, CO: Autonomous Learning Publications and Specialists.

Bloom, B. S., (Ed.). (1956). *Taxonomy of educational objectives: The classification of educational goals. Handbook I: Cognitive domain.* New York: Longmans, Green.

Brasefield, J. (1970). *Liberté: A simulation of the French Revolution*. Lakeside, CA: Interact.

Brooks, J. A. (1987). Taba teaching strategies: Effects on higher level cognitive functioning of academically gifted students. (Doctoral dissertation, North Carolina State University, 1988). *Dissertation Abstracts International, 49*(10-A), A2908.

Bruner, J. S. (1983). *Child's talk: Learning to use language*. New York: Oxford University Press.

Bruner, J. (1985). Models of the learner. *Educational Researcher, 14*(6), 5–8.

Carin, A. A., & Sund, R. B. (1980). *Teaching science through discovery* (4th ed.). Columbus, OH: Merrill.

Ceci, S. J. (1990). *On intelligence—more or less: A bio-ecological treatise on intellectual development*. Englewood Cliffs, NJ: Prentice-Hall.

Christensen, M. (1994). An investigation of gifted students' perceptions involving competitive and non-competitive learning situations. In N. Colangelo, S. G. Assouline, & D. L. Ambroson (Eds.), *Talent Development, Vol. 2: Proceedings from the 1993 Henry B. and Jocelyn Wallace National Research Symposium on Talent Development* (pp. 505–507). Dayton: Ohio Psychology Press.

Christie, A. (1934). *Murder on the Orient Express*. New York: Dodd, Mead.

Christie, A. (1939). *And then there were none*. New York: Dodd, Mead.

Clark County School District. (1979). *The Venture independent study contract form*. Las Vegas, NV: Author.

Clark, B. (1986). *Optimizing learning: The integrative education model in the classroom*. Columbus, OH: Merrill.

Clark, B. (1992). *Growing up gifted* (4th ed.). New York: Merrill.

Clarke, J. H. (1990). *Patterns of thinking: Integrating learning skills in content teaching*. Boston: Allyn & Bacon.

Clarke, H. J., MacPherson, B. V., & Holmes, D. R. (1982). Cigarette smoking and locus of control among young adolescents. *Journal of Health and Social Behavior, 23*, 253–259.

Cohen, E. (1986). *Designing groupwork: Strategies for the cooperative classroom*. New York: Teachers College Press.

Coleman, L. J. (1985). *Schooling the gifted*. Menlo Park, CA: Addison–Wesley.

Costa, A. (Ed.). (1985). *Developing minds*. Alexandria, VA: Association for Supervision & Curriculum Development.

Costa, A. L., Hanson, R., Silver, H. F., & Strong, R. W. (1985). Other mediative strategies. In A. L. Costa (Ed.), *Developing minds* (pp. 166–169). Alexandria, VA: Association for Supervision and Curriculum Development.

Csikszentmihalyi, M. (1988). Society, culture, and person: A systems view of creativity. In R. Sternberg (Ed.), *The nature of creativity* (pp. 325–339). New York: Cambridge University Press.

Damon, W. (1984). Peer education: The untapped potential. *Journal of Applied Developmental Psychology, 5,* 331–343.

Day, M. (1980). *Stock market.* Lakeside, CA: Interact.

De Paola, T. (1989). *The art lesson.* New York: Putnam.

Dewey, J. (1956). *The child and the curriculum and the school and society* (2nd ed.). Chicago: University of Chicago Press. [Original work published in 1900]

Deyhle, D. (1983). Between games and failure: A micro-ethnographic study of Navajo students and testing. *Curriculum Inquiry, 13,* 347–376.

Dunn, R. S., & Griggs, S. A. (1988). *Learning styles: A quiet revolution in American secondary schools.* Reston, VA: National Association of Secondary School Principals.

Dunn, R. S., & Price, G. E. (1980). Learning style characteristics of gifted students. *Gifted Child Quarterly, 24*(1), 33–36.

Durham Public Schools. (1992). *Curriculum goals for academically able students.* Unpublished document available from C. June Maker, Department of Special Education and Rehabilitation, University of Arizona, Tucson.

Durkin, M. (1971). Reviewing the concept development task. In Institute for Staff Development (Eds.), *Hilda Taba teaching strategies program: Unit 1.* Miami, FL: Institute for Staff Development.

Ennis, R. H. (1964). A definition of critical thinking. *The Reading Teacher, 18,* 599–612.

Ennis, R. H., & Millman, J. (1971). *The Cornell critical thinking test: Manual for level x and level z.* Urbana: University of Illinois.

Feldhusen, H. J. (1993). Individualized teaching of the gifted in regular classrooms. In C. J. Maker & D. Orzechowski–Harland (Eds.), *Programs for the gifted in regular classrooms* (pp. 263–273). Austin, TX: PRO-ED.

Feldhusen, J. F. (1985). Parents' perceptions of gifted children's educational needs. *Roeper Review, 7*(4), 249–252.

Feldhusen, J., & Kolloff, M. (1978). A three-stage model for gifted education. *Gifted Child Today, 1,* 53–58.

Foster–Harrison, E. S. (1994). *More energizers and icebreakers: For all ages and stages* (Book 2). Minneapolis, MN: Educational Media.

Frasier, M. M., & Passow, A. H. (1994). *Toward a new paradigm for identifying talent potential.* Storrs, CT: National Research Council for the Gifted and Talented.

Fulghum, R. (1988). *It was on fire when I lay down on it.* New York: Villard Books.

Gage, N. L. & Berliner, D. C. (1979). *Educational psychology.* Chicago: Rand McNally.

Gallagher, J. J. (1985). *Teaching the gifted child* (3rd ed.). Boston: Allyn & Bacon.

Gallagher, J. J., Aschner, M. J., & Jenné, W. (1967). *Productive thinking in classroom interaction.* Reston, VA: The Council for Exceptional Children.

Gallagher, J. J., Shaffer, F., Phillips, S., Addy, S., Rainer, M., & Nelson, T. (1966). *A system of topic classification.* Urbana: University of Illinois, Institute for Research on Exceptional Children.

Gallagher, S. A., Stepien, W. J., & Rosenthal, H. (1992). The effects of problem-based learning on problem-solving. *Gifted Child Quarterly, 36*(4), 195–200.

Gamberg, R., Kwak, W., Hutchings, M., & Altheim, J. (1988). *Learning and loving it: Theme studies in the classroom.* Portsmouth, NH: Heinemann.

Gardner, H. (1992). Assessment in context: The alternative to standardized testing. In B. R. Gifford & G. O'Connor (Eds.), *Changing assessments: Alternative views of aptitude, achievement, instruction* (pp. 77–119). Boston: Kluwer Academic.

Gardner, H. (1983). *Frames of mind: The theory of multiple intelligences.* New York: Basic Books.

Gardner, H. (1994). Five forms of creative activity: A developmental perspective. In N. Colangelo, S. G. Assouline, & D. L. Ambroson, (Eds.), *Talent development, Vol. 2: Proceedings from the 1993 Henry B. and Jocelyn Wallace National Research Symposium on Talent Development* (pp. 3–17). Dayton, OH: Ohio Psychology Press.

George, W. C., (1976). Accelerating mathematics instruction. *The Gifted Child Quarterly, 20,* 246–261.

Getzels, J., & Csikszentmihalyi, J. (1967). Scientific creativity. *Science Journal, 3,* 80–84.

Getzels, J. , & Csikszentmihalyi, J. (1976). *The creative vision: A longitudinal study of problem finding in art.* New York: Wiley.

Gipson, F. (1956). *Old Yeller.* New York: Harper.

Goodman, K. S. (1989). Whole-language research: Foundations and development. *Elementary School Journal, 90,* 207–221.

Graves, N., & Graves, T. (1990). *What is cooperative learning? Tips for teachers and trainers* (2nd ed.). Santa Cruz: Cooperative College of California.

Guilford, J. P. (1967). *The nature of human intelligence.* New York: McGraw-Hill.

Guilford, J. P. (1975). Varieties of creative giftedness, their measurement, and development. *The Gifted Child Quarterly, 19*(2), 107–121.

Haensley, P. A., & Roberts, N. M. (1983). The professional productive process and its implications for gifted students. *Gifted Child Quarterly, 27,* 9–12.

Heath, S. B. (1982). Questioning at home and at school: A comparative study. In G. Spindler (Ed.), *Doing the ethnography of schooling* (pp. 102–131). New York: Holt, Rinehart & Winston.

Hoerr, T., the faculty of the New City School. (1994). *Celebrating multiple intelligences: Teaching for success.* St. Louis, MO: The New City School.

Hollingworth, L. (1926). *Gifted children.* New York: Macmillan.

Howley, A., Howley, C. B., & Pendarvis, E. D. (1985). *Teaching gifted children: Principles and strategies.* Boston: Little, Brown.

Isaksen, S. G., Dorval, K. B., & Treffinger, D. J. (1994) *Creative approaches to problem solving*. Dubuque, IA: Kendall Hunt.

Isaksen, S. G., & Parnes, S. J. (1985). Curriculum planning for creative thinking and problem solving. *Journal of Creative Behavior, 19*(1), 1–29.

Isaksen, S. G., & Treffinger, D. J. (1985). *Creative problem solving: The basic course*. Buffalo, NY: Bearly Limited.

Institute for Staff Development (Ed.). (1971a). *Hilda Taba teaching strategies program: Unit I*. Miami, FL: Author.

Institute for Staff Development (Ed.). (1971b). *Hilda Taba teaching strategies program: Unit II*. Miami, FL: Author.

Jacobs, H. H. (1989a). The growing need for interdisciplinary curriculum content. In H. H. Jacobs, (Ed.), *Interdisciplinary curriculum: Design and implementation* (pp. 1–11). Alexandria, VA: Association for Supervision & Curriculum Development.

Jacobs, H. H. (1989b, Fall). Interdisciplinary curriculum options: A case for multiple configurations. *Educational Horizons, 68*, pp. 25–27, 35.

Jung, C. G. (1923). *Psychological types*. London: Routledge & Kegan Paul.

Kaplan, S. N. (1974). *Providing programs for the gifted and talented: A handbook*. Ventura, CA: Superintendent of Schools.

Kaplan, S. N. (Ed.). (1979). *Inservice training manual: Activities for developing curriculum for the gifted/talented*. Ventura, CA: Superintendent of Schools.

Kaplan, S. N. (1986). Qualitatively differentiated curricula. In C. J. Maker (Ed.), *Critical issues in gifted education: Vol. I. Defensible programs for the gifted* (pp. 117–134). Austin, TX: PRO-ED.

Kaplan, S. N., & Gould, B. T. (1987). *Developing competencies related to a differentiated curriculum for the gifted-talented*. Burbank, CA: National State Leadership Training Institute for the Gifted-Talented.

Keirsey, D., & Bates, M. (1978). *Please understand me: An essay on temperament styles*. Del Mar, CA: Prometheus Nemesis Books.

Kersh, M. E., Nielsen, M. E., & Subotnik, R. F. (1987). Techniques and sources for developing integrative curriculum for the gifted. *Journal for the Education of the Gifted, 11*(1), 56–68.

Khatena, J. (1978). *The creatively gifted child: Suggestions for parents and teachers*. New York: Vantage Press.

Khatena, J., & Fisher, S. (1974). A four-year study of children's responses to onomatopoeic stimuli. *Perceptual and Motor Skills, 39*, 1062.

Koberg, D., & Bagnall, J. (1976). *The universal traveler: A soft-systems guide to creativity, problem-solving, and the process of reaching goals*. Los Altos, CA: William Kaufmann.

Kohlberg, L. (1966). Moral education in the schools: A developmental view. *The School Review, 74*, 1–29.

Krathwohl, D. R., Bloom, B. S., & Masia, B. B. (1964). *Taxonomy of educational objectives: The classification of educational goals. Handbook II: Affective do-main.* New York: David McKay.

Langer, J. A. (1992). Speaking of knowing: Conceptions of understanding in academic disciplines. In A. Herrington & C. Moran (Eds.), *Writing, teaching, and learning in the disciplines* (pp. 69–85). New York: Modern Language Association.

Langer, J. A. (1994). Teaching disciplinary thinking in academic coursework. In J. N. Mangieri & C. C. Block (Eds.), *Creating powerful thinking in teachers and students: Diverse perspectives* (pp. 81–109). Fort Worth, TX: Harcourt Brace College Publishers.

Langer, J. A., & Applebee, A. N. (1988) *Speaking of knowing: Conceptions of learning in academic areas.* Final report to U. S. Department of Education, Office of Educational Research and Improvement, Grant No. G008610967. Albany: State University of New York. (ERIC Document Reproduction Service No. ED 297 336)

Lawrence, G. (1979). *People types and tiger stripes: A practical guide to learning styles.* Gainesville, FL: Center for Applications of Psychological Type.

Lewis, B. A. (1991). *The kid's guide to social action: How to solve the social problems you choose—and turn creative thinking into positive action.* Minneapolis, MN: Free Spirit.

Li, A. K., & Adamson, G. (1992). Gifted secondary students preferred learning style: Cooperative, competitive, or individualistic? *Journal of Education for the Gifted, 16,* 46–54.

Lohman, D. F. (1994). Spatially gifted, verbally inconvenienced. In N. Col-angelo, S. G. Assouline, & D. L. Ambroson (Eds.), *Talent development, Vol. 2. Proceedings from the 1993 Henry B. and Jocelyn Wallace National Research Symposium on Talent Development* (pp. 251–264). Dayton, OH: Ohio Psychology Press.

MacKinnon, D. W. (1962). The nature and nurture of creative talent. *American Psychologist, 20,* 273–281.

Maker, C. J. (1982a). *Curriculum development for the gifted.* Austin, TX: PRO-ED.

Maker, C. J. (1982b). *Teaching models in education of the gifted.* Austin, TX: PRO-ED.

Maker, C. J. (1986). Developing scope and sequence in curriculum. *Gifted Child Quarterly, 30,* 151–158.

Maker, C. J. (1992). Intelligence and creativity in multiple intelligences: Identification and development. *Educating Able Learners, 17*(4), 12–19.

Maker, C. J. (1993). Gifted students in the regular classroom: What practices are defensible and feasible? In C. J. Maker & D. Orzechowski–Harland (Eds.), *Programs for the gifted in regular classrooms* (pp. 413–434). Austin, TX: PRO-ED.

Maker, C. J., & Nielson, A. B. (1995). *Teaching models in education of the gifted* (2nd ed.). Austin, TX: PRO-ED.

Maker, C. J., Nielson, A. B., & Rogers, J. A. (1994). Giftedness, diversity, and problem solving: Multiple intelligences and diversity in educational settings. *Teaching Exceptional Children, 27*(1), 4–19.

Margulies, N. (1991). *Mapping inner space: Learning and teaching mind mapping.* Tucson, AZ: Zephyr Press.

Martin, S., McMillan, D., & Hillam, C. (1988). *More brain boosters.* Palo Alto, CA: Monday Morning Books.

McCarthy, B. (1990). Using the 4MAT system to bring learning styles to schools. *Educational Leadership, 48*(2), 31–37.

McTighe, J. & Lyman, F. T. (1988). Cueing thinking in the classroom: The promise of theory-embedded tools. *Educational Leadership, 45*(7), 18–24.

Meeth, L. R. (1978). Interdisciplinary studies: Integration of knowledge and experience. *Change, 10,* 6–9.

Milgram, R. M., Dunn, R. S., & Price, G. E. (1993). *Teaching and counseling gifted adolescents: An international learning style perspective.* Westport, CT: Praeger.

National Academy of Science. (1991). *To the moon and beyond* [videocassette]. Washington, DC: Author.

National Council of Teachers of Mathematics, Commission on Standards for School Mathematics. (1989). *Curriculum and evaluation standards for school mathematics.* Reston, VA: Author.

Nickerson, R. Perkins, D. N., & Smith, E. (1985). *The teaching of thinking.* Hillsdale, NJ: Lawrence Erlbaum.

Nielsen, M. E. (1989, Fall). Integrative learning for young children: A thematic approach. *Educational Horizons 68,* pp. 18–24.

Noller, R. B., Parnes, S. J., & Biondi, A. M. (1976). *Creative action*book: *Revised edition of creative behavior workbook.* New York: Charles Scribner's Sons.

Nunes, S., & Himler, R. (1988). *Coyote dreams.* New York: Atheneum.

Ogle, D. M. (1986). K–W–L: A teaching model that develops active reading of expository text. *The Reading Teacher, 39,* 564–570.

Onosko, J. J., & Newmann, F. M. (1994). Creating more thoughtful learning environments. In J. N. Mangieri & C. C. Block (Eds.), *Creating powerful thinkers in teachers and students: Diverse perspectives* (pp. 27–49). Fort Worth, TX: Harcourt Brace College Publishers.

Parnes, S. J. (1966). *Programming creative behavior.* Buffalo: State University of New York at Buffalo.

Parnes, S. J. (1967). *Creative behavior guidebook.* New York: Charles Scribner's Sons.

Parnes, S. J. (1975). *Aha: Insights into creative behavior.* Buffalo, NY: DOK Publishers.

Parnes, S. J. (1977). Guiding creative action. *The Gifted Child Quarterly, 21,* 460–476.

Passow, A. H. (1989, May/June). Designing a global curriculum. *Gifted Child Today, 12*(3), pp. 24–26.

Perkins, D. N. (1986). *Knowledge as design*. Hillsdale, NJ: Erlbaum.

Perkins, D. N. (1989). Selecting fertile themes for integrated learning. In H. H. Jacobs (Ed.), *Interdisciplinary curriculum: Design and implementation* (pp. 67–76). Alexandria, VA: Association for Supervision & Curriculum Development.

Perkins, D. N. (1992). *Smart schools: From training memories to educating minds*. New York: Free Press.

Piaget, J. (1972). *The epistemology of interdisciplinary relationships*. Paris: Oganization for Economic Cooperation and Development.

Piaget, J. & Inhelder, B. (1969). *The psychology of the child*. New York: Norton. (Original work published 1952)

Polette, N. (1984). *The research book for gifted programs: K-8*. O'Fallon, MO: Book Lures.

Presseisen, B. (1985). Thinking skills: Meanings, models, materials. In A. Costa (Ed.), *Developing minds: A resource book for teaching thinking* (pp. 43–48). Alexandria, VA: Association for Supervision & Curriculum Development.

Quattrone, D. F. (1989, Fall). A case study in curriculum development: Developing an interdisciplinary curriculum. *Educational Horizons, 68*, pp. 28–35.

Reis, S. M., & Schack, G. D. (1993). Differentiating products for the gifted and talented: The encouragement of independent learning. In C. J. Maker & D. Orzechowski–Harland, D. (Eds.), *Critical issues in gifted education: Programs for the gifted in regular classrooms* (pp. 161–186). Austin, TX: PRO-ED.

Renzulli, J. S. (1977). *The enrichment triad model: A guide for developing defensible programs for the gifted and talented*. Mansfield, CT: Creative Learning Press.

Renzulli, J. S., & Reis, S. M. (1985). *The schoolwide enrichment model: A comprehensive plan for educational excellence*. Mansfield Center, CT: Creative Learning Press.

Resnick, L. (1987). Learning in school and out. *Educational Researcher, 16*, 13–20.

Restow, R. S., Edeburn, C. E., & Restor, G. L. (1985). Learning preferences: A comparison of gifted and above-average middle grades students in small schools. *Roeper Review, 8*(2), 119–124.

Ricca, J. (1984). Learning styles and preferred instructional strategies, 4th–6th grade regular vs. gifted students. *Gifted Child Quarterly, 28*(3), 121–126.

Risemberg, R., & Zimmerman, B. J. (1992). Self-regulated learning in gifted students. *Roeper Review, 15*(2), 98–101.

Robinson, A. (1990). Cooperation or exploitation? The argument against cooperative learning for talented students. *Journal for the Education of the Gifted, 14*(1), 9–27.

Robinson, A. (1991). *Cooperative learning and the academically talented student*. Storrs, CT: National Research Center on the Gifted and Talented.

Rogers, K. (1993). Grouping the gifted and talented: Questions and answers. *Roeper Review, 16*(1), 8–12.

Rogoff, B. (1990). *Apprenticeship in thinking: Cognitive development in social context.* New York: Oxford University Press.

Root–Bernstein, R. S. (1987). Tools of thought: Designing an integrated curriculum for lifelong learners. *Roeper Review, 10*(1), 17–21.

Ross, J. D., & Ross, C. M. (1976). *The Ross Test of Higher Cognitive Processes.* Novato, CA: Academic Therapy Publications.

Rothman, R. (1989, May 17). What to teach: Reform turns finally to the essential question. *Education Week, 8*(34), pp. 1, 8, 10.

Roukes, N. (1982). *Art synectics.* Worcester, MA: Davis.

Rowe, M. B. (1986). Wait times: Slowing down may be a way of speeding up. *Journal of Teacher Education, 37*(1), 43–50.

San Diego City Schools, School Services Division. (1991). *GATE Curriculum Framework 1991–1996.* San Diego, CA: Author.

Schack, G. (1988). Methodologies of the disciplines: A key to differentiated education for the gifted. *Roeper Review, 10*(4), 219–222.

Schiever, S. W. (1986). *The effects of two teaching/learning models on the higher cognitive processes of students in classes for the gifted.* Unpublished doctoral dissertation, University of Arizona, Tucson.

Schiever, S. W. (1991). *A comprehensive approach to teaching thinking.* Boston: Allyn & Bacon.

Schlichter, C. L. (1986). Applying the multiple talent approach in mainstream and gifted programs. In J. S. Renzulli (Ed.), *Systems and models for developing programs for the gifted and talented* (pp. 352–389). Mansfield Center, CT: Creative Learning Press.

Schlichter, C. L., Hobbs, D., & Crump, W. D. (1988). Extending Talents Unlimited to secondary schools. *Educational Leadership, 45*(7), 36–39.

Scruggs, T. E., & Mastropieri, M.A. (1988). Acquisition and transfer of learning strategies by gifted and nongifted students. *Journal of Special Education, 22,* 153, 166.

Scruggs, T. E., Mastropieri, M. A., Monson, J., & Jorgensen, S. (1985). Maximizing what gifted students can learn: Recent findings of learning strategy research. *Gifted Child Quarterly, 29* (4), 181–185.

Shacal, N., & Rachmel, S. (1993). *Gifted children information booklet.* Jerusalem, Isreal: Ministry of Education and Culture.

Sharan, S., & Shacar, H. (1988). *Language and learning in the cooperative classroom.* New York: Springer.

Sharan, Y., & Sharan, S. (1992). *Expanding cooperative learning through group investigation.* New York: Teachers College Press.

Shore, B. M., Cornell, D. G., Robinson, A., & Ward, V. S. (1991). *Recommended practices in gifted education: A critical analysis.* New York: Teachers College Press.

Short, K. G., & Armstrong, J. (1993). Moving toward inquiry: Integrating literature into the science curriculum. *The New Advocate*, 6, 183–193.

Short, K. G., & Pierce, K. M. (1990). *Talking about books: Creating literate
communities.* Portsmouth, NH: Heinemann.

Shulman, L. S. (1968, September). Psychological controversies in the teaching
of science and mathematics. *The Science Teacher*, 35, 34–38, 89–90.

Silverman, L. (1986). Parenting young gifted children. *Journal of Children in
Contemporary Society*, 18(3), 73–87.

Sisk, D. (Ed.). (1979). Simulation games and other innovative curriculum.
Gifted Child Quarterly, 23(2).

Smith, K. (1992, October). Presentation at Research in Language and Literacy
Weekend Series: Literacy Research Informs Teaching/Literacy Teaching
Informs Research. University of Arizona, Tucson.

Smith, L. H., & Renzulli, J. S. (1984). Learning style preference: A practical
application for classroom teachers. *Theory into Practice*, 23, 44–50.

Spearman, C. (1904). General intelligence, objectively determined and measured. *American Journal of Psychology*, 15, 201–293.

Spearman, C. (1927). *The abilities of man.* New York: Macmillan.

Spier, P. (1980). *People.* New York: Doubleday.

Stanford, G., & Stanford, B. D. (1969). *Learning discussion skills through games.*
New York: Citation Press.

Starko, A. J. (1988) Effects of the Revolving Door Identification Model on
creative productivity and self-efficacy. *Gifted Child Quarterly*, 32, 291–297.

Start, K. B. (1989, July). *The tyranny of age.* Keynote address at the 8th World
Conference on the Education of Gifted Children, Sydney, Australia

Start, K. B. (1992, July). *CHIP—Children of high intellectual potential: The issues,
not the rhetoric, in the mainstream school.* Paper presented at the 2nd Asian
Conference on Gifted Children, Taipei, Taiwan.

Stedman, L. (1924). *Education of gifted children.* Yonkers-on-Hudson, NY: World
Book.

Stepien, W. J., Gallagher, S., & Workman, D. (1993). Problem-based learning
for traditional and interdisciplinary classrooms. *Journal of Education for the
Gifted*, 16(4), 338–357.

Steffy, J. (1975). *Boxcars.* Lakeside, CA: Interact.

Steptoe, J. (1980). *Daddy is a monster . . . sometimes.* New York: Lippincott.

Sternberg, R. J. (1985). Human intelligence: The model is the message. *Science*,
230(4730), 1111–1118.

Sternberg, R. J. (1988). *The triarchic mind: A new theory of human intelligence.*
New York: Viking.

Sternberg, R. J. (1990). *Metaphors of mind: Conceptions of the nature of intelligence.*
Cambridge, MA: Cambridge University Press.

Sternberg, R. J., & Davidson, J. E. (1986). *Conceptions of giftedness.* New York:
Cambridge University Press.

Sutton, S. (1985). *Learning through the built environment: An ecological approach to child development*. New York: Irvington Press.

Taba, H. (1962). *Curriculum development: Theory and practice*. New York: Harcourt, Brace & World.

Taba, H. (1964). *Thinking in elementary school children* (USOE Cooperative Research Project No. 1574). San Francisco, CA: San Francisco State College. (ERIC Document Reproduction Service No. ED 003 285)

Taba, H. (1966). *Teaching strategies and cognitive functioning in elementary school children* (USOE Cooperative Research Project No. 2404). San Francisco, CA: San Francisco State College.

Taylor, C. W. (1967). Questioning and creating: A model for curriculum reform. *Journal of Creative Behavior, 1*, 22–23.

Taylor, C. W. (1968). The multiple talent approach. *The Instructor, 77*, 27, 142, 144, 146.

Taylor, C. W. (1986). Cultivating simultaneous student growth in both multiple creative talents and knowledge. In J. S. Renzulli (Ed.), *Systems and models for developing programs for the gifted and talented* (pp. 307–351). Mansfield, CT: Creative Learning Press.

Taylor, C.W., Allington, D., & Lloyd, B. (1990). Multiple creative talent totem poles: Their uses and transferability to non-academic situations. In C. W. Taylor (Ed.), *Expanding awareness of creative potentials worldwide* (pp. 35–55). Salt Lake City, UT: Brain Talent-Powers Press.

Taylor, C.W., Ghiselin, B., & Yagi, K. (1967). *Exploratory research on communication abilities and creative abilities*. Final report, U.S. Air Force Grant AF-AFOSR-144-63. Salt Lake City: University of Utah.

Taylor, D. (1990). Teaching without testing: Assessing the complexity of children's literacy learning. *English Education, 22*, 4–74.

Taylor, D. (1991). *Learning denied*. Portsmouth, NH: Heinemann.

Thinking in the classroom: Resources for teachers, Vol. 2: Experiences that enhance thoughtful learning. (1991/1993). Victoria, British Columbia: Ministry of Education and Ministry for Multiculturalism & Human Rights.

Tierney, R. J., Readence, J. E., & Dishner, E. K. (1990). *Reading strategies and practices: A compendium* (3rd ed.). Boston: Allyn & Bacon.

Torrance, E.P. (1972). Can we teach children to think creatively? *Journal of Creative Behavior, 6*(4), 236–262.

Torrance, E. P. (1979). *The search for Satori and creativity*. Buffalo, NY: Creative Education Foundation.

Treffinger, D. J. (1975). Teaching for self-directed learning. *The Gifted Child Quarterly, 19*, 46–59.

Tucson Unified School District Gifted and Talented Education. (1993). *G.A.T.E. Curriculum Scope and Sequence*. Tucson, AZ: Author.

United States Department of Education. (1976). Program for the gifted and talented. *The Federal Register, 41*, 18665–18666.

VanTassel-Baska, J. (1982). Results of a Latin-based experimental study of the verbally precocious. *Roeper Review, 4*(4), 35–37.

VanTassel-Baska, J. (1994). The national curriculum development projects for high ability learners: Key issues and findings. In N. Colangelo, S. G. Assouline, & D. L. Ambroson (Eds.), *Talent Development: Proceedings from the 1993 Henry B. and Jocelyn Wallace National Research Symposium on Talent Development,* (pp. 19–38). Dayton, OH: Ohio Psychology Press.

VanTassel–Baska, J., Feldhusen, J., Selley, K., Wheatley, G., Silverman, L., & Foster, W. (1988). *Comprehensive curriculum for gifted learners.* Boston: Allyn & Bacon.

VanTassel-Baska, J., Landrum, M. S., & Peterson, K. (1992). Cooperative learning and gifted students. *Journal of Behavioral Education, 2*(4), 405–414.

Vygotsky,. L. S. (1978). *Mind in society: The development of higher psychological processes* (M. Cole, V. John–Steiner, S. Scribner, & E. Souberman, Eds.). Cambridge, MA: Harvard University Press.

Ward, V. S. (1961). *Educating the gifted: An axiomatic approach.* Columbus, OH: Merrill.

Ward, V. S. (1985). Giftedness and personal development: Theoretical considerations. *Roeper Review, 8,* 6–10.

Watson, G., & Glaser, E. M. (1964). *Watson-Glaser critical thinking appraisal: Manual for forms ym and zm.* New York: Harcourt, Brace, Jovanovich.

Wheaton, B. (1980). The sociogenesis of psychological disorder. *The Journal of Health and Social Behavior, 21,* 100–124.

Williams, F. E. (1972). *A total creativity program for individualizing and humanizing the learning process.* Englewood Cliffs, NJ: Educational Technology Publications.

Williams, F. E. (1986). *The second volume of classroom ideas for encouraging thinking and feeling.* East Aurora, NY: DOK Publishers.

Williams, F. E. (1990). *Classroom ideas for encouraging thinking and feeling, Vol. 3: Curriculum units,* (James West, Ed.). Buffalo, NY: DOK Publishers.

Wills, H. (1971). Diffy. *Arithmetic Teacher, 18*(6), 402–405.

Womack, J. G. (1966). *Discovering the structure of social studies.* New York: Benziger Brothers.

Wood, D. (1991). Aspects of teaching and learning. In P. Light, S. Sheldon, & M. Woodhead (Eds.), *Learning to think: A reader* (pp. 97–120). New York: Routledge.

Zimmerman, B. J., & Martinez-Ponz, M. (1990). Student differences in self-regulated learning: Relating grade, sex, and giftedness to self-efficacy and strategy use. *Journal of Educational Psychology, 82*(1), 51–59.

Author Index

Subject Index

NATIONAL UNIVERSITY
LIBRARY   SAN DIEGO